Digital Media Production for Beginners

Written for the non-specialist media producer, this book offers a practical and engaging guide to basic digital media production using modern equipment and software.

As media production tools and software become more pervasive and traditional media jobs scarcer, today's media professionals are now expected to be content creators across multiple forms of media, often working with little more equipment than a smartphone. In this accessible manual, Griffey explains how well-crafted media can help sell products, bolster subscriptions, and influence public opinion—and how to go about crafting it in a landscape of high-speed social media consumption. Topics covered include the basics of photography, film, video, and audio production, as well as animation and building websites. Readers will learn not just how to shoot or record content, but also how to edit, compress, and share it, considering the most appropriate file types, equipment, software, and platforms to use for each scenario. After reading this book, students will understand best practices associated with almost every area of media production and possess the essential skills to get the job done.

This book is an essential companion for students in communication disciplines, including PR, advertising, journalism, and marketing, looking for a solid grounding in digital media production to prepare them for the competitive job market.

Julia V. Griffey is Associate Professor of Interactive Digital Media and Media Production at Webster University, USA.

Digital Media Production
for Beginners

Julia V. Griffey

Routledge
Taylor & Francis Group

NEW YORK AND LONDON

Designed cover image: Golubovy/iStock via Getty Images

First published 2025
by Routledge
605 Third Avenue, New York, NY 10158

and by Routledge
4 Park Square, Milton Park, Abingdon, Oxon, OX14 4RN

Routledge is an imprint of the Taylor & Francis Group, an informa business

Library of Congress Cataloging-in-Publication Data
Names: Griffey, Julia, author.
Title: Digital media production for beginners / Julia Griffey.
Description: 1st. | New York : Routledge, 2025. | Includes
    bibliographical references and index.
Identifiers: LCCN 2024023954 (print) | LCCN 2024023955 (ebook) |
    ISBN 9781032611457 (hardback) | ISBN 9781032611433
    (paperback) | ISBN 9781003462200 (ebook)
Subjects: LCSH: Digital media. | Mass media.
Classification: LCC QA76.575 G75 2025 (print) | LCC QA76.575
    (ebook) | DDC 006.7—dc23/eng/20240528
LC record available at https://lccn.loc.gov/2024023954
LC ebook record available at https://lccn.loc.gov/2024023955

ISBN: 978-1-032-61145-7 (hbk)
ISBN: 978-1-032-61143-3 (pbk)
ISBN: 978-1-003-46220-0 (ebk)

DOI: 10.4324/9781003462200

Typeset in Galliard
by Apex CoVantage, LLC

Contents

1 Introduction

The importance of media production skills

Media production is a broad term that refers to the creation of video, audio, graphics, photography, and even interactive content like websites and apps. Many of us produce media daily thanks to the camera and related apps built into our smartphones which reflects a dramatic shift in media production behavior. It wasn't too long ago that media production was only done by media specialists. Until about the 1990s, only photographers were expected to take photos, graphic designers to design graphics, and videographers to shoot video. But now these roles have blurred. While these specialties still exist, oftentimes such a high degree of specialized know-how is not needed to get the job done.

In many situations, a non-media-specialist is required to be a media producer. For example, PR agencies, which were once focused on strategy and relationship building, are now creating images and video for social media channels. Were these PR professionals trained as film makers and photographers? Probably not. But they have likely learned a whole lot on the job. Organizations need employees that understand the power of a compelling image and spend time crafting the right shot prior to posting it on Instagram. Clearly, we are now working in an era where even non-production focused jobs need a more refined set of media production skills than what is required to take a selfie with an iPhone.

Any occasion where media is being used in the fields of advertising, marketing, PR, or journalism, there is always some communication objective. For example, is an image being used to sell a product, or encourage us to subscribe to a newsletter, or simply feel a certain way about a personality? When the media is poorly crafted it will fail at meeting these goals. A good product photo can make the product more appealing and lead to more sales. A compelling social media graphic can yield more web visitors. A well-shot and edited video can increase engagement. Those working in traditional communication fields such as journalism, PR, advertising, or marketing are now expected to not just conceive and strategize about these creative media projects, they are oftentimes expected to actually produce them. Some knowledge of how to

DOI: 10.4324/9781003462200-1

use the technology as well as best practices are needed by anyone working in these fields.

So, why now? What has changed?

There are a few factors that have changed the landscape of media production which now requires almost any communication professional to also be a media producer. The cost of the equipment has decreased substantially. When cameras cost thousands of dollars, they were only entrusted to people who *really* knew how to use them. Up until the 2000s, most photos were taken with a film camera. Film was expensive as was the cost of getting it developed. Even when digital cameras emerged (in the late 1980s and early 1990s), they were expensive and had limited resolution. The quality of photo we can now take with the average iPhone is almost ten times as good as the early digital cameras. Now that media producing equipment is so cheap and readily available, there is no reason why everyone can't use it.

The channels in which media is distributed have changed. The web was only invented in 1991! Prior to the web, media was distributed via print, television, and radio. These channels were expensive. Graphics and advertising on the web really didn't take off until the mid- to late 1990s and social media platforms did not arrive until the mid-2000s. These emerging media channels offer new opportunities for advertisers, journalists, PR agencies, and marketers. And what makes these distribution channels different from traditional ones is the speed at which the media now gets distributed and consumed. When an opportunity emerges, content needs to be created and shared quickly.

Consider how the marketing team at 360i handled the power outage at the Superbowl XLVII in 2013. While viewers were waiting for the lights to come back on, they sent out a clever tweet: "Power Out? No Problem. You can still dunk in the dark." The tweet went viral, making headlines in over 100 countries, garnering thousands of likes, retweets, and shares. It was retweeted over 10,000 times in one hour. They also won several advertising and marketing awards for this quick-thinking tweet ("Oreo's Super Bowl Tweet: 'You Can Still Dunk In The Dark'" 2013).

Do you think they called a professional photographer to come in and take the perfect shot of an Oreo cookie in order to get a professional graphic designer to compose several variations of the image before deciding which one to post? Absolutely not. A small team of people from Oreo's agency came up with the idea and designed and captioned it and got the tweet approved within minutes.

Was the image brilliant? Not really. But the timing and execution was brilliant. The production of the graphic could have been done by almost anyone who had a clever idea and some fundamental media production skills.

So, what's the point?

Basic media production skills are incredibly valuable for all types of professionals, and no longer relegated to the domain of "production" people. With the emergence of new media channels and the accessibility of production equipment, it is essential for anyone in a creative or communication-oriented field to have a basic understanding of media production. This includes knowledge of technology, design principles, storytelling techniques, and distribution methods.

What is covered in this book

This book covers the basics of media production skills across multiple forms of media, including photography, image editing, vector-based graphics, image compositing, audio recording and editing, shooting and editing video, web development, writing, and soliciting audience feedback. In each chapter, we will look at the evolution of this form of media production and how we have arrived where we are today. We will cover basic techniques as well as best practices. Additionally, this book addresses the importance of understanding communication objectives when creating media content and provides real-world examples to illustrate its impact.

Within each chapter, I've integrated a related "industry voice" to add another perspective on the topics. These voices include professionals across the media production fields to give you some authentic practitioner insight spoken in their own words. At the end of each chapter, there are questions for review as well as some suggested activities that will help you apply what you have learned and develop your own media production skills. By the end of this book, you will have a solid foundation in media production skills that will be valuable for any career path you choose.

Reference

"Oreo's Super Bowl Tweet: 'You Can Still Dunk In The Dark.'" 2013. *Huffington Post*. 2013. https://www.huffpost.com/entry/oreos-super-bowl-tweet-dunk-dark_n_26 15333.

2 Photography

In the previous chapter, you learned that in the workplace, non-photographers are often needed to take pictures. Why? Well, the speed and volume at which digital content often needs to be produced requires companies and organizations to obtain and share pictures quickly. The public is no longer satisfied waiting for tomorrow's newspaper to see a photograph of breaking news. We crave immediate visual information which can create a challenge for organizations whose job it is to supply this content, because while almost anyone can pull out their iPhone and snap a photo, the quality may not be great, and the image may not communicate the intended message.

Good-quality photos are always highly coveted, whether they are part of a website, social media campaign, article, or e-commerce site. Photographic images have become the universal language that people all over the world can connect with. When they are successful, they will be what the viewer notices first, and can compel them to act. Poorly composed and executed photographs will be simply ignored or will discredit the message you are trying to communicate.

In this chapter, we will discuss the power of photography, as well as what makes a photo "good." We will also cover the history of photographic technology and how it has evolved over the past two centuries. We will investigate some of the settings on a modern camera and the effect each of them has on the resulting image that is generated. Finally, we'll review a few valuable tips to help you maximize your photography results no matter the type of camera you use.

The power of good photography

The attention-grabbing and staying power of photographs is undeniable. It's a biological fact that we respond to visual data faster than other types of information, and memories about what catches our eye will stick around longer too. Words are processed by our short-term memories, and our brains can only hold onto about seven pieces of text-based information. Images, on the other hand, "go directly into long-term memory where they are indelibly etched"

DOI: 10.4324/9781003462200-2

(The Media Education Center 2021). For these reasons, photographs have the potential to be a highly effective communication medium. And, of course, the better the photograph, the higher its potential to resonate with our audience.

Photographs are simply a much more efficient way to communicate than the written word as the human brain processes images a staggering 60,000 times faster than text (The Media Education Center 2021). There is clearly some truth to the statement "a picture is worth a thousand words," as a photo can convey a message or emotion with just one glance, whereas it may take several sentences to describe the same thing in text. Efficiency of communication is of utmost importance online as users' attention spans have declined from 12 seconds to only eight seconds since the year 2000 (McSpadden 2015).

When images are nestled within blocks of text, they tend to catch our attention first. That's why, as you scroll through your Instagram feed, you often find yourself pausing at a beautifully curated photo of food, rather than delving into lengthy paragraphs that attempt to describe it. "The mere presence of an image in a social media post helps the post stand out from the majority of text-only posts and, as a result, attracts more attention" (Li and Xie 2020). The challenge for content creators is that anyone who consumes media is bombarded with hundreds of competing images every day. Your photograph must be compelling enough to make someone stop, look, and engage with what you are trying to say. A powerful image should evoke emotion, tell a story, or provide information that words alone cannot.

Good photography is especially important when it comes to selling products. When shopping online, shoppers are unable to physically touch and interact with items like they can in a store. As a result, high-quality product photos are critical for consumers to make informed purchasing decisions. In fact, photography "significantly influences consumers' purchase decisions and market behaviour" (Szulc and Musielak 2022).

When promoting a business or organization, building trust is crucial. The quality of your photographs plays a significant role in conveying credibility and professionalism, ultimately making it easier for potential customers to trust your offerings. The simple act of including a photograph can enhance user trust. Studies have shown that integrating a photo of an employee on a company website significantly increased user trust. A similar effect occurs when including a picture of the author within an online article; the credibility is increased (Riegelsberger, Sasse, and Mccarthy 2003).

"Images are the heart and soul of social media" (Butow et al. 2020). In addition to building trust between the viewer and the brand, good photography can also increase reach and engagement. On X (the platform formerly known as Twitter), "the inclusion of an immediately viewable image in a Tweet increases the number of retweets by 119.15% and the number of likes by 87.26%" (Li and Xie 2020). In addition, the quality of the photograph impacts the engagement as "professionally shot pictures consistently lead to higher engagement" (Li and Xie 2020).

The evolution of photography

Photo technology has evolved significantly over its almost 200-year history. The camera has evolved from a plain box that projected fleeting images to the high-tech minicomputers found in today's DSLRs and smartphones. Understanding a bit about the history offers photographers valuable insight into the evolution of the medium and the techniques used by trailblazing photographers. This knowledge helps them build their own unique style by learning from the past and understanding the context and purpose of different photographic styles. Furthermore, a historical perspective can help liberate photographers from current trends by unveiling a vast array of creative possibilities that have been explored throughout the history of photography. It also fosters a deeper appreciation for the art form, enabling photographers to contribute to the ongoing evolution of photographic expression in a more informed and conscious manner.

Camera obscura

Long before the emergence of the earliest cameras, humans had begun experimenting with image projection. In fact, the origins of photography can be traced back to the invention of the "camera obscura" in the 11th century. A camera obscura is a darkened chamber with a small hole on one side. When the sunlight reflected off the objects outside the camera obscura and passed through the hole in the device, a reflection of the outdoor scene would be projected on the inside wall of the chamber. Although the reflected visuals were upside down and reversed, they could be traced to construct precise drawings of real subjects such as buildings and monuments. The camera obscura was primarily viewed as a tool to aid artists in creating realistic renderings of the

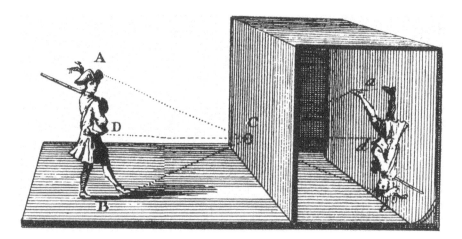

Figure 2.1 Camera obscura

outside world. It didn't document images, and the entire chamber needed to be moved to capture different scenes (until smaller, portable versions were made in the 16th and 17th centuries), nevertheless it was an exciting innovation because "for the first time there was proof positive that the sun could be used to imprint its energy" (Gustavson and House 2011, p. 2; see also Turner 1987). And it inspired researchers to experiment with ways to record images (Wills and Wills 1980, p. 11).

Creating permanent images

It was not until images were able to be stored for posterity that the field of photography truly started in earnest. In the early 1800s, French inventor Joseph Nicéphore Niépce revolutionized photography by successfully capturing permanent images with a camera obscura onto metal sheets. His method was driven by the realization that coating a metal plate with an asphalt like substance called bitumen would harden when exposed to light. After an eight-hour exposure time, he would wash the plate with oil of lavender to dissolve the unhardened areas to create a permanent image (Wills and Wills 1980, p. 12). Because this method required such a long exposure time, the types of images that could be captured were limited. Subjects needed to remain motionless for eight hours to produce an accurate photograph.

Advancements in photographic prints

While Niépce's methodology was an exciting innovation, it was not a practical means of generating photographic images due to the long exposure time required. But his success fueled other innovators to craft their own means of recording visuals. He even formed a collaboration with Louis Daguerre which ultimately led to their creation of the daguerreotype—an essential predecessor to modern film. To make a daguerreotype, a copper plate was thinly coated with silver, exposed inside a camera, fumed with a mercury vapor to make it visible, and then further treated with chemicals to remove the plate's light sensitivity. Daguerreotypes represented a remarkable improvement in photographic image production as it decreased the exposure time to 10–60 minutes (Gustavson & House 2011, p. 18).

Around the same time, another photographic process was being developed by an Englishman, William Henry Fox Talbot. The technique he developed, the calotype, was more of a precursor to the modern photographic process as he captured the negative image of the subject from which he made positive prints. He did this by placing subjects on light sensitive paper and exposing it to light. Then he affixed the image by using a salt solution. From these negatives, he was able to make positives by contact printing using sheets of the original light sensitive paper. While the Talbot technique was much more reproducible, it lacked the quality of the daguerreotype (Gustavson & House 2011, p. 19).

By the mid-1800s, the concept of capturing a negative from which a positive image could be generated became a standard technique. And the most common method for doing so was on emulsion plates, silver plates that were coated with a light-sensitive emulsion. They were exposed to light and then "developed" in a dark room, just like film. Emulsion plates were the superior choice to daguerreotypes due to their affordability, short exposure time of only two or three seconds, and enhanced light sensitivity. However, this higher level of sensitivity required that they get developed quickly for optimal results. The entire development process needed to be complete before the plate dried. As a result, field photographers in the late 1800s often carried chemicals with them and traveled in wagons that could also serve as a darkroom.

Major technological improvements to the photographic process came with the invention of the dry plate and the flexible negative. In 1871, Richard Maddox, an English doctor, discovered that gelatin coated with silver halide was light sensitive and could be used to create a negative. This type of negative (which he termed a "dry plate,") could then be used to produce multiple positives via contact printing. Dry plates were much more convenient than wet plates as they could be stored rather than made as needed and did not need to be developed immediately after exposure. Maddox's dry plate provided a foundation from which many others made improvements (Wills and Wills 1980, p. 23). Another important innovation was the flexible negative. Up until this point, plates were made of glass which broke easily. A flexible roll of sensitive material offered another advantage in that it could be rolled up and advanced through a camera (Wills and Wills 1980, pp. 23–24).

During this era of photographic reproduction experimentation, the types of photographs that could be taken were quite limited. The longer exposure times meant that any movement within the scene would create a blurry image. In addition, very few people had access to this type of technology. Nevertheless, the public marveled at its potential as a "shortcut to art." Some experts even predicted that painting would soon be dead (Vallencourt 2016). But as the turn of the century neared, this attitude would begin to change.

Additional technological advancements of the late 19th century

In the late 1800s, camera technology improved substantially. The revolutionary camera with bellows that allowed the photographer to adjust the distance between the lens and the plate at the back of the camera, ushered in an era of brighter and more focused imagery, drastically improving the quality of photographs (Gustavson and House 2011, p. 42). And the introduction of a camera with tapered bellows made the device smaller and even more portable (Gustavson and House 2011, p. 41).

These technological advancements had an impact on the types of photographs that could be taken. Up until the mid-1800s, photography was used primarily for taking portraits. Toward the later part of that century, cameras became more lightweight and portable. At the same time, the railroad system was expanding rapidly, facilitating cross-country travel, and cities were also becoming more industrial and congested. The culmination of these factors sparked a fascination with the world outside these metropolitan centers, inspiring a generation of landscape photographers towards the late 1800s. People such as William Henry Jackson and Ansel Adams established their own reputations by immortalizing stunning vistas from America's Wild West into lasting photographs. The images they captured not only informed the public about these exotic locals, they also helped establish photography as an art form in its own right.

Cameras for everyone

Prior to the late 1800s, photography was too expensive for everyday people. But this changed with the emergence of the Kodak company and its signature inexpensive and accessible camera (Gustavson and House 2011). The Kodak camera was unique in that it was a self-contained box camera that used rolled film. It was also simple to operate, with one small lens and no focusing adjustment. This camera had a generous capacity of 100 exposures, so the owner could take multiple shots with it. After shooting all the film, they would then return it to the factory for developing and printing out prints. "Its simplicity greatly accelerated the growth of amateur photography, especially among women, to whom much of the Kodak advertising was addressed" (Vallencourt 2016).

The birth of photojournalism

During the 1930s, photographers began to break away from traditional staged portraits and landscapes and started shooting candid shots of life as it happened. The new, small 35mm cameras facilitated this type of shooting as they were very portable and could be quickly reloaded with small film cassettes. They also allowed for a wider variety of shots, and faster shutter speeds meant that photographers could capture action better than ever before. 35mm film revolutionized the industry with its easy-to-manage design compared to larger format film. It soon became a new standard for high-end still photography cameras.

This new way of capturing moments caught on quickly, especially during the Great Depression and World War II. Photographers were hired by the U.S. government to visually document impoverished framers to help promote Roosevelt's New Deal. During World War II, photojournalists captured gripping images of war unlike anything most people had ever seen. Iconic mages such as Dorthea Lange's "Migrant Mother" and Joel Rosenthal's "Raising the Flag on Iwo Jima" (1945) are perfect examples of this new style of journalistic photography as they not only captured poignant moments in American history, but also demonstrated the power to convey truth through images ("Farm Security Administration/Office of War Information Black-and-White Negatives" n.d.).

Figure 2.2 Dorthea Lange's *Migrant Mother, Circa 1936*

Advancements in camera technology

Technological improvements in cameras during the early 20th century made photography increasingly accessible while giving photographers even more control over the images they created. In 1936, the first 35mm SLR (single lens reflex) camera made its debut, allowing for many more manual adjustments and gave the photographer the ability to preview their subject in real time. The emergence of the SLR camera was followed by the invention of faster films in the late 1940s which allowed photographers to take photos more quickly. The 1950s and 1960s saw a boom in camera technology with advancements such as automated exposure controls, electronic flashes, and even motorized film. The Japanese company Nikon raised the bar on SLR cameras even further, by releasing a version with interchangeable lenses and other accessories (Gustavson and House 2011, p. 267). These high-tech innovations helped establish the company as a leader in photographic technology.

The wonder of instant images

In 1948, as 35mm cameras were becoming the norm, Polaroid released their groundbreaking Model 95 shortly before the holiday shopping season.

Through its revolutionary chemical process, this camera could develop its own film and produce a photographic print in under a minute. Although it weighed 4 pounds, comparable to "professional" cameras, it was still devoured by consumers, outselling the company's predictions (Bonanos 2012). By 1963, Polaroid made a number of improvements to its technology, releasing a new model, the Automatic 100. By 1970, Polaroid cameras were extremely pervasive due to their low price, ease of use, and the privacy they afforded the photographer since the film did not need to be sent out to be developed.

The introduction of smart cameras

With the advent of "point and shoot" cameras in the late 1970s, photography became even more accessible. These automatic devices calculated shutter speed, aperture, and focus so that casual photographers could easily produce high-quality photos without worrying about technical settings. Nevertheless, professionals and experienced amateurs still opted for SLR cameras where they had more control over their images.

The digital age

Digital photography began to make its presence known toward the end of the 20th century, leading us into a new age of imaging technology. These point-and-shoot cameras stored images on digital media instead of film. Digital cameras that incorporated the capabilities of the SLR cameras became known as DSLR cameras.

While Kodak produced the first digital camera in 1975, it wasn't until 1991 when a fully digital camera became available to consumers, the Dycam Model 1 (Gustavson and House 2011, p. 446). Its maximum resolution was 320 × 240 pixels and it retailed for $995. Other manufacturers quickly followed, and with each version came improved image quality and additional features such as LCD (liquid crystal display) screens and larger storage capacity. These early digital photographs were not high enough quality for printed media. It would not be until the later part of the decade until digital cameras could yield this level of resolution.

A camera in every pocket

The 2000s saw a massive shift in the photography landscape with the introduction of digital cameras that could fit in your pocket. However, the real game changer was when Apple released the iPhone in 2007. This device included an advanced camera and photo-editing software, combining two of the most important components of any good photography system—capturing and editing. Today, almost everybody has a camera in their pocket at all times and photography is no longer limited to the professional photographer or serious hobbyist.

Naturally, as smartphone photography has improved, the sales of DSLR cameras have decreased significantly (Richter 2023). Today, many companies and organizations take all their photographs on smartphones as modern cameras within smartphones have integrated features that were once exclusive to DSLRs. With that said, DSLR cameras still offer a level of control that iPhones have yet to achieve (Kieldsen 2022).

How a DSLR camera works

Because DSLR cameras are now the standard tool for capturing photographic images, it is essential for any photographer to understand how they work. While many features native to a DSLR camera are now integrated within a smartphone, it's helpful to know your way around a DSLR before trying to master comparable features within your camera phone. Operating a DSLR camera is not overly complicated. You can simply use the "Auto" setting, press the shutter release button halfway to focus and then all the way to take the picture. However, understanding some basic controls and functions will allow you to have the greatest amount of control over the images you capture.

Parts of a DSLR camera

While there are several different manufacturers of DSLR cameras, the following components can be found on all:

Viewfinder: the small window that you look through to frame your shot.

Lens: the part of the camera that takes light and focuses it onto the sensor. One hallmark of a DSLR camera is that the lenses are interchangeable. For example, to capture subjects that are far away, the photographer may switch to a zoom lens.

Shutter release button: the button you press to take a picture. It will open and close the shutter, allowing light to reach the sensor.

Display: a screen (typically on the back of the camera) that allows you to quickly review your images and make adjustments to settings. The display also acts as an interface through which you can modify some of your camera's settings.

Dial: the wheel located on top of the camera that lets you quickly adjust the shutter speed, aperture, and other settings. The most common settings you will select on the dial are: "A" or automatic and "M" for manual. Using your camera in manual mode will give you the greatest amount of control—allowing you to make further adjustments that you see fit. In Automatic mode, the camera will make these decisions for you.

Sensor: the part of the camera that you can't see, but is probably the most crucial component since it actually captures the image. It converts light into digital data which can be stored as an image file.

Battery: the power source for your camera. A battery charger is always included with a digital camera.

Memory card: the device that stores images from your camera. It should be inserted into the side of the camera when you want to take pictures, and removed when you are done shooting. You can insert the memory card into your computer to copy the images onto your hard drive or (better yet) on some type of cloud-based storage. If your computer does not have a built-in memory card reader, you can get an external one that plugs into your computer via USB.

DSLR camera settings and their effect

You can modify some of the camera settings on exterior dials and buttons; however, some settings must be accessed through menus in the display.

Resolution

Resolution refers to the number of pixels that are incorporated into each image. The higher the resolution, the more detail that is captured within an image. If you want to print an image at a large scale, you will need ample resolution to be able to achieve a crisp print. However, if you will just be using an image for a social media post or a product image, a lower resolution will suffice. Therefore, depending on what you are shooting, you may want to adjust the resolution on the camera.

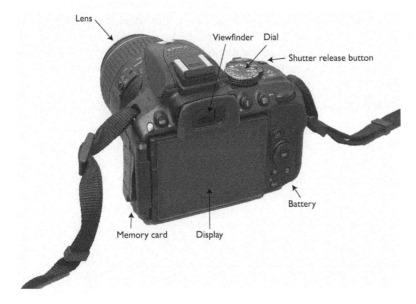

Figure 2.3 DSLR camera

Megapixels (MPs) or millions of pixels are the most commonly used measure to gauge how well a digital camera performs, primarily based on its image sensor. Therefore, a 20 MP camera can produce images of up to 20 million pixels. Higher-quality cameras will have the ability to capture more pixels in each image.

Image format

The file format refers to how data in a digital file is compressed and saved. There are several different digital image file formats; however, the few that are most often created by digital cameras are RAW, TIFF, and JPEG. Many cameras will give you a choice of which format to capture images in. RAW format is the least compressed and the most versatile, giving you more data to work with when editing. TIFF is a bit more compressed than RAW but still provides a good amount of detail. JPEG is the most used image format because it is highly compressed and easy to share on social media or via email. Since you can always convert your images to JPGs or TIFFs, it's best to shoot in RAW format when you can.

White balance

The white balance setting helps your camera adjust for different light sources, such as sunlight or artificial lighting. Most DSLR cameras have automatic white balance settings where you choose the type of lighting in your shooting environment and your camera adjusts to make the colors in your image look most realistic. You can also set your white balance manually by taking a picture of something that is white and then telling your camera to modify its reproduction of the light in the scene based on this white as a reference point. If you don't set this correctly, colors can appear off in your photos.

Settings to consider when shooting in manual mode

Any DSLR camera will allow you to shoot in either Manual or Automatic mode. If you are shooting in manual mode, you will need to focus your own images—the camera will not do it for you. You must also select Manual mode if you want to adjust shutter speed, aperture, and ISO as well as many other settings. However, before you make these types of adjustments, you should have some understanding of what they do.

Shutter speed

The shutter speed is the amount of time that the shutter remains open and light is allowed to hit the sensor. This setting will affect how motion appears (or doesn't appear) in an image, as well as how much light is captured. A slow shutter speed is 1 second. A very fast shutter speed is 1/2000 of a second.

A DSLR camera will offer many other shutter speeds between these two settings.

If you take a picture of a moving object at a slow shutter speed, the object will appear blurry. Conversely, if you take the same image at a high shutter speed, the object will be completely frozen in time. If you are shooting in low-light conditions (or your scene isn't particularly bright), a slower shutter speed might be necessary to allow for more light to enter the camera and create an evenly exposed image.

Aperture

The aperture setting on a DSLR camera controls how much light is allowed through the lens by changing the shutter blade positions. The F-stop is the measurement of the size of a lens aperture. A wider (lower number, e.g., f/2) aperture will allow more light to enter. Conversely, a narrower (higher number, e.g., f/22) aperture will reduce the amount of light.

There are a few reasons why you might want to adjust the aperture on your camera. One reason might be to control the amount of light that is being allowed through the lens. Let's say you are shooting at a very fast shutter speed. You may want to lower the aperture to allow in more light, balancing out the reduction of light caused by the fast shutter speed.

Aperture plays a pivotal role in setting the depth of field, which is how far away objects are from each other to appear acceptably sharp. If you choose a smaller opening (higher aperture number), it will result in a deep depth of field, meaning everything is in focus. A larger opening will result in a shallower depth-of-field, meaning that the objects in the background will be more blurred.

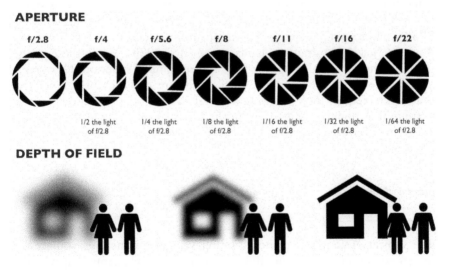

Figure 2.4 Aperture vs. depth of field

ISO

The ISO setting on the camera determines how sensitive your camera is to light. The lower the ISO, the less sensitive it is to light, and images will be darker. The higher the ISO, the more sensitive it is to light, and images will appear brighter.

Choosing the right ISO can be tricky because too low of an ISO will result in a dark image, while too high of an ISO will result in a grainy (also known as "noisy") image. Generally speaking, you want to keep your ISO at its lowest setting unless the light is very poor and you need to boost it.

Settings on an iPhone that mimic the behavior of a DSLR

Modern iPhones have a lot of features that mimic the behavior of a DSLR and can be still used to take stunning photos, often with a professional-level quality, as you can now control shutter speed, aperture, and ISO just as you would on a traditional DSLR. However, the terms used to describe these settings vary. For example, shooting in "portrait mode" produces an image with a shallower depth of field. To further enhance the capabilities of an iPhone, you can attach special lenses.

Taking good photographs

Now that we all have cameras in our pockets, and we can readily *take* pictures, it doesn't necessarily mean the photos we take will be any good. Then, again, what is good photography? The definition is somewhat subjective and has evolved significantly of the course of the medium's history. What was once seen as "good" quickly becomes a cliché and falls out of favor. Kodak's instructional books on good photography published in the 1930s encouraged photographers to capture subjects posed in front of windows or "gazing at dramatic landscapes" (Beil 2020). While these images now look hokey and dated, they were the epitome of superior photography at the time. Just like fashion, photo trends are cyclical. Instagram filters that make pictures look like they were taken in another era suddenly look current and modern again. Despite the fact that our taste in photography has changed over time, there are still many traits that are shared by "good" photographs.

Start with the basics

Subject

The subject of your photo should be relevant to the message you are trying to communicate. Be mindful of any details or elements that may distract from it. "There are no substitutes for simplicity and clear action" (Company, n.d.).

Focus

At least one part of your image should be in focus, and the focus of your image should align with your communication goal. It could be a particular element in an image, or it could be the entire scene. Think about what emotion you want the viewers to feel or the point you want them to understand when they look at the image and make that the focus of your image.

Composition

Composition means how the elements of your photo—the people, objects, and background—come together to form a visual. There are a few techniques that photographers use to create a compelling composition.

- **Leading lines**. Leading lines are directional elements in a composition that help draw the viewer's eye toward the main subject or deeper into the image. Examples of leading lines include paths, staircases, railings, or rivers.
- **Rule of thirds**. The rule of thirds is a guideline for creating balanced and interesting compositions. Divide your frame into three sections both horizontally and vertically, creating nine equal squares. Position elements within the frame along these imaginary lines or at their intersections. If the subject is in motion, you want to leave the empty space in the direction the subject is facing. The result is that the composition feels more balanced and open.
- **Rule of odds**. The rule of odds states that an odd number of objects in a composition is naturally more interesting to look at than an even number. The human eye tends to move around the objects, looking for relationships between them and trying to make sense of the arrangement.
- **Negative Space**. Negative space (sometimes referred to as "white space") is the empty area around the main subject in the composition. It can be used to create balance, emphasize a focal point and provide breathing room.
- **Balance**. Balance in a composition means that the visual weight of the elements is evenly distributed. When the elements are balanced, there's less tension and stress for the viewer. There are many types of balance such as symmetrical, asymmetrical, and radial.

Shot angle

If you want your photos to stand out in a social media feed, experiment with the angle of your shots. We typically see the world at eye level. To capture a more interesting perspective, try shooting from above or below the subject or capturing it from an unconventional angle. A strategic position can exaggerate distances making for a more dramatic image.

Background

A busy background within an image can be visually confusing and detract from your communication goal. The best way to avoid this is to always search for a plain, contrasting background that won't distract the viewer from your main subject. Photographers often stage their product shots within a white photo cube to get a crisp and clean background to keep the emphasis of the image on the product itself.

Lighting

Light is one of the most important elements for any photograph. The quality of light is determined by the intensity (how bright or dark it is), direction (where it's coming from), and color (how warm or cool it is). You can use natural light, artificial light sources, and other features in the environment to dramatically alter the look of your photographs. You can also reflect and diffuse light to create soft, even lighting that won't overwhelm your subject.

- **Natural light**. Natural light is light provided by the sun or the moon. It tends to be softer and more flattering than artificial light. Whenever possible, take advantage of natural light. However, direct sunlight can create dramatic shadows which can hinder (or enhance) the quality of your photographs. When shooting outdoors, mid-morning or late afternoon sun produces a more subtle, warmer light. If you're shooting indoors, try to find the best available natural light and use white reflectors or bounce boards to add extra fill if needed.
- **Artificial light**. When shooting indoors or at night, you will most likely have to rely on artificial light. Artificial light is usually more intense and harsher than natural light, but if used correctly it can still create great photographs. The benefit of artificial light is that it can be controlled. You can dial it up or down depending on your needs which is something you can't exactly do with the sun.

Additional Tips

Secure your camera

If the camera moves while you are taking a picture, it will result in a blurry image. To avoid this, you should always make sure that your camera is securely mounted or held in place with a tripod. This will also help you maintain the desired composition and framing of your shot. DSLR cameras offer convenience with their tripod mount holes on the bottom, allowing you to easily and securely attach them to a tripod. Smartphone users can also benefit from shooting in this manner using an attachment that screws into a tripod and holds the device firmly while shooting. You can also get unconventional tripods without a screw mount that work quite well for securing a smartphone.

Taking several shots

"The expert never takes just one shot" (Company n.d.). To maximize your chances of capturing a stunning shot, take multiple photos in different angles and perspectives. Experiment with different settings on the camera and make adjustments to your shooting environment. With practice and experimentation, you will eventually gain confidence in your photography skills and maybe even develop your own unique style.

Be patient and alert

Have you ever noticed that some of the best photographs are ones that seem to capture a perfect and fleeting moment in time? This is a result of a photographer being poised and ready to shoot at any moment. These shots can't be had by staging your subject(s). They are reliant on patience of the photographer to simply observe and shoot.

Tell a story

The most interesting snapshots are ones that tell a story. A great photograph captures a moment in time and conveys emotion, atmosphere, and character. Don't just focus on capturing the subject, but also consider the surrounding elements and how they contribute to the overall story of the image. By adding layers of meaning, you can create a more impactful and memorable photograph.

Create context

When shooting products, consider adding props to create a sense of context and help tell a story. For example, if you are shooting a product for camping gear, add in elements such as tents or campfires to convey the intended use of the product. This not only creates an interesting visual but also helps your audience imagine themselves using the product in their own lives. The prop should not distract from the main subject. "Props can have some prominence in a photo, but should not confuse consumers, as they will misunderstand props as the main product" (Do and Forsström n.d.).

Every photographic technology has its own visual language by professor and photographer Kathleen Sanker

Photographic technologies have evolved in direct relationship to our human understanding of the world around us—particularly in relationship to our perceptions of time. A photographic practitioner often chooses the type or style of their image-making methods based on how it represents or illustrates their intended message and perspective. Every technology or style has its own visual language, marks, and signature characteristics, creating a language, mood, tone, and narrative unto itself. The grain of film, the pixelation of older digital technology, the fingerprint on a contact print are all examples of this. For instance, large format film photographers typically made a few exposed sheets of film, capturing deliberately intentional images of relatively still environments with a strong discernment for exposure and composition. Smartphone camera photographers by contrast may capture many frames in a very short session of far less formal imagery, with less concern for exposure accuracy, and a composition less informed by training and education, often all while in motion themselves.

Tips for taking good photos by professional photographer by Jennifer Silverberg

Take a lot of photos, change your exposure, vary your focal distance, you know, experiment! More than anything, take your time, especially in the beginning. Be intentional in your process and go back and really look at the images and learn from them as you go. More than ever, we're surrounded by images. Study them. Analyze them, dissect, and talk about what's good about them, what's bad about them, what's working for you, what isn't. You're going to learn and grow more if you're truly honest with yourself and analytical in the process. The smarter you are in your approach, the more skilled you can become. You don't have to be an artist to start. You have to be smart and pay attention.

Study questions

1) How does the incorporation of photos into a social media post affect engagement?
2) What are the qualities of "good" photography?
3) What are some techniques you can use to create eye-catching photographs?
4) Describe what aperture, shutter speed, and ISO mean and how it is set on a camera. What effect do they have on the image you produce?
5) What are the typical file formats of the images you pull off of a DSLR camera? How do you choose which one to use?

Exercises

1) Share an image with the class that you saw online (on any website or social media) that caught your attention. Why did it stand out to you? What qualities of the photo made it stand out?
2) Share a product photo that made you not want to purchase the product? What was it about the photo that left a bad impression?
3) Visit a professional photographer's online portfolio. Discuss what settings on the camera they might have used to achieve various images.
4) Analyze ten images that you found on Instagram that you feel are striking. What qualities did they possess?
5) Experiment with a DSLR camera. Try taking the following shots and discuss what you learned from this exercise.

   a. a portrait with a high aperture setting
   b. the *same* portrait with a low aperture setting
   c. an action shot with fast shutter speed
   d. the *same* action shot with slow shutter speed
   e. a landscape with higher aperture setting
   f. the *same* landscape with low aperture setting

References

Beil, Kim. 2020. *Good Pictures: A History of Popular Photography*. Stanford, CA: Stanford University Press. https://library3.webster.edu/login?url=https://search. ebscohost.com/login.aspx?direct=true&db=e000xna&AN=2450230&site= ehost-live&scope=site.

Bonanos, Christopher. 2012. *Instant: The Story of Polaroid*. New York: Princeton Architectural Press. https://worldcat.org/title/785071814.

Butow, Eric, Jenn Herman, Stephanie Liu, Amanda Robinson, and Mike Allton. 2020. *Ultimate Guide to Social Media Marketing*. Irvine, CA: Entrepreneur Press. https://library3.webster.edu/login?url=https://search.ebscohost.com/login.aspx?direct=true&db=nlebk&AN=2516921&site=ehost-live&scope=site.

Company, Eastman Kodak. n.d. "How to Make Good Pictures: A Guide for the Amateur Photographer." https://worldcat.org/title/2974797.

Do, P. H., and Forsström, M. (n.d.). *The Impact of Product Photography on Consumer Attention and Perception*.

"Farm Security Administration/Office of War Information Black-and-White Negatives." n.d. Library of Congress. https://www.loc.gov/collections/fsa-owi-black-and-white-negatives/about-this-collection/. Accessed May 31, 2023.

Gustavson, Todd, and George Eastman House. 2011. *500 Cameras: 170 Years of Photographic Innovation*. New York: Sterling Signature. https://worldcat.org/title/757518833.

Kieldsen, Sam. 2022. "5 Things a DSLR Still Does Better than an IPhone." TechRadar. https://www.techradar.com/features/5-things-a-dslr-still-does-better-than-an-iphone.

Li, Yiyi, and Ying Xie. 2020. "Is a Picture Worth a Thousand Words? An Empirical Study of Image Content and Social Media Engagement." *Journal of Marketing Research* 57 (1): 1–19. https://doi.org/10.1177/0022243719881113.

McSpadden, K. (2015). "You Now Have a Shorter Attention Span than a Goldfish." *Time.* Available from: http://time.com/3858309/attention-spans-goldfish/. Accessed August 13, 2018.

Media Education Center. (2021). Using Images Effectively in Media. *21st Century Psychology: A Reference Handbook.*

Richter, Felix. 2023. "Smartphones Wipe Out Decades of Camera Industry Growth." Statista. https://www.statista.com/chart/15524/worldwide-camera-shipments/.

Riegelsberger, Jens, M Angela Sasse, and John D. Mccarthy. 2003. "Shiny Happy People Building Trust? Photos on e-Commerce Websites and Consumer Trust." http://www.bizrate.com.

SZULC, Radosław, and Katarzyna Musielak. 2022. "Product Photography in Product Attractiveness Perception and E-Commerce Customer Purchase Decisions." *Scientific Papers of Silesian University of Technology. Organization & Management/Zeszyty Naukowe Politechniki Slaskiej. Seria Organizacji i Zarzadzanie,* no. 166.

Turner, Peter. 1987. *History of Photography.* New York: Exeter Books. https://worldcat.org/title/17359903.

Vallencourt, Margaret. 2016. "The History of Photography." *Britannica Guide to the Visual and Performing Arts.* New York: Britannica Educational Publishing in association with Rosen Educational Services. https://worldcat.org/title/930893913.

Wills, Camfield, and Deirdre Wills. 1980. *History of Photography: Techniques and Equipment.* New York: Exeter Books. https://worldcat.org/title/7172233.

3   Pixel-based image editing

In the preceding chapter, we delved into the creation of photographs and how to capture the most compelling imagery. However, even when you manage to snap the perfect photograph, you may need to make some adjustments in an image-editing program. Knowing how to edit photographic images is essential for anyone who is trying to communicate a specific message on any of the multitudes of platforms used by advertisers, marketers, and strategic communicators.

In this chapter we will cover the essential elements of photographic image manipulation which includes understanding how to adjust color balance and contrast, eliminate unwanted elements, and add special effects. We will also explore the basics of image sizing and resolution.

While image editing is an essential skill for appropriately sizing your images and improving the look of your photos, it can also be used to create images that do not exist in reality. "Photoshopped" images have raised ethical questions as image manipulation can be used to mislead people into believing something untrue. It is important for media producers to use image editing responsibly and ethically, ensuring that the image is not misleading or false. Image editing should be used to enhance, rather than distort, the truth of an image.

The evolution of image editing

Image editing has come a long way since the early days of photography. In the past, photographers would manually manipulate negatives in darkrooms to achieve desired effects and retouch photographs with paint and airbrushing. But, with the advent of digital technology, image editing has become much more accessible and sophisticated. Today, anyone with a computer can edit photographic images using various software programs such as Adobe Photoshop.

Adobe Photoshop has become synonymous with image editing. It is the most widely used software for image manipulation and compositing, with a substantial range of tools and features that allow for precise editing. While

DOI: 10.4324/9781003462200-3

there are now some powerful alternatives available, it is still the leading program of its kind, and its invention marks the origin of digital image editing.

Photoshop was conceived in 1987 by Thomas and John Knoll, who were both students at the University of Michigan. They were inspired to create a program that would allow them to display grayscale images on a computer display. When looking for investor, they caught the attention of a company called Barneyscan, which had invented a new machine called a Barneyscanner that "could make digital copies from 35mm slides and display them on the screen of a Macintosh computer" ("The Time-Travelling Camera: A Short History of Digital Photo Manipulation" 2021). Their scanner wasn't as well received by consumers as they had hoped because photographers "couldn't do much with the photos digitized with the scanner" (Zhang 2018). Executives at Barneyscan saw Photoshop as a solution for allowing consumers to edit their scanned slides, so they stuck a deal with the Knoll brothers who received royalties for the sale of their product which came bundled with the scanner.

Fortunately for the Knolls, the licensing deal that they made with Barneyscan allowed them to retain the rights to the software and shortly thereafter they presented their idea to Adobe co-founder John Warnock, who was impressed and decided to purchase the license from the brothers. The first version of Photoshop was released in 1990 (which coincided closely with the advent of the first consumer-level digital camera), and it has been continuously updated and improved since then ("The History of Photoshop" 2023).

As digital imagery became more commonplace (sourced initially from scanned material then eventually from digital cameras), and computer processing power increased, Photoshop became a more pervasive image-editing tool used across industries. Although it remains an essential tool for photographers, graphic designers, and anyone working with digital images there are now several clones and competitors.

Digital photographic images

Before we delve into the techniques of image editing, it is essential to understand the basics of digital photographic images. A digital photographic image is a two-dimensional representation of an object or scene created using pixels (picture elements). If you zoom in far enough when previewing a digital photographic image on your computer screen, you'll see that your image is like a mosaic formed by small tiles, which are called pixels. A pixel can be only one color. The more pixels that you have in an image, the better the resolution and, therefore, the quality of the image. Because digital photographic images are comprised of pixels, they are often called pixel-based images or bitmap images or raster images.

Properties of pixel-based images

Before you start editing pixel-based images, you should have a good understanding of their unique properties and how you intend to use the image. The settings you choose in your editing process should be dictated by the specific end use of the image. One major factor that will dramatically affect how you edit your image is whether you will be using the image for print or online. Images intended to be viewed on a screen have different properties from those used in print. Another factor is the specific online platform in which an image is to be used. Different ones have different proportion and size requirements.

Proportion

Images used in different contexts are required to be specific proportions. For example, Instagram images are usually 1:1 (square), while Facebook cover photos are 16:9. When preparing your images for these uses, you must ensure that the proportions of the image are accurate or else your image will appear distorted.

Most image editing programs will have some type of cropping tool where you can specify your target proportion while making your crop. The program will then only allow you to make selections in this configuration to ensure your resulting image is accurately proportioned.

Resolution

Image resolution is a critical aspect of image editing, fundamentally influencing the quality and clarity of the finished product. Measured in DPI (dots per inch), resolution refers to the number of dots or pixels along a linear edge of an image. A one inch by one inch, 300 dpi image contains 900,000 pixels whereas a 1 inch by 1 inch 72 dpi image only contains 5184 pixels. As you might imagine, the 300dpi image is going to be very crisp and clear, but its file size will be quite large.

High-resolution images, often required for print media, typically have a resolution of 300 DPI, ensuring fine details are captured for a sharp, high-quality print result. In contrast, images intended for screen viewing typically require a lower resolution of around 72–96 DPI. This is due to the pixel density of standard computer, tablet, and smartphone screens. Saving images intended for screen viewing at a higher resolution than necessary can result in larger file sizes without any perceptible increase in image quality, potentially slowing down webpage loading times and negatively impacting the user experience. Website owners who want to optimize their site for search engines pay close attention to image file size as "images are often the largest contributor to overall page size," and therefore page load time. And Google favors sites with fast load times ("Google

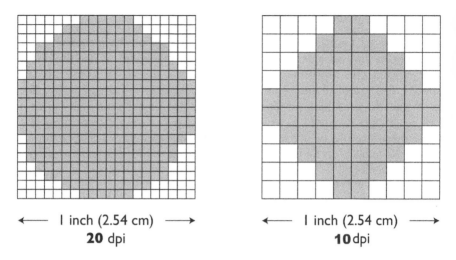

←—— I inch (2.54 cm) ——→   ←—— I inch (2.54 cm) ——→
20 dpi   **10** dpi

Figure 3.1 Higher resolution images can represent more precise detail

Image SEO Best Practices" n.d.). Therefore, understanding and correctly adjusting image resolution based on the intended use is a crucial skill in image editing.

Color mode

Understanding the difference between CMYK and RGB color modes is also fundamental. CMYK stands for cyan, magenta, yellow, and key (black) and is used primarily in print media. This is a subtractive color model, meaning the colors get darker as more colors are added, simulating the way inks blend on paper. On the other hand, RGB, which stands for red, green, and blue, is an additive color model used for on-screen images, where colors get brighter as more are added, imitating the way light combines to produce various colors. In an RGB image, colors are produced by mixing light, which means a wider color gamut (or range of colors) can be achieved, making it ideal for digital platforms. Conversely, a CMYK image is produced by mixing pigments, which has a narrower color gamut. Therefore, when you are working in an image-editing program to create images for the screen, you should always be working in RGB color mode. If you are working on an image for print, and thus in CMYK mode, you want to avoid using out-of-gamut colors which are colors that may look fine on a computer screen but can never be achieved by the four printing inks (cyan, magenta, yellow, and black).

Bit depth

Bit depth is often referred to as "color depth" or "pixel depth." It is the number of bits used to represent each pixel in an image. A bit is a number that is either one or zero. When you have one bit you can represent two different possibilities:

one or zero. With two bits there are four possibilities. The higher the bit depth, the more colors can be represented and the better the image quality. Most digital images have a bit depth of 8 bits per color channel: red, green, and blue. With eight bits you can represent 256 different levels of each color channel: red, green, and blue. And the net result is that you can produce over 16 million different colors total ($256 \times 256 \times 256 = 16,777,26$ different colors).

Some image formats support 16 bits per color channel which adds exponentially more potential colors (281 trillion). If you are editing images for high-quality printing, it makes sense to edit your images in this higher bit depth. However, if you are saving an image that will only be viewed on a screen, you will definitely want to reduce the bit depth to 8 bits per color before saving.

Image format

When preparing your digital images for print or web, selecting the correct image format is critical. But, before we get into the nitty gritty of different image formats, one major difference between formats you should be aware of is the type of compression it supports: lossy or lossless. Lossy compression is where the file size of the image is reduced by removing some information. This can result in a lower-quality image, but also a smaller file size. On the other hand, lossless compression preserves all of your original image data, so there is no change to quality or resolution (it will be a larger file size than its lossy counterpart though).

For print, TIFF (Tagged Image File Format) is widely recognized as the gold standard due to its high quality and lossless compression, preserving all the details of the original image. However, this results in a larger file size, which is less of an issue for print but would be problematic for web use. In addition, web browsers do not support TIFF images.

For web use, JPEG (Joint Photographic Experts Group) and PNG (Portable Network Graphics) images are most common. JPEGs are ideal for complex images like photographs, allowing for a balance between image quality and file size through adjustable compression rates. JPEGs achieve a smaller file size via lossy compression which means that information within the image is discarded when it is saved as a JPEG. If you save an image as a JPEG with a large amount of compression, you cannot open it and improve the quality by retrieving the information that was lost.

Another popular file format used in screen-based media is PNG. PNGs excel in preserving transparency and are excellent for simpler images with fewer colors, such as logos or icons. This is because PNG compression is lossless so the file size is typically not as small as a JPG. Unlike JPG files, PNGs support transparency. Therefore, if you want areas of your image to be transparent, PNG format is a good option.

Another web-friendly file format is a GIF (Graphics Interchange Format). GIF files will only display up to 256 colors total, so they can be used for simple images with fewer colors. Like the PNG file format, they also support areas of transparency. Another fun feature of the GIF image format is animation, which is perfect for creating dynamic images to use on websites, marketing emails, or social media. We will discuss animated GIFs in greater detail in a later chapter.

The WEBP image format, developed by Google, is another option that is optimized for web use. This format combines the best features of JPEG and PNG file types. Similar to JPEG, WebP offers efficient compression algorithms, ensuring high-quality images while maintaining relatively small file sizes. Like PNG, WebP supports transparency, making it a versatile choice for web designers. Furthermore, WebP also supports animation, akin to the GIF format. Its superior compression and quality characteristics make it an excellent choice for modern web applications, although its usage may be limited by the fact that not all web browsers currently support WebP.

Fortunately, all of these aforementioned image formats are quite common. Almost any image-editing software will allow you to save your edited image in any of these formats at resolutions suitable for print or screen.

Manipulating pixels in a pixel-based image

When you take a picture from a digital camera, or obtain a digital image from another source, your image has a certain number of pixels distributed in a certain way. But for different types of projects, you often need your images to be different proportions and different resolutions. As we discussed earlier, you can easily crop out a portion of your image at a specific proportion and specify your desired resolution.

Usually, when you crop out portions of an image, you are asking the computer to discard the pixels you don't need. Anytime you get rid of excess pixels, you are downsampling. Another instance of downsampling is when you lower an image's resolution while maintaining its physical size. For example, if you needed to use some product pictures from a print catalog with a resolution of 300 dpi on the web at 72 dpi, and want to keep them the same physical size, you would need to downsample the image.

Upsampling is the opposite of downsampling. It is increasing the resolution an image and adding pixels. There is never a good reason to upsample an image. In order to increase the resolution of an image, the computer needs to generate more pixels. For as clever as computers can be, they don't do a great job at figuring out what pixels to generate. Image-editing software will allow you to upsample an image, and although it will technically be higher resolution, it will not look crisp and clear. It's impossible to increase the quality of an image via upsampling.

Another manipulation you may need to do is to change the resolution of an image while keeping the same number of pixels in an image. If you increase the resolution of an image and want to keep the pixel count the same, you will need to make the physical size of the image smaller. Image-editing programs will allow you to see how you are changing (or not changing) the overall number of pixels when you edit your image size.

Sourcing pixel-based images

Taking your own photographs (or hiring someone to take them for you) is one way of obtaining images that you can use for various marketing and promotion pieces. However, using your own photographs is not always feasible. For example, what if you need an image of an ocean wave but you live in the middle of the country? When you find yourself in this type of situation, your best bet is to get an image from a stock image site.

It is never a good idea to use a random image you find in a Google Images search in your professional work. If you take an image from a Google search and use it in your work, the owner of the image may come after you. It is not uncommon for stock image companies to contact individuals who use their images without permission and/or without paying for them and demand payment. If you are on a budget, always respect copyright and look for free images or royalty-free images whenever possible. Additionally, you should always make sure to give credit to any image creators that allowed you to use their work in your project.

There are several royalty-free stock photo websites such as Shutterstock, iStockPhoto, FreePix, Pond5, Yay Images, Dreamstime, 123RF, and many others. A quick Google search will also yield a wide variety of royalty-free images. The images on these sites are tagged with keywords, so if you are searching for an image of an ocean wave, you should have a wide variety of results. Once you select one, oftentimes the sites will display additional images that are similar in nature to the one you have selected.

Some issues to be aware of when comparing stock image databases:

- Some sites offer individual downloads for purchase, some offer subscriptions where you can download a certain number of images per month or year, and some offer both.
- Some stock image sites work on a credit system, where you can purchase credits for downloads.
- The quality of the photos is not always equal on every stock image site. Before investing in a subscription, be sure to assess the quality of the images available.
- Some images have different levels of permission associated with them. So be sure that you have the appropriate rights for your end use.
- Some images may be available on multiple stock image sites. If you are planning on using a stock image in your advertising or branding, you may want to do a reverse image search on Google to see where else it has been used.

Always make sure that you are following the terms outlined by each provider when using their stock imagery to ensure that your project does not get flagged for copyright violation.

Pixel-based image-editing software

Oftentimes you will want to manipulate or enhance an image to achieve an optimal look. This is when you need to use an image-editing program. Typically, Adobe Photoshop is recommended for image editing, but it can be a bit pricey for a hobbyist or a solopreneur. Fortunately, there are several other programs you can use to edit your images that have similar features to Photoshop, some of which are even free.

In the corporate world, however, you should expect to see Adobe Photoshop, and for many positions you will be expected to know how to use it, as it is the leading professional image-editing program and the flagship program in Adobe's Creative Cloud. This powerful program contains a collection of tools and features that allow users to manipulate images for web, print, and video production. You can use it to perform simple tasks such as cropping or resizing images to more complex edits like removing blemishes from a photo, adjusting the color balance and contrast, or adding special effects. But, because it so comprehensive, it may be a bit overwhelming for a casual user.

If you need image-editing capabilities and Photoshop is not in your budget, consider using a free alternative like GIMP (GNU Image Manipulation Program). GIMP is an excellent alternative to Adobe Photoshop for digital image editing tasks, offering a wide array of tools that allow you to manipulate images, including color adjustment, cropping, resizing, and adding special effects. Its key strength lies in its open-source nature, making it freely accessible to all, and its functionality can be extended further with a vast range of plugins. Additionally, GIMP supports a variety of file formats, including JPEG, PNG, TIFF, and even Photoshop's native PSD files. While its interface might feel less polished than Photoshop's, its extensive tutorial database can help beginners and intermediate users navigate the software and leverage its powerful features. GIMP stands as a robust and cost-effective solution for both basic and complex image editing tasks.

Photopea.com is an online image-editing platform that serves as another good alternative to Adobe Photoshop, especially for users who don't want to install another program on their computer and are on a budget. Photopea operates directly in your web browser, eliminating the need for hefty downloads or installations. One of its standout features is its compatibility with various file formats, including PSD files, enabling users to open and edit Photoshop files without needing the actual software. While it may not have the extensive feature set of Photoshop, it still boasts a wide array of tools for common tasks such as cropping, resizing, color adjustment, and layer manipulation. Its interface is nearly identical to Adobe Photoshop, but

Figure 3.2 Editing the same image in Photoshop (left) and Photopea.com (right)

because it runs inside of a browser and the free version features omnipresent advertising on the sidebars, it can be a little disorienting and distracting. Nevertheless, its convenience and cost-effectiveness make it a valuable tool for digital image-editing tasks.

Canva is another exceptional tool for digital image manipulation, particularly for those seeking a user-friendly platform. Like Photopea.com, it's entirely web-based. But, unlike Photopea.com (as well as Photoshop or GIMP), Canva is primarily a graphic compositing tool, focusing on integrating bitmap images with text and other graphic elements. It does not have the extensive editing capabilities of Photoshop or even GIMP or Photopea. But what Canva does offer is an expansive library of templates, fonts, and images intended to assist image editors with less design experience. Users can manipulate elements like color, size, and layout, and can also upload their own images for editing. Its drag-and-drop interface makes it easy to use. The downside to Canva is that unless you pay for a subscription, some design templates and fonts are restricted. Export options are limited as well on a free plan. Nevertheless, Canva is a great choice for basic image-editing tasks and we will dive into its compositing capabilities in a subsequent chapter.

Common image-editing tasks

Image-editing programs allow you to enhance and transform pixel-based images in many different ways. Basic tasks typically include cropping, which trims an image down to focus on a particular area or subject, and resizing, which alters the dimensions of the image to fit specific requirements. Color correction is another prevalent task, which involves adjusting the hue, saturation, and brightness to improve the overall color balance and make the image more visually striking. Other common tasks include removing unwanted elements from an image, retouching to correct blemishes or imperfections, enhancing the contrast or brightness of an image or an area of an image. Many of these tasks are required in order to achieve a suitable image for a particular platform or medium as they often require specific formats and sizes for the optimal viewing experience. While Photoshop is being referenced below as the tool for these types of edits, keep in mind that other programs have similar tools and even use the same language to describe each of the tasks.

Cropping images

One of the most common tasks done in image-editing programs is cropping. Cropping an image involves changing the size or shape of an image by eliminating certain elements in order to focus attention on a particular area. It can be used to enhance the impact of a photograph or graphic, as well as remove any unnecessary distractions from within the frame. The Crop tool can be used to select and reshape your image frame if you create a crop area that is a different proportion from your original image.

To use the crop tool in most image-editing programs, you simply select it and click and drag around the area of the image that you want to keep. You get a preview of the selected crop area before you confirm it. If you would like your cropped area to be a specific proportion or resolution, you can specify these settings prior to using the tool.

Resizing images

Resizing images in any image-editing program is a fairly straightforward process. If you are using Photoshop, you would simply open the image you wish to resize and navigate to the "Image" menu at the top of the screen, then select "Image Size" from the dropdown menu, which will open a new dialog box. In this dialog box, you'll see fields for "Width" and "Height," allowing you to specify the dimensions of your image. It's important to ensure that the "Constrain Proportions" box is checked to maintain the original aspect ratio of the image, preventing it from becoming distorted. After entering your desired dimensions, click "OK," and Photoshop will resize your image. If you want to preserve the original file, be sure to save your work under a new name.

Color and contrast adjustments

Photoshop (as well as the other image-editing programs) offers various tools and techniques to enhance the overall look of digital images. One of the most common adjustments is the brightness and contrast settings which you can adjust with a simple set of sliders. For more precise manipulations, you can use the "Levels" and "Curves" options, found under the "Adjustments" menu. These tools allow for detailed control over the tonality and color balance of an image, adjusting its highlights, midtones, and shadows. The "Color Balance" adjustment, on the other hand, modifies the color mix in the entire image, making it possible to give a warm or cool tone to your image. The "Hue/Saturation" adjustment enables you to change the hue (color), saturation (intensity of color), and lightness of the entire image or of individual colors within the image. The Selective Color tool provides the ability to precisely adjust specific colors in an image. For instance, you can effortlessly fine-tune the reds in a picture using this tool, without impacting other colors present. This allows for greater control and customization of the image's color composition. Lastly, the Color Lookup tool is a powerful feature that enables you to apply stunning color grades to your images. By utilizing predefined lookup tables, you can enhance your images with unique and captivating looks. It is somewhat like Instagram filters but with many more options. To access this tool, simply navigate to Image > Adjustments > Color Lookup.

If you want to apply a different amount of an adjustment to different areas of your image or you want to be able to turn the adjustment on or off, you can do so using an adjustment layer. In Photoshop, these adjustment layers are found under the "Layer" menu. The options mimic what you would see under the Image > Adjust menu, but you are applying them through the context of a layer mask. This makes the adjustment non-destructive because you can easily remove the layer mask to return to your unadjusted version of your image. Another neat feature of layer masks is that you can apply a gradient to the mask. So, if you wanted to apply a greater degree of color correction to one part of your image than another, you can specify variable strengths of the mask to different parts of the image. For example, you could use an adjustment layer to darken the sky in a landscape photograph without affecting the trees or other elements of the scene.

If you are looking for a quick and easy way to color correct your image in a manner similar to an Instagram filter, check out some of Canva's filters. This is one of the ways in which Canva excels in its image-adjustment capabilities. Just upload your image to Canva and apply one of the built-in filters. Canva even allows you to control the sensitivity of the filter effect while also allowing you to add in more standard color correction techniques like enhancing the brightness and contrast.

Retouching

Retouching in Photoshop is a skillful process that can help improve the appearance of an image or remove unwanted elements. This technique is often used in portrait photography to enhance the subject's features or to remove blemishes and other distractions. Tools such as the "Spot Healing Brush," "Patch," and "Clone Stamp" are frequently employed for retouching purposes. For instance, the "Spot Healing Brush" works by replacing the selected area with pixels from the surrounding area, making it an excellent tool for quick fixes on small areas. The "Patch" tool allows you to select

Figure 3.3 Blemishes can be easily retouched using image editing programs

and replace a larger area by matching the texture, lighting, and shading from the sampled pixels. "Clone Stamp," on the other hand, copies pixels from one area and allows you to paint them onto another area, offering more control for detailed retouching.

Removing elements in an image

One of the key features of Photoshop is its ability to selectively remove elements from a digital image. This feature is especially useful when there are unwanted objects or a background within a frame that you want to eliminate. Selecting is required if you want to extract one part of an image and paste it into another. The "Lasso," "Magic Wand," and "Quick Selection" tools are designed for this purpose. The "Lasso" tool lets you draw around the object you wish to remove, creating a selection that matches the shape you drew. But it works in different modes. There is a freeform lasso tool that creates a selection based on how you drag your mouse. The polygonal lasso tool allows you to click around your desired selection. And the magnetic lasso tool creates a selection line close to where you drag your mouse and where it detects areas of highest contrast between pixels. The "Magic Wand," on the other hand, selects areas based on color and tone, which is ideal for removing elements that are relatively uniform in color. The "Quick Selection" tool is apt for larger and more distinct objects; it creates an adjustable round brush which you can use to "paint" over the object, and Photoshop will intelligently select it. Once the object is selected using any of these tools, you can copy and paste the selected area, delete the selected area or do something more creative such as selecting the "Edit > Fill > Content Aware" command which can be used to fill the selected area with surrounding pixels, effectively removing the object while maintaining the background integrity.

As you can see, selections play a major role in Photoshop. You can store selections, invert them, and even smooth them out. If you want to make a selection with a softer edge, you can feather it. By refining the edges of your selection, you can create a more realistic and seamless result. Feathering allows for a smooth transition between the selected area and the rest of the image, making it appear more natural.

Adding text to an image

All pixel-based image-editing programs incorporate a type creation tool. This tool allows you to add text on top of your images using any font installed on your computer. The software will also allow you to customize the text size, font style, color, and alignment.

When adding type, it is important to make sure that the words are legible and readable; this means using an appropriate font size for both desktop and mobile devices. You should also consider the color contrast between your background and text overlays to ensure readability.

Applying filters

Filters within image-editing programs can be used to dramatically change the look of an image. In image-editing programs like Photoshop, however, you have far more control over the look and feel of each filter effect. You can choose from a range of filters, such as "Blur," "Sharpen," "Smudge," and "Diffuse." With each filter, you can adjust the strength, opacity, amount, tolerance, and other parameters to create unique looks for your images. Some of the filters are extreme in their behavior and can turn your image into a charcoal sketch or even an oil painting. Applying the same filter effect to a group of images can be an effective method of creating unity among originally disparate images.

Creating images from filters

Although, in most cases, we start with an image when working in an image-editing program, it's possible to create imagery from a blank canvas. Photoshop and other image-editing programs come with a wide range of filters that can be applied to an empty canvas. These filters are great for creating abstract designs, patterns, and shapes quickly. By experimenting with different combinations of color, opacity, scale, offset, and other parameters associated with each filter effect you can create interesting graphic elements in no time. Furthermore, many of the filter effects can be combined with multiple layers to create more sophisticated abstract images as well as realistic textures.

Exporting images

When saving images for final use, be sure to use the right file format and size as choosing the wrong file format or size can lead to distorted appearance and slow loading times, both of which can detract from your message.

If you are preparing images for a social media channel, research the recommended proportions and resolutions before saving and uploading your image to that platform. If you are generating images for a website or blog, ask the person in charge of the site what is desired proportion, size and format. Oftentimes it is necessary to create a few different sizes and proportions of an image so that a responsive website can display the appropriate one for the device that has accessed the site.

Another consideration is naming convention. Your organization may have a preferred method of naming images to help your team locate them in the future. Sometimes images need to be named in a specific way so that the code in a web page will automatically display them.

Before you export your final image, ensure that you save the higher-resolution version first, even if you only need a lower-resolution version. By doing so, you'll have the advantage of working with a higher-quality image if you need to make further edits. With more pixels at your disposal, you'll have the ability to create more precise and refined edits if you need to do so in the future.

When saving your image in various file formats, you can specify your desired amount of compression. When in doubt, compress your images as much as possible without the image looking any worse (blurry or pixelated). And, if you have your choice of image formats, let the nature of your image dictate the final file format. JPEG files are usually best for photographs while GIFs or PNGs are more suitable for logos (or images with limited number of colors). Understanding the strengths of each type of image format will help you make an informed choice when saving out your resulting image. Image format may also be specified by a client or the platform to which you are uploading the image.

The ethics of image editing

A frequent issue that arises with image editing is that digital image manipulation also allows users to create graphics that don't exist in real life. As with any type of media production, it's important to use these tools responsibly and ethically so as not to mislead viewers or misrepresent reality. Image-editing software should be used to enhance the quality and creativity of images, not manipulate them to deceive or misinform.

It can be a fine line between enhancing the quality of an image versus deceiving people. In product photography, for example, it is common to use image-editing software to retouch small imperfections and enhance the overall appearance. However, it becomes unethical if these edits are used to significantly alter the product's appearance or misrepresent its features. As a retailer you will only hurt yourself by altering your product pictures to an extent that it deceives buyers. When shoppers receive a product that doesn't look like the photograph, they will likely complain and leave negative reviews.

Photojournalists also have a responsibility to accurately represent the events they document and should avoid using image-editing software to manipulate or falsify images. Excessive manipulation of photographic imagery has been grounds for termination which was exactly the fate of a *Los Angeles Times* photographer in 2003 when he combined an image of British soldier with an image of an Iraqi civilian. These two subjects were actually photographed on separate occasions, but he combined them into one composite image because he liked the way they looked (NewsHour 2015). There are some occasions where photo manipulation is considered acceptable in the field of photojournalism. Renowned photojournalist Steve McCurry believes that some photo manipulation is acceptable if "the truth and integrity of the picture [are] maintained" (Laurent 2016).

When editing original images, it is important to consider the potential impact on cultural sensitivities or perpetuating stereotypes. Image-editing tools should not be used to alter an individual's appearance in a way that reinforces harmful societal prejudices. *Time* magazine "ignited a firestorm" when a photographer digitally altered a photograph of O.J. Simpson making him look darker complected than he really was (NewsHour 2015). Be mindful and respectful of the subject matter when working with digital images, especially if they are depicting real people or sensitive issues.

Image-editing missteps cannot only deceive and offend, but they can also discredit your brand and shift the focus from the image's intended message to an editing fail. A prime example of this type of mishap was Kim Kardashian and Kylie Jenner's 2019 Instagram promotion of their new fragrance. Their post was flooded with comments, but not for the reason the entrepreneurs had hoped. Instead of commenting on the fragrance or the brand, viewers couldn't stop mocking the image that had been digitally altered to give each woman an extra toe (Brinsford 2019).

"Anyone can manipulate the truth" by professional photographer Zachary Kaufman

Digital editing tools are practically limitless and highly accessible. Previously, our concerns with over-editing and manipulation were largely based on the actions and intent of the photographer. Now, once a photograph is distributed electronically, anyone can make wholesale edits to the image, and very easily add or subtract content from the original photograph and reshare it. Therefore, the notion that a photograph captures truth, which is something that the medium has enjoyed since its inception, is no longer. Photography is being redefined in this post-truth era.

Study questions

1) List one pro and one con of the four common image formats found on the web: JPG, GIF, PNG, and WEBP.
2) Explain which image-editing tools are free and which ones are not and what it means to be an open-source program.
3) Why is upsampling an image never recommended?
4) Explain why a 5″ x 7″ 150 dpi image does not have twice as many pixels as a 5″ x 7″ image that is 300 dpi.
5) Explain the advantages of adjustment layers.

Exercises

1) You and a partner give each other an assignment to search for a specific image for an imaginary project, e.g., a panda standing on hind legs. Find three legal stock image sources for this image and determine which one is the most affordable.
2) Open an image in Photopea.com and perform all of the editing tasks outlined earlier in this chapter.
3) Explain how Canva is different than Photopea.com.
4) Challenge yourself to remove a mustache from a subject's face. Does your edit look believable? What tools did you use to achieve it?
5) How do you know whether you have the legal right to use an image in a composition or not?

References

Brinsford, James. 2019. "Kim Kardashian and Kylie Jenner Mocked after 'Photoshop Fail Gives Them 6 Toes'; The Keeping Up with the Kardashians Have Had a History of Photoshop Fails and Their Latest Has Left Their Fans Cringing." *Daily Mirror*, August.

"Google Image SEO Best Practices." n.d. Google Search Central. https://developers. google.com/search/docs/appearance/google-images. Accessed May 31, 2024.

Laurent, Oliver. 2016. "Steve McCurry: I'm a Visual Storyteller Not a Photojournalist." *Time*, May 30.

NewsHour, PBS. 2015. "What Happens When Photoshop Goes Too Far?"

"The History of Photoshop." 2023. https://link.gale.com/apps/doc/A772193626/ITOF?u=edenweb_main&sid=ebsco&xid=67321823.

"The Time-Travelling Camera: A Short History of Digital Photo Manipulation." 2021. Science and Media Museum.

Zhang, Michael. 2018. "The Story of How Photoshop Was First 'Barneyscan XP.'" PetaPixel. https://petapixel.com/2018/05/25/the-story-of-how-photoshop-was-first-barneyscan-xp/.

4 Vector-based graphics

Vector-based images are inherently different from pixel-based images. Instead of being comprised of small squares of color, vector image files are made up of points, lines, curves, and shapes that are based on mathematical equations. Because of their unique composition, vector-based graphics have different qualities and uses as well as strengths and weaknesses when compared to pixel-based graphics.

Learning to work with vector-based graphics is crucial for professionals in the field of digital design, marketing, and similar industries. This is largely due to their unique properties and use for so many different purposes and processes. Vector graphics are most commonly used to create logos, illustrations, icons, and other graphic elements for the screen and print. They are also used in animations, games, and even computer-aided design (CAD). As such they play a key role in branding and marketing strategies across various industries.

In this chapter we will discuss what vector-based images are, how they differ from pixel-based images, and delve into their origins and history. We will also discuss their many uses and advantages in different contexts. Lastly, we will explore the essential software utilized in crafting these images, along with the distinctions between vector-based file formats and the optimal scenarios for their application.

What are vector-based graphics?

When you save a vector-based graphic, it is stored on the computer as points and lines and not a collection of individual picture elements (pixels) which means that they tend to be smaller in size than pixel-based images. Imagine an image of a circle that is created and stored as a vector-based graphic. The computer would just need to store the mathematical equation of the circle along with its color. However, if this image of a circle was saved as pixel-based image, the computer would need to store the color information for thousands or even millions of pixels. When it comes to pixel-based images, the computer doesn't care if it's storing colored pixels that produce a colorful photograph or a simple circle; they are all pixels.

DOI: 10.4324/9781003462200-4

Figure 4.1 The Vetrex: a stand-alone video game console that supported vector-based graphics [Jzh2074 / CC BY-SA 4.0 (via Wikimedia Commons)]

Vector-based graphics are a versatile and efficient way to render images composed of flat areas of color and basic shapes. By providing descriptions of points, lines, and shapes, they offer precise control over the final output. However, when it comes to photographic images, which often feature intricate details and a wide range of color variations, vector graphics may not be the most suitable choice. The level of detail and complexity involved in accurately representing photographic images can be better achieved through rendering as pixel-based graphics.

Because vector-based graphics are stored on the computer as mathematical equations, the computer can simply regenerate the graphic at any scale which makes them always look crisp and clean at any size. Since they are scalable without a loss of quality, companies create logos and other brand imagery as vector files so that they can be used on a business card and letterhead, but also on larger surfaces, such as the corporate jet.

Origins of vector-based graphics

The origins of vector-based graphics date back to the emergence of the first computers in the 1940s. Early computers had very limited memory and could not display a pixel-based image. Therefore, vector graphics were the solution for displaying visuals on a computer. In fact, the U.S. Department of Defense used them to create and store mapping data ("The Guide to Vector Design" n.d.).

An MIT computer scientist named Ivan Sutherland is credited with further popularizing vector-based graphics. In 1963, he released the first vector-based graphics program called Sketchpad, which enabled people to draw and manipulate vector graphic line drawings on a computer and "foretold the future of interactive and graphical computing" (Markoff 2023). The program could detect the position of the user's light pen and store the positions and shapes formed by the light pen in the computer as mathematical information. This marked the beginning of widespread use of vector images in computer graphics (Brock 2023).

In the late 1970s, software developers saw the potential in vector-based graphics to create technical drawings for architecture and product design. By the early 1980s the first version of AutoCAD was released which became (and is still to this day) a dominant technical drawing software ("Computer-Aided Design" n.d.).

Another discipline that embraced vector-based graphics is the video-game industry. Some of the earliest video games like Atari's Asteroids, released in 1979, were made possible with vector graphics. The brightly colored blobs on the screen were stored as mathematical equations. The simplicity of the design could be efficiently described with vector graphics and the primitive gaming system was powerful enough to render them fast enough to keep up with game play (Nicoll, 2019, p. 50).

The special properties of vector-based graphics were so appealing to one gaming company that they built an entire gaming console around vector-based graphics technology. The Vectrex, released in 1982, was a unique video-game console developed by General Consumer Electronics. Unlike other consoles that used raster graphics and were connected to televisions, the Vectrex had its own built-in monitor that used an electron gun to create wireframe lines and shapes directly on the screen's surface. In contrast, most video-game consoles plugged into televisions employed "rasterscan" cathode ray tubes (CRTs), where images were painted row-by-row, forming a series of pixels. The Vectrex's innovative use of vector graphics represents a clever implementation of the technology to support quick rendering times required by video games. Interestingly, the Vectrex's packaging of a display with the video-game console marked the first portable all-in-one video game console (Nicoll 2019).

By the 1980s, when personal computers were making their debut, software companies that made programs for these new machines began to develop vector-based drawing programs. These new applications allowed users to draw, manipulate, and store vector images on their own computers instead of mainframe machines. The late 1980s saw the birth of Aldus Freehand (which later

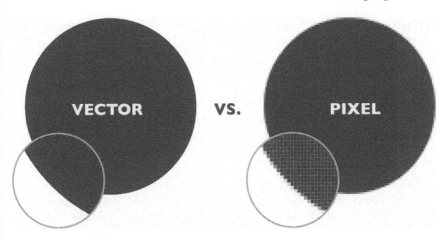

Figure 4.2 Vector vs. pixel-based graphics

became Macromedia Freehand and is now discontinued), Adobe Illustrator, and Corel Draw. Both Corel Draw and Adobe Illustrator are still used today.

Vector-based graphics played a prominent role in the early days of the World Wide Web. The "lightness" of the format seemed well suited for display within a web browser; however, early browsers only supported bitmap image formats like JPGs and GIFs. In the late 1990s, a company called Macromedia released a program entitled Flash which allowed vector graphics to be embedded in webpages. This gave designers the ability to create animation and other interactive elements on websites that were scalable and still looked crisp and clear no matter how large they became. Flash fell out of favor in the early 2010s (shortly after its acquisition by Adobe) as Apple refused to support the technology on their smartphone browsers. They claimed the technology was "a sluggish battery drain, ripe for hacking," which forced web developers to modify their sites and Adobe to reinvent Flash (Bedingfield 2020).

In the late 1990s, the World Wide Web Consortium (W3C) introduced the SVG (scalable vector graphic) format. SVG is an XML-based vector image format that can be used in webpages and other documents. The language allows for a range of graphic elements such as charts, diagrams, text, clippings, and more. It was revolutionary in that it was a non-proprietary vector-based file format. Although it was not initially very well known or popular, it eventually gained support when people began to see the benefit in integrating SVG files within a web page ("SVG Files" n.d.).

Today, vector-based graphics are still used in a variety of applications including graphic design for logos, print media, and technical drawings. They are also frequently used within video game development and 2D and 3D animation software. For modern laser cutting and etching tools, vector-based graphics are the preferred file type.

Vector-based graphic software

When it comes to creating and editing vector-based graphics, there are a variety of software programs available. They range in price from free to a bit pricey. Some of the more popular programs are Adobe Illustrator, Corel Draw, Inkscape, and Vectr.com.

Adobe Illustrator is a flagship vector-based design software used primarily by design professionals. It's a powerful program with a wide range of tools for creating shapes, logos, icons, and more. One of its greatest strengths is that it integrates seamlessly with other Adobe software. For example, if you are using Adobe's page-layout program Adobe InDesign and you want to integrate vector-based graphics, you can import your images in the native Adobe Illustrator file format as opposed to saving the file as something more generic. Any subsequent changes you make to the Illustrator file will be reflected on the embedded file within Adobe InDesign document. Because Adobe Illustrator is part of the Adobe Creative Cloud, and is considered a professional-level graphic program, you should expect to see it being used at most marketing, design, and advertising firms.

Corel Draw is another powerful vector-based design software that has been a staple in the industry for a considerable time. It is widely utilized by professionals and hobbyists alike, although it may not enjoy the same level of popularity as Adobe Illustrator within the design community. While Corel Draw offers comparable functionality to Illustrator, what sets it apart is its user-friendly and intuitive interface, making it an ideal choice for beginners who may find the learning curve less daunting.

An interesting and powerful free and open-source alternative to Adobe Illustrator and Corel Draw is Inkscape. Inkscape, a versatile vector-based graphics editor, offers a wide range of features comparable to its commercial counterparts. Its popularity has soared among hobbyists and students due to its cost-free availability. Moreover, the open-source nature of the program ensures constant evolution, with independent developers consistently crafting new plug-ins to further enhance its capabilities.

Another free alternative for creating vector-based graphics is vectr.com. This is a web-based application that allows users to create vector-based images and share them with others. It's a great way for hobbyists or students to get their feet wet with vector-based graphics without spending any money or installing any software.

Best uses of vector-based graphics

Most designers who create graphics for a living work in both vector-based drawing programs as well as bitmap image editors. Sometimes it's tricky to decide when to use what program. Some projects should always be created in a vector-based drawing tool like logos, icons, typefaces, and illustrations that don't require photographic or textured elements. But sometimes it comes down to personal preference or the style of the project.

Vector-based drawing programs can be used to create other types of projects like posters and flyers for print or web/social media graphics. However, the style of project should dictate the type of software that is used. A composition that is photographically based would more easily be made in Photoshop. Or you could do all your image compositing in Photoshop, then bring it in to Illustrator to add the type on top of the image as Illustrator has more sophisticated type-manipulation tools than Photoshop.

Some designers use Adobe Illustrator for interface design. An interface design is a mockup of key screens within an interactive application (website, app, etc.). These graphics are given to developers to provide a visual direction. Adobe offers another program, Adobe XD, that interfaces nicely with Adobe Illustrator, specifically for the purpose of visualizing interactive applications. An interface or user experience designer can import vector-based completed screens or graphic elements into Adobe XD and from there build a prototypical interactive application.

Another use for vector-based graphics is in character design. Adobe Illustrator as well as other vector-based drawing programs are powerful tools to create comic-book art and animation. A vector-based illustration imports seamlessly into a vector-based animation program such as Adobe Animate or Toon Boom Harmony. Characters and props drawn in vector-based drawing programs can also be imported into a game-making application like Unreal Engine or Unity.

Vector-based graphics have become highly coveted by people who own Cricut and laser-cutting and etching machines. These machines are equipped with a knives or lasers that cut out shapes from cardstock or other material or etch designs into plastic, glass, or wood. The mathematical precision of the vector-based art provides clear and efficient cutting and etching instructions. If the operator knows how to create vector-based graphics they can have these machines cut and etch out their own, original art.

Another use for vector-based graphics is as a starting point for a 3D model. You can simply import your vector-based graphic into a 3D modeling software like Blender and use it to build a three-dimensional shape. One typical operation is an extrusion where you add thickness to the two-dimensional shape. Another common modeling task that begins with a 2D vector-graphic is to do a rotation where you build a 3D model by rotating a profile around a center. A classic example of this type of model is a martini glass as it possesses the rotational symmetry that could be reproduced using this technique. After you use your 2D vector-based graphic as a basis for your 3D model, it works like any other three-dimensional model. It can then be used in games, in a 3D animation or turned into a physical object by 3D printing it.

With native support for vector-based graphics in web browsers, they now play a more significant role in web-based interactive content. These graphics can serve as static visual elements or be manipulated through user interaction. Just imagine having a color slider beneath your vector-based graphic, allowing you to change its color as you move your mouse. This can easily be achieved using JavaScript, a client-side scripting language that can detect the user's mouse position and dynamically adjust the vector graphic's parameters accordingly. By harnessing the power of JavaScript and vector-based graphics, developers can create captivating visualizations, games, and artistic experiences that run seamlessly within web browsers.

Tools and techniques used in vector-based drawing programs

While different software programs may use different names and interfaces, the fundamental principles underlying the concepts, tools, and techniques employed in the creation and modification of vector-based graphics remain consistent. The following concepts are commonly used in vector-based drawing programs.

Vector objects

At the core of vector-based graphics is the concept of a "vector object." A vector object consists of lines and curves (paths) that are connected to form a closed or open shape.

Strokes and fills

Every shape or line in a vector-based drawing program can either have a stroke, a fill, both, or none. Fills are the inside of a vector-based graphic and can be solid colors, gradients, or patterns. Strokes can vary in thickness and can be a simple straight line, a dashed line, or even a patterned line. When an object has no stroke or fill applied to it, it still exists—it is just invisible.

Layers

The order in which you create objects in a vector-based drawing program dictates their stacking order. More recent objects appear in the foreground. Of course, you can easily change that stacking order, but complex illustrations can be comprised of a lot of objects which can be challenging to arrange. For this reason, vector-based drawing programs allow users to place shapes on different layers which can then be grouped and organized together. This makes it easier to work with intricate drawings by allowing you to focus on one layer at a time or to move entire layers in front or behind other layers.

Transformations

Every vector-based drawing program will allow you to transform your objects in many ways. There are tools that facilitate moving, rotating, scaling,

reflecting, and distorting your objects. It's also possible transform and duplicate at the same time. Imagine creating a flower by drawing one petal and
then rotating the petal around a center point and duplicating it at the same
time. It would be a quick way to generate a lot of petals around a common
origin point.

Primitives

Primitives are basic shapes that you can draw quickly and easily without having
to freehand them. Common primitives include circles, squares, polygons, and
stars. Once the primitive is drawn, it can then be distorted or manipulated in
some way using the transformation tools.

Drawing

Vector-based drawing programs naturally have many different drawing tools
that allow you to create both open and closed shapes that are more complex
than basic primitives. Most vector-based drawing software offers a variety of
freeform drawing tools like pencils and brushes. However, you can also draw
in a more controlled manner using a pen tool where you click and drag to
establish anchor points (points that are on the path) and handles (lines that
dictate the shape of the curve). These types of paths are often described as
"bezier curves."

Editing shapes and paths

Regardless of the tool you used to create the object, everything you create in
a vector-based drawing program can be manipulated by moving the anchor
points or the handles. This allows you to fine tune the shape of your object.
You can also add and remove anchor points and change curve points to corner
points and vice versa. There are also more basic object-editing tools such as
the scissors (to cut objects) and the eraser (to remove a portion of an object).

Align and distribute

Alignment tools allow you to quickly align multiple objects relative to each
other in a variety of ways. This can be useful for creating complex symmetrical designs or arranging objects on a page in an organized manner. Distribute tools are used when you want to create equal amounts of space between
a series of elements.

Boolean operations

Boolean operations are a way of combining or subtracting two shapes to create one new shape. You can use these tools for creating complex shapes from
simple ones, and you can also use them to delete sections of the object that

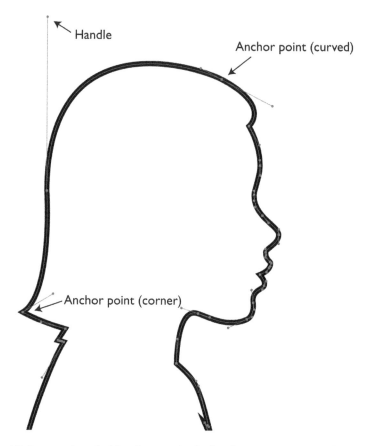

Handle

Anchor point (curved)

Anchor point (corner)

Figure 4.3 A vector-based object is comprised of anchor points and handles

you don't want. Let's say for example, you wanted to draw a bullet shape. You could align a rectangle and circle horizontally with the circle at the top of the rectangle. Then you would simply union the two objects together to make a bullet shape.

Text

Vector-based programs also allow you to add text to your designs. You can adjust the font, size, color, kerning, tracking, and leading of your text. You can also manipulate the shape of the lettering by distorting it or setting it on a path. If you are integrating text within a design and you want that design to be printed, it's always a good idea to convert the text to outlines prior to sending your design to the printer. Turning your text into outlines will prevent the text from being edited; however, it ensures that the shapes of your letters will not change. If you leave the text as text and your printer does not have the font you used, the software will replace your font with whatever it thinks is the closest similar font which may not look the way you want it to look.

Vector-based file formats

Compared to pixel-based graphics, vector-based images do not come in as many different file formats. The most common ones are AI (Adobe Illustrator), CDR (Corel Draw), EPS (Encapsulated Postscript), PDF (Portable Document Format), and SVG (Scalable Vector Graphics).

The two leading vector-based drawing programs, Adobe Illustrator and Corel Draw, each have their own proprietary file format: AI for Adobe Illustrator files and CDR for Corel Draw files. If you are a user of these programs, it's absolutely fine and expected that you would save your illustrations in these formats. Saving your work in one of these formats ensures that the full features of the illustration stay intact. For example, an AI file can contain embedded typefaces, color swatches, and other elements that may not be retained if the illustration is saved in another format. Fortunately, when it comes to AI files, you can open and reference them in other Adobe Programs. But, if your intended audience is not an Adobe Creative Cloud user, you will need to save your work in a more universal file format.

The EPS (Encapsulated Postscript) format was originally created by Adobe as a universal vector-based image format. The intention was to allow users of different design programs to share files without worrying about compatibility issues. For example, a printer who is not using Adobe Creative Cloud may request an EPS version of your file. If you are trying to import your illustration into another non-Creative Cloud program, you may need to convert your file to EPS. The EPS file format is not as common as it used to be. PDF and SVG files have really taken over as the go-to generic vector-based graphic file formats.

PDF files (Portable Document Format) are becoming increasingly popular as a type of vector-based file format. This is due to their ability to include both raster and vector elements and the fact that they can be easily shared between different programs and platforms. They can also be viewed within a web browser. A drawback of PDF files for vector-based images is that they don't have full support for transparency effects. Nevertheless, PDF files are a great way to share your vector-based illustrations with others.

The SVG (Scalable Vector Graphic) format was introduced by the World Wide Web Consortium in 1998 as an XML-based vector image format that could be used on webpages and other documents. It is a universal file format that supports transparency, text, and animation effects. SVG files are the only vector-based file format that can be used within a web or mobile application due to its ability to work with HTML5 and other programming languages.

Vector to pixel and pixel to vector conversion

Converting a vector-based graphic to pixels (also known as rasterizing) is necessary if you need to use the image in an environment where vector images are not supported. This could include integration on certain parts of web-pages, or to embed within specific applications that only support pixel-based images, or for certain types of post-production processes. The conversion of a vector-based graphic to a pixel-based image is quite simple. One way is to simply open the vector-based file in a pixel-based image-editing programs like Adobe Photoshop. The program will either convert it to pixels at any size you desire or retain the vector-based properties of the image, put it on its own layer, and integrate it into the image composition. Another way to convert a vector-based image to a pixel-based image is to export it as a bitmap graphic directly from the vector-based drawing program.

The opposite process of converting a pixel-based graphic to a vector-graphic is often not as easy. This is because many pixel-based images don't lend themselves well to being described with vectors. Some programs like Adobe Illustrator will attempt to do this with their "Live Trace" tool, but it is often a hit-or-miss process. Naturally, the simplest images to convert from pixels to vectors are ones with minimal numbers of colors and simple shapes.

Sometimes the easiest (and only) solution for converting pixels back into vectors is to redraw the image yourself in a vector-based program. This may take longer to accomplish, but you are guaranteed that your result will be accurate and ready for production. If you use the auto trace feature to create a vector-based graphic from a pixel-based graphic, you may notice that the bitmap tracing tools generate an excessive number of vertices when creating the vector-based graphic. It may look acceptable at certain sizes, but if you scale it up, the borders could look very jagged. This is another reason why you may want to redraw the vector-based graphic yourself.

Design tips when creating vector-based graphics

Having a solid understanding of how to effectively utilize the tools in a vector-based drawing program is undoubtedly crucial. However, it is merely the initial phase in crafting a vector-based graphic that aligns with your specific requirements. In order to elevate your vector-based designs to align with your communication goals, a bit of design strategy goes a long way.

Logo design

While most companies hire professional designers to create logos, it is possible for a hobbyist or budding designer to create their own logo in a vector-based program. The goal of a logo is to visually communicate the essence of the company, organization, or product it represents. It is usually a combination of the name and some type of graphic element. Sounds simple, right? It is, but designing a *good* logo can be challenging.

A good logo should possess several key qualities. Firstly, it should be simple, eschewing intricate details for a design that can be easily recognized at a glance. This simplicity also ensures that the logo remains recognizable across various sizes and mediums. Secondly, it should be versatile, functioning well in monochrome as well as in color, and looking just as striking on a business card as on a large billboard. A good logo is also unique and creative, setting the brand apart from its competitors and making it memorable to the target audience. Lastly, it should be timeless, retaining its relevance and appeal over the years, even as trends change.

To achieve these lofty goals, you need to have a deep understanding of the industry, the brand's identity, and the intended audience. Visual research can be a helpful strategy when you are trying to create a logo. It involves studying the logos of other companies in similar industries and pinpointing design elements that resonate with you. This can help guide your own logo creation process by giving you a better idea of what works well in terms of aesthetics, messaging, and overall impact. You may also notice logo design commonalities within the industry that you can either embrace or ignore.

A productive next step in the logo development process is to make some rough sketches. It may be tempting to jump right into your vector-based drawing program, but sketching will help you home in on some ideas and prevent you from staring into a blank computer screen. Once you have some concepts on paper that look interesting, you can bring them into your vector-based drawing program and start recreating your concept using the drawing tools within the program.

Be mindful of the shapes and typography you use within your logo as it should be appropriate for the brand it's representing. Would you use Comic Sans for a law-firm logo? I wouldn't think so. Also, any shape or iconography within the logo should also be brand appropriate. Would pointy aggressive shapes be appropriate for a spa's logo? Probably not. After you land on appropriate text and shapes or icons, think about ways in which they can be seamlessly integrated. Could a representative symbol replace one of the letters in the organization's name? Think about ways in which you can combine letters and shapes to make a simple yet visually distinct logo.

When finalizing the logo design, critically think about size, shape, and detail. Because a logo will be used at multiple sizes, it's important to consider how the details of your design will look when scaled up or down. Imagine if your logo incorporated a giraffe with the name of the company running through the middle of the giraffe's body. In order for the logo to fit on a business card, the giraffe would need to be scaled down quite a bit which would make the text very small and possibly not legible at that scale.

Color selection is a crucial factor to consider in logo design. The colors used in a logo not only define the brand's visual identity but also convey meaning that can resonate with audiences. Colors carry inherent symbolism, and it becomes important to align these meanings with the brand's values and message. For instance, in Western culture, the color green often symbolizes money and health. Therefore, if you were tasked with designing a logo for a financial institution, incorporating green into the design would likely be appropriate as it would evoke a sense of financial stability and trust. In other parts of the world, green is associated with disease, so it would be a terrible color choice for health-related logos in that culture.

By carefully considering the shapes, type choice, and colors, designers can create logos that effectively communicate the desired message and connect with their target audience on a deeper level. It may take many iterations to arrive at a satisfactory logo design. Keep in mind that the more options you explore, the more likely you will be to come up with an effective logo.

Flyer and poster design

A vector-based drawing program is an excellent choice when designing a flyer or poster if the intended look is non-photo-realistic. But, before you even get started working in the software, you should have absolute clarity about the purpose of the piece you are making. Think about the last time you looked at a flyer or a poster. How long did you study it before moving on? Probably not very long. This is why developing an information hierarchy is important. An information hierarchy is a design strategy of making the most important piece of information most prominent, the second-most important piece of information less prominent and so on. The idea is that, if the most important piece of information catches a viewer's attention, then they will seek further information within the piece.

But how do you get a passerby to look at the poster in the first place? The use of striking imagery, unusual scale, unconventional colors and patterns are all design techniques that could be employed to catch a viewer's attention. Also, think about the context in which the flyer will be posted. What do the surrounding flyers tend to look like? What would be striking within this context?

Since the objective of a flyer or poster is to convey information, it is critical for the text to be readable. Decorative type styles, very small text, and poor contrast between the text and the background impair the legibility of your flyer or poster.

Advertisements

If you plan to use a vector-based drawing program to create an online or print ad, you'll need to keep a few things in mind. First, you want to think about how much space is available and what proportion of that space will be. Advertising platforms like Facebook will provide standards for dimensions. Then set your document size accordingly in your software.

To help guide the design of your ad, ask yourself what the key message should be and what you want your viewer to do? Online ads should have a clear call to action, e.g., sign up, enroll, buy now. Clearly and efficiently communicate the product or service being offered with minimal text, within a visually interesting and engaging design. In addition, the aforementioned tips pertaining to an information hierarchy as well as type legibility apply here as well.

Oftentimes companies create a series of ads for a campaign. If you plan to communicate a similar message in advertisements across multiple publications, consider how you can make them visually cohesive with consistent typography, color, and layout so that viewers can associate the message with the same brand.

Infographics

An infographic is a visual representation of information or data, using elements such as charts, graphs, and images to present complex information in a concise and engaging manner. They are often created in vector-based drawing programs due to their frequent use of iconography, simple illustrations, charts, and graphs. These graphics are becoming increasingly popular due to their ability to make complex information more understandable and visually appealing.

Infographics are widely used across various industries and fields for their ability to condense complex data into a highly digestible and visually appealing format. They are often found in business reports, academic research, marketing materials, and news articles to aid in the comprehension of intricate data or processes. The effectiveness of infographics stems from their ability to leverage visual learning; by converting numerical or text-based data into visual elements, they facilitate rapid understanding and engagement. With the surge in digital media, infographics have also found a significant place in social media marketing, where they are used to capture audience attention and convey key messages swiftly and effectively.

The rise in popularity of infographics is striking. Between the years of 2010 to 2012, searches for "infographics" on Google increased over 800% (Crane 2016, p. 18) and their popularity has not waned. The production of infographics is increasing by 1% every day (Crane 2016, p. 19). The popularity of infographics can be seen as a response to the increasingly overwhelming amount of data that is being collected by almost any system we touch. Infographics make "enormous spreadsheets and piles of statistics far friendlier to the average user."

While there are a number of user-friendly applications such as Piktochart, Easel.ly, Capzle, and Creately that allow creators to build infographics through a drag and drop interface, none will provide the versatility, control, intricate detailing, and scalability of a vector-based drawing program like Adobe Illustrator. Most of these programs are geared towards building a specific type of infographic whereas a full-fledged vector-based drawing program will facilitate the creation of any type of infographic you can imagine.

There are several features built into a vector-based drawing program that are useful in the creation of infographics. For example, Illustrator has the ability to create charts and graphs based on data sets, making it an efficient tool for building these types of displays without having to manually draw each individual element. Additionally, the ability to create custom symbols in Illustrator allows for greater creativity as well as a more efficient design process. In Illustrator, you can design a master symbol that you might use in various instances within your infographic. Once you edit a master symbol, all instances are updated throughout the infographic.

Before you commence the creation of your infographic, you should have a clear understanding of the story you are trying to tell. If you are not clear about what you are trying to communicate, the infographic will not do you any favors. The content you want to convey will shape the nature of the infographic you produce. There are several different categories of infographics, including statistical, process, comparison, geographic, hierarchical, list, and timeline-based. Investigate these different types and see which one best aligns with the story you want to tell.

Since the objective of an infographic is to aid in the understanding of (oftentimes) complex information, the design choices you make should serve to clarify information as opposed to detract from it. Color choices can be critical in supporting this goal. Embrace a color's inherent association to make your infographics easily understandable. Color can also be distracting. Use your highest contrast color combinations for areas of greatest importance. Excessively bold lines and borders draw attention away from the more important elements within the infographic.

Symbols are often used throughout infographics to represent complex ideas or processes. When creating symbols, keep in mind that they should be simple and easily understood. Overly complicated or abstract symbols can create confusion and hinder the infographic's effectiveness and should not change meaning within the infographic.

When it comes to typography, make sure to use a legible font that is appropriate for the content being presented. Avoid using too many different fonts or styles as it can create a cluttered and confusing design. Instead, use hierarchy and contrast to guide the viewer's eye through the information in a logical and organized manner. Incorporating too much text can also be overwhelming and take away from the visual aspect of the infographic, so use text sparingly and only when necessary.

Most importantly, since infographics are based on facts and numerical data, it is crucial to ensure accuracy in the information being presented. Any incorrect or misrepresented data can undermine the credibility of the entire infographic. Take the time to fact-check and verify all data sources before including them in your design.

Sourcing vector graphics

If creating vector-based graphics from scratch is not ideal, the internet offers a vast selection of pre-made vector elements that can and easily be added to your design. You can open these designs in a vector-based drawing program and apply different styles and colors to the elements. And, of course, because they are vectors, you can use them at any scale.

Stock websites like iStockphoto, Shutterstock, and Adobe Stock and offer an array of vector-based artwork created by professional designers. Most of the pixel-based stock image sources mentioned in the previous chapter will also offer vector-based images as well. Prices for these stock images vary depending on complexity and usage rights. Free vector-based clip art can be found online as well. Sites like Vecteezy, Freepik, and Pikbest offer a large collection of free vector-based graphics. Just make sure to check the usage rights prior to using them in your design.

The beauty of a vector graphic by art director Leila Mitchell

The art of vector graphics lies in navigating complexity to craft simplicity. The designer as artist pushes and pulls anchor points to sculpt the most refined shapes. The designer as engineer uses precision and math, knowing the design is resilient to resolution regardless of scale. Creating a vector logo reminds me of sketching a parti in architecture. Just a few elements can define multiples spaces, solid and void harmony, and dynamic movement with line. Through a thoughtful approach at the concept and design development phases, a great vector logo has the ability to create a rich ecosystem of branded elements.

Study questions

1) Explain how vector-based graphics are different from pixel-based graphics.
2) Why is it easier to convert a vector-based graphic to pixels than vice versa?
3) What are the most common vector-based graphic file formats and what are the pros and cons of each?
4) Name and describe a design strategy you might use to help enhance your communication goal when designing a project with vector-based graphics.
5) Explain why early video-game developers were interested in vector-based graphics.

Exercises

1) Design a logo for a band using a vector-based drawing program. Have the class guess what type of music your band plays.
2) Explore each of the vector-based graphic drawing and design tools listed in the chapter. What can you create by combining the elements you make using each of these tools and techniques.
3) Research and compare different stock image websites to determine which one offers the best options for vector-based graphics.
4) Use a vector-based drawing program to create a timeline graphic showcasing major events in your life or a significant historical event.
5) Convert a vector-based graphic to a pixel-based graphic, then convert a pixel-based graphic to a vector-based graphic.

References

Bedingfield, Will. 2020. "Flash Is Finally Dead. This Is Why We Should All Mourn Its Passing." Wired. https://www.wired.co.uk/article/flash-obituary-adobe.

Brock, David C. 2023. "The Tremendous VR and CG Systems—of the 1960s and How Computer Graphics Pioneer Ivan Sutherland Helped Instigate It All." IEEE Spectrum. https://spectrum.ieee.org/sketchpad.

"Computer-Aided Design." n.d. https://www.computerhistory.org/revolution/computer-graphics-music-and-art/15/216. Accessed November 30, 2024.

Crane, Beverley. 2016. "Infographics : A Practical Guide for Librarians." Lanham, MD: Rowman & Littlefield. https://worldcat.org/title/929854378.

Markoff, John. 2023. "A Tech Industry Pioneer Sees a Way for the U.S. to Lead in Advanced Chips." *International New York Times*, January 12.

Nicoll, Benjamin. 2019. *Minor Platforms in Videogame History*. Games and Play. Amsterdam: Amsterdam University Press. https://library3.webster.edu/login?url=https://search.ebscohost.com/login.aspx?direct=true&db=nlebk&AN=2251023&site=ehost-live&scope=site.

"SVG Files." n.d. Adobe. https://www.adobe.com/au/creativecloud/file-types/image/vector/svg-file.html. Accessed November 30, 2024.

"The Guide to Vector Design." n.d. https://www.coreldraw.com/en/learn/guide-to-vector-design/history-of-vector-graphics/. Accessed November 30, 2023.

5   Compositing images

Image compositing is a process of combining two or more images and/or text into a single visual output. This technique allows for the creation of unique and imaginative compositions that would be impossible to capture in a single photograph or illustration. Image compositing has become a vital tool for visual communicators, enabling us to attract attention, project an image and engage with an audience.

In addition to understanding the technique of assembling disparate graphic elements on different layers, effective image compositing also requires a bit of design know-how. A poorly designed composited image will fail to live up to its intended purpose. In this chapter, we will not only discuss the technical aspects of image compositing such as software and technique, but also some of the basic design principles and how they can be used to help with your communication goal. But, before we get too deep into the how-to, we will also discuss the evolution of composited images and learn how innovative designers advanced this form of communication.

While composited images can be standalone pieces of art, within the context of this book, we are focusing on how to use image-compositing techniques for commercial purposes, such as advertising, marketing, and editorial design. In these areas, the final output is intended to have a specific purpose and function—whether it's promoting a product or conveying a message. Therefore, the process of creating a composite image goes beyond just merging different elements together; it also involves careful planning, conceptualization, and execution to achieve the desired result.

Where are composited images used?

Composited images can be found in a wide range of mediums, including advertising, social media, film and television, newspapers and magazines, and websites. They have become an essential part of the visual language used to convey messages and ideas. Whether it's creating a striking social media banner or showcasing multiple products in a single advertisement, image compositing allows for endless possibilities in visual communication.

DOI: 10.4324/9781003462200-5

The evolution of composited images

Image compositing has been around since the early days of photography, where photographers would combine different negatives to create a single print. However, the practice of compositing photographic imagery with text and bold, colorful graphics did not become a graphic technique until the early 20th century when "a brief flowering of creative art in Russia had an international influence on twentieth-century graphic design and typography" (Meggs 1998, p. 262).

Before the days of the Internet and social media, governments funded the creation of propaganda posters to promote their political ideologies and manipulate public opinion. These posters often combined various visual elements, such as photographs, illustrations, and text to convey a powerful message. During the Russian Revolution in the early 20th century, poster artists such as El Lissitzky and Alexander Rodchenko pioneered creative image compositing techniques to create these types of propaganda posters that would inspire action and loyalty from the masses. El Lissitsky was a prominent designer for the Russian propaganda publication *USSR in Construction*. Through his work in the magazine, Lissitsky strove to create a sense of narrative in the graphics, experimenting with "montage and photomontage for complex communications messages" in ways never seen before (Meggs 1998, p. 267). Alexander Rodchenko, another significant designer at the magazine, "delighted in contrasting bold, blocky type and hard-edged shapes against the softer forms and edges of photomontages" (Meggs 1998, p. 269). His graphic experimentations were a deliberate effort to innovate graphic communication for the 20th century. Due to their unique style and pioneering methods, their posters "have often been regarded as works of art" (Taylor 2013).

The Bauhaus, an influential modernist design movement and school founded in 1919 in Weimar, Germany, by architect Walter Gropius, championed the marriage of art, craft, and technology. It produced some of the most well-known and prolific professional designers and educators of the 20th century, many of whom had a significant impact on image compositing and the development of modern graphic design. A young Hungarian instructor named László Moholy-Nagy "made significant progress in terms of integrating photography into the design arts" (Eskilson 2019, p. 220). He coined the term "typophoto," referring to the objective integration of word and image to "communicate a message with immediacy," and later experimented with photomontages which he believed was "a new expression that could become both more creative and more functional than straightforward imitative photography" (Meggs 1998, p. 281).

Another innovator in the evolving practice of image compositing was Swiss designer Herbert Matter who was best known for his Swiss travel posters of the 1930s. Like Moholy-Nagy, Matter applied his knowledge of photography to graphic design, playing with "montage, dynamic scale changes and an

Figure 5.1 America Calling - Take Your Place in Civilian Defense Propaganda Poster
by Herbert Matter - 1941

effective integration of typography and illustration" (Meggs 1998, p. 298).
The effects of his unexpected combinations are striking and iconic.

In the mid-20th century, creative image compositing permeated American
advertising and editorial design. New York-based art director and professor
Alexy Brodovitch inspired a generation of creative editorial designers with
his unconventional teaching methods, dumping piles of paper, photographs,
and type proofs onto a table and encouraging his students to "do something
brilliant" (Meggs 1998, p. 346). Students like Otto Storch and Henry Wolf,
who later became art directors at *McCall's* magazine and *Esquire*, respectively,
transformed boring magazines into eye-catching works of art with their creative compositions.

The late 1970s ushered in a new style of image composition: the graphic
design movement of détournement, whereby "appropriated elements of the
mass media were reinterpreted as to undermine the original intent" (Eskilson
2019, p. 323). The concept was to combine familiar ideas into something new
and different, and it went hand and hand with the rise of punk culture. The
crude collage posters and album covers created in this style had a raw, edgy
aesthetic that captured the rebellious spirit of the punks at the time.

When personal computers with graphic applications emerged in the late 1980s, image-compositing techniques became more accessible to the general public, and new possibilities emerged in graphic design. Today, image compositing has become an integral part of the creative process for many designers and artists who often borrow techniques from the early pioneers while adding a new level of sophistication, as they can now easily combine multiple images, manipulate them, and create seamless compositions.

How to create a composited image

Creating a composited image can be accomplished in either pixel-based or vector-based software. Popular applications for image compositing include Adobe Photoshop and Illustrator, but, as we already covered, there are also many alternatives available to both. Since the nature of creating a composited image involves bringing together disparate graphic elements, your first step should be to assemble these assets that will be incorporated into the final composition. This could include photographs, illustrations, text, and other graphic elements such as logos or icons. Once you have these elements, the next step is to begin the process of layering and blending them together to create a cohesive and visually appealing composition that aligns with your communication goal.

Software for creating composited images

Your first decision when creating a composited image is to identify the software you want to use. Since composited images can be created either in a pixel-based or vector-based program, you have a few different options. So how do you decide? Oftentimes it doesn't matter and can be dictated by personal preference. Generally, though, if your final output will be primarily photographic in nature, you should use a pixel-based program such as Photoshop. On the other hand, if your final output contains a vector-based background without any blending of photographic elements, it makes sense to use vector-based programs like Adobe Illustrator. Or, for example, if your final output does not require multiple layers and will primarily be text-based, a vector-based program would be more suitable. Finally, if your composite image does not need to be a specific number of pixels, a vector-based program might make more sense. As you learned in an earlier chapter, it is simple to export an image created in a vector-based program as a pixel-based image. All you have to do is specify the number of pixels you want the program to generate when you export it. So, if your final output must be pixel-based, either a vector- or a pixel-based program will work. But, since converting a pixel-based composition into vectors is not usually feasible, if your final composition must be vector-based, you should work in a vector-based program.

Some designers prefer to use Adobe InDesign to create a composite image as it allows for precise control over typography and placement of graphic elements. While this program is primarily used for layout of print media, you can certainly export your resulting composition in a format that can be viewed on a screen. Adobe InDesign's strength is in laying out multiple page documents but you can certainly create a standalone composite image in this program.

If you don't have access to the Adobe Creative Cloud, Canva (www.canva.com) is a great web-based program to make composited images comprised of both vector- and pixel-based elements and text. You can make projects with pre-made elements or upload your own vector or pixel images. Canva offers templates in appropriate proportions for various social media platforms as well as other end uses. You can also export your final composition at various resolutions based on the requirements of the desired output. Keep in mind, however, that while Canva is a powerful, verstile (and free) tool for image compositing, it does not offer the editing and compositing capabilities of a professional-level graphics program.

Setting up your image composition

The most important step in creating your image composition is to set it up in the correct proportion and resolution. If you are building your composition in a vector-based program, then resolution is not relevant, unless, of course, you integrate pixel-based images. You must ensure that the resolution of the pixel-based image is high enough to be integrated into the composition at your desired finished size. On the other hand, if you are building your composition in a pixel-based program, it's best to start your composition working at the desired proportion and resolution (or higher). You should not later increase the number of pixels in your composition, because this will result in a loss of image quality due to pixel interpolation (or upsampling)—meaning that the software will be forced to create new pixels to fill in gaps. We discussed the problems associated with upsampling in a previous chapter.

Working with layers

Layers are a fundamental concept in image compositing and can be thought of as transparent sheets stacked on top of each other. Each layer can contain different elements of your composition, such as text, images, or graphics. These layers can be individually edited, moved, and adjusted without affecting the content of the other layers. This flexibility allows for non-destructive editing, meaning you can make changes to one aspect of your composition without permanently altering the overall image. In essence, layers serve as the building blocks of your composite image, allowing for a high degree of control and precision in your design process.

Layers also aid in the organization of your composition as you can clearly see the "stacking order" of the layers that indicate which items are in the foreground and which ones are in the background. Layers can also be grouped which can further assist you in organizing all the elements in your composition. Finally, layers can be hidden which can help you to better focus on one aspect of the composition or locked so that you don't inadvertently move an element on a layer.

Both Adobe Photoshop and Illustrator include layers as a fundamental component of their functionality, but they work slightly differently in each application. In Photoshop, whenever you add a new element to the composition, it is automatically placed on a new layer. In Illustrator, objects (which can be modified independently) are automatically contained within the same layer unless you manually create a new one. However, both programs allow for extensive layer management and customization, including the ability to group, merge, and adjust the opacity of layers.

In Photoshop, there are several ways to integrate images into your composition. You can simply copy from one source (another Photoshop document, a screen shot, or elements from other open programs) and paste them into your active composition. But, you can also incorporate new elements by using the Place -> Embedded command and select the image file from your computer that you want to integrate in your composition. The advantage of embedding elements into a Photoshop document (as opposed to simply copying and pasting) is that any edits you make to the source files will update in the composite image. Adobe Illustrator has a similar embedding function.

Although the function of layers is to keep elements independent, oftentimes, to create a particular look, we want the layers to interact with one another. A blending mode is one way you can get a layer to interact with what's below it. Every blending mode uses some mathematical operation and/or logic to determine how to interact with the pixel below it. For example, the "Multiply" blending mode does what its name implies: it multiplies the colors of the pixels below it with the color value in each pixel on the layer. This is a way to achieve a darker look. Conversely, the "Screen" blending mode can be thought of as the opposite of the multiply blending mode. It multiplies the inverse of the blend and base colors and the result is always a lighter color ("Blending Mode" n.d.). These are just two examples of blending modes that are available in Photoshop but there are many others. Some of the blending modes are used more often than others and have become a bit of a cliché, but used in conjunction with one another, they can be a quick method for creating a unique look and feel. Adobe Illustrator also has blending capabilities. But, in Illustrator, you can apply a blending mode to either an object or an entire layer.

Another important aspect of layer management in a pixel-based image editor is the use of layer masks. Layer masks allow you to hide or reveal certain parts of a layer, giving you more control over how elements blend together. They can also be used to create effects like vignetting (creating a darker overlay on background areas of an image to draw focus to the subject of the image). Masks are created in a pixel-based editing program by adding a mask to a layer and then painting on the mask with white (for total transparency) or black (for opaque effect), depending on if you want to hide or reveal parts of the layer. If you created a black to white gradient on a layer mask, you would create a gradual amount of transparency throughout the layer. In vector-based programs, masks work a little differently. Instead of layer masks, you have clipping masks. In Illustrator, you can use one object to mask out another by converting it to a "clipping mask."

While Canva does not have layers per se, it does maintain every item that you introduce into your project so that you can move it independently and change the stacking order. You just need to select the element and move it forward, backwards, etc. Clearly, pixel-editing programs offer much more precise control when manipulating layers; however, Canva is great for people who are new to compositing images or simply want the process to be more intuitive and don't need that level of control.

Adding text

Text often plays a large role in image compositing, whether it's a title, caption, or other important information. Adobe Photoshop and Illustrator both have robust text creation and editing tools that allow for a high degree of customization and creativity. In Photoshop and Illustrator, you can simply use the Type tool to add text to your composition. Both programs let you adjust tracking, kerning and spacing of your text. However, Illustrator allows for much more creative treatments of text. For example, Illustrator allows you to flow text into shapes or set text along a path. You can even transform text into shapes, warp the shape of your text, and create 3D effects. These features give designers a wide range of options when it comes to adding text to their composite image.

In Canva, adding text is also a simple process. You can use drag and drop one of the text elements into your project and edit it as needed. While not as robust as the text options in Photoshop and Illustrator, Canva offers a variety of font choices and basic editing tools like alignment and spacing.

Adding areas of color

Another important aspect of image compositing is adding areas of color, whether it's a background or a specific element within the composition. In Photoshop and Illustrator, you can use the Paint Bucket tool to fill an entire layer with solid colors or gradients. You can also use the shape tools to create geometric shapes that can be filled with color.

In Canva, adding areas of color is also a simple process. You can use the Elements tab to browse and add various shapes and backgrounds, which can then be customized with different colors or patterns. Canva also offers a variety of shape tools for creating geometric shapes that can be filled with color.

Design principles for effective image compositing

Understanding the technical aspects of image compositing is important, but in the end, what matters is whether or not your composited image helps you achieve your desired communication goal. Once you have chosen the software and assembled the elements you want in your composited image, it's time to focus on the design aspect to make sure your composite image is visually interesting and effectively communicates your message.

Good design of a composite image begins with having an understanding of how you want the viewer to interact. Do you want them to better understand your brand? Show up at an event? Make a purchase? Once you have a clear objective in mind, you can weigh every design decision against this goal. The design decisions you make can have a major impact on how your message is received and how your audience responds.

Color

Color plays a vital role as a design element in composite images. It can evoke certain emotions and set the tone for your message. When choosing colors for your composited image, consider the overall color palette and how it will complement or contrast with the elements you have chosen to (or must) include. You should always take into account any existing branding guidelines that you need to adhere to when selecting colors. Be mindful of the inherent qualities of a color and associations. For example, blues are often associated with trust and stability while reds can evoke passion and excitement.

Typically, composited images are comprised of carefully chosen colors that complement each other, which is referred to as the color palette. There are various techniques you can use to create a suitable color palette. Referring to a color wheel and choosing complementary colors (colors opposite each other on the color wheel) can help create a dynamic contrast in your composition. Triads, where three colors are evenly spaced on the color wheel, can create a harmonious and balanced palette. Analogous colors, which are adjacent to each other on the color wheel, can create a more subtle and cohesive look. There are also several online tools that can help you build a color palette. For example, Adobe Color is a great resource for creating and exploring color schemes. These tools will typically specify colors in RGB mode (the amount of red, green, and blue light used to generate each color) or its corresponding hexadecimal value (a six-digit code comprised of letters A–F and numbers 0–9 used in HTML coding). Either of these numbers can be entered into your graphics program to generate the color.

While it's tempting to want to use all the beautiful colors available in our graphics applications, it's important not to overwhelm the viewer with too many colors and to ensure that they work harmoniously together. Limit the number of colors you integrate into your composition. A more controlled color palette will make your composition feel more unified. Ultimately, the color choices you make should support your overall message and help create a cohesive visual experience for the viewer.

Typography

Like, color, typefaces have inherent qualities that can evoke certain emotions or associations. Serif fonts are often seen as more traditional and formal, while sans-serif fonts tend to be viewed as more modern and casual. Choosing the right font for your composition can have a significant impact on how your message is perceived.

Using too many different typefaces in one composition can create a chaotic and disorganized feeling. However, it's perfectly acceptable to mix two to three typefaces within a more text-heavy composition in order to create "typographic contrast." Typographic contrast refers to the use of different typefaces to convey hierarchy and emphasize certain elements. For instance, a bold sans serif header can be employed to break up lengthy blocks of body text set in a serif typeface. This deliberate difference in appearance draws attention and enhances readability.

Avoid making all your text the same size. Incorporate hierarchy in your text by varying the size and weight of different elements to help the viewer prioritize what to read. The largest, most dominant text element should get a viewer's attention and help her decide if she wants to read more. The following text should naturally flow from left to right, aligning with our natural reading pattern. You may want to create a secondary and even tertiary level of text, again, to help the reader quickly absorb important details and decide whether or not to read more.

Alignment of your text can have a significant impact on legibility. Justifying text (aligning it along the left and right margins) can sometimes have a negative impact on readability, particularly if there are large gaps between words or awkward "rivers" of white space. Center or right-aligned paragraphs can pose challenges for readability too. The varying horizontal starting points after each line break make it harder for readers to locate the beginning of each line. In general, left alignment is the preferred choice for paragraphs, as it offers the best readability and flow.

Lines

When we refer to lines in design, we can either mean actual lines (sometimes called rules) or implied lines. Actual lines are the physical elements of a composition, such as borders, outlines, and strokes. Implied lines refer to how elements are placed in relation to each other and how we perceive them visually. For instance, a row of objects can create an implied line that guides our eye from one element to another.

Lines play a crucial role in directing the viewer's attention and creating visual interest. Horizontal lines often convey feelings of calmness and stability, while diagonal lines can create a sense of action or movement. Vertical lines tend to feel more formal and powerful. Straight lines bring a sense of order and tidiness to an image, while crooked or curved lines can be used to create tension or haphazard energy.

When using actual lines in your composition, be mindful of their thickness and color. Bold, thick lines can overwhelm the content and make it difficult to read or see the most important aspects of your composition. Thin, delicate lines can be all you need to define different areas of your composition.

With implied lines, think about how you want the viewer's eye to travel through the image. For instance, a series of objects angled in the same direction can create an implied diagonal line that leads to a prominent focal point. Given that viewers naturally tend to "read" an image from left to right, top to bottom, it is advantageous to organize your composition accordingly. So, as you arrange elements in your composition, think about how the viewer's eye may be traveling. You want to make sure that the most important elements are placed in such a way as to be seen first and then have the viewer's eye travel logically through the rest of the image.

Composition

The composition of your image refers to how all the elements are arranged and presented within the frame. A well-composed image will direct the viewer's eye to the most important elements, draw them in to read more once you have caught their attention. Good composition helps ensure that viewers absorb the intended message quickly and are not confused by what you are trying to communicate. Contrast, alignment, balance, proximity, scale, space, and repetition are all techniques you can use to help you capture a viewer's attention and efficiently communicate your intended message.

Contrast

Contrast refers to the varying relationships between elements within an image and can be achieved through color, size, texture, or placement of elements. Applying contrast is a great strategy for drawing attention to the most important information in the composition.

Let's say, for example, you want a viewer to see the words "FALL SALE" first when looking at your composite image. Consider how you can use contrast to draw attention to these words. They can be larger than all the other elements in the image. Or, they could be a different color or font than everything else in the composition. You could also incorporate more whitespace around these words to really set them off from the rest of the composition. All of these techniques are common methods that designers use to create contrast.

Alignment

Alignment is another key aspect of a well-designed composite image. A composite image with haphazardly placed pieces of text and graphics can create an unintentional visual distraction, pulling the viewer's attention away from your intended focal point. When aligning elements, consider using a grid or guidelines to help ensure consistency and cohesiveness. Both Adobe Photoshop and Illustrator allow you to turn on grids and guides and "snap" elements to these objects. You can also employ the alignment tool to ensure elements are aligned vertically and/or horizontally. Good alignment makes it easier for the viewer to follow the flow of information from one element to the next.

Keep in mind that alignment doesn't necessarily mean everything has to be perfectly centered or evenly spaced. In fact, sometimes a slight misalignment can create visual interest and draw attention to an element. However, be intentional with your alignment choices and avoid creating a cluttered and chaotic composition.

Balance

One of the most important design principles in compositing is balance. This refers to the distribution of visual elements within the composition, and how they interact with each other. A balanced image will feel harmonious and stable. If your composition incorporates an element with a lot of visual weight in the bottom right corner, for example, you may want to balance it out with another element of similar weight in the opposite corner. This helps to create a sense of equilibrium and avoids an image that feels lopsided or unbalanced.

Balance can also be achieved through symmetry or asymmetry. A symmetrical composition has equal visual weight on both sides of the image, while an asymmetrical composition has different elements on either side that still create a sense of balance. This can be achieved by manipulating color, size, or placement.

Proximity

Proximity in design means keeping related elements close together. For example, if your composition includes all your company's social media handles, they should probably be grouped together in close proximity. By doing so, you are telling your viewer that these items are related. Conversely, unrelated elements should be spaced further apart. This helps to avoid confusion and allows for a more organized and easy-to-follow composition.

Scale

Scale refers to the size of elements within your composition, and it is a natural way to communicate their relative importance. For example, a large title at the top of your composition will likely be perceived as more important than smaller text or images below. Using varying scales can also create visual interest. Scaling an element beyond the bounds of the composition in a way that keeps the object recognizable but forms a striking silhouette can be an effective way of drawing attention to your composition and/or elements within it.

Scaling is a fairly intuitive task in any graphics application as there are both scale tools as well as dialog boxes where you can enter precise scaling amounts to apply to an object. If you are scaling an object manually, it's easy to inadvertently distort an object by not applying a proportional scale. To avoid this common mishap, be mindful of how the program you are using scales objects. Some programs will scale elements proportionally by default, whereas others will require you to hold down the Shift key as you click and drag a handle to scale an item proportionally.

Space

The use of space in your composition can also have a significant impact on how it is perceived. The negative space, or the area around and between objects, can create its own form and balance within an image. It can also be used to guide the viewer's eye towards important elements. By intentionally leaving empty areas in your composition, you can create a sense of calm and simplicity, allowing the viewer to focus on the most important elements in your image.

Repetition

Lastly, repetition is another design principle that can be used to create cohesion and consistency within your composition. Repeating certain elements or

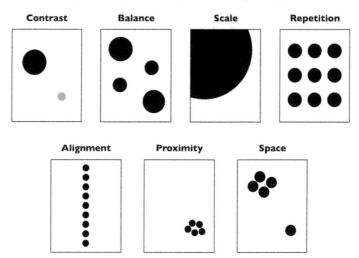

Figure 5.2 Design principles

patterns throughout your image can help tie everything together and make it feel unified. This could be through the use of a specific color, shape, or font. Repetition also creates visual rhythm and helps guide the viewer's eye through the composition.

There are few tools in Adobe Photoshop and Illustrator that can help you repeat elements in regular intervals. For example, the "Transform Again" and "Duplicate" functions allow you to easily create multiple copies of an element with consistent spacing between them. The Distribute command will equally space elements within a given area. These tools can save you time and eliminate the guesswork in laying out equally spaced repeated elements to create a more professional-looking composite image.

Saving composite images

Regardless of what program you use to create your composited image, you will have the opportunity to save your image in an uncompressed and fully editable format. If you are using Photoshop, for example, saving your image as a PSD file ensures that all the layers, type, and even color corrections are still editable. In Adobe Illustrator, the corresponding, fully editable format is a .AI file. If you are working in Canva, you can always go back and make edits to any composition you created that is stored within your Canva account.

If you want to export your composition for use as a social media graphic, flyer, advertisement, etc. you will need to save it in a more universally understood format. If you are preparing a composite image for print, you will typically just save the document as a PDF file. But if the image is intended to go on the web, you will most likely want to save it as a JPEG or a PNG image (if there are areas of transparency). Assuming you have set up your composition in the appropriate proportion, you will just need to make sure that you choose an appropriate resolution setting. Generally, a resolution of 72 pixels or dots per inch (dpi) is sufficient for images displayed on the web. However, if your composite image will be printed at a larger size or in high quality, the resolution should be higher (typically 300 dpi).

Remember when you are working on your composite image to always save your work frequently so that you don't lose any progress in case of a computer crash or other unexpected issue. If you are working in Canva, this is not an issue as the program automatically saves your work to the Cloud after each edit you make. Also, if you are working with large and complex images, it may be a good idea to save different versions of your composite image at different stages in the process. This way, if you decide later on that you preferred an earlier version, you won't have to start from scratch. Finally, always make sure to save your final composite image (the compressed and lower resolution version) under a new name or as a separate file so that you don't accidentally overwrite your original composition.

Image compositing as a form of storytelling by designer and professor Noriko Yuasa

Compositing graphics is about more than just blending visuals; it's about storytelling. It is the process of arranging images and text to convey a message. Through careful placement and juxtaposition, we can evoke emotions and provoke thoughts, engaging our audience. It's about creating meaningful connections through our work.

Study questions

1) How can you use contrast in a composite image to help you more efficiently communicate your message?
2) What effect can repetition have on a composite image?
3) Why might you want to save different versions of your work when creating a composite image?
4) Explain a visual hierarchy and how you can create one within a composite image.
5) How are layers useful when creating a composite image.

Exercises

1) Create a Pinterest graphic to promote your latest recipe on your blog using Canva. The goal of your Pinterest graphic is to get viewers to click on the image to learn how to make it. This graphic should use scale in an effective way.
2) Design a flyer for your upcoming event using Adobe Illustrator that integrates bitmap imagery. Utilize the design principles of balance and proximity to create an eye-catching composition that will draw in potential attendees.
3) Use Photoshop to create three different composite images comprised of both bitmap and vector-based images that will be used as META (Facebook and Instagram) ads promoting a company of your choice's latest product. Each of these images share the same goal of getting a viewer to purchase the product. They should also contain the same (or very similar) design elements. The challenge is to construct them in the three different proportions suggested by the META platform: 1500px × 1500px, 1800px × 3200px, and 1910 × 1000 pixels.
4) Use Canva to create a social media graphic for some type of consulting business featuring an inspirational quote with a corresponding, visually appropriate image. This image could be in the background or integrated somehow with the quote. Choose a typeface for your quote and a dominate color for your composition that reflects the sentiment of the message and the personality of the business.

5) Using any program you prefer, create a composite image designed to go on a home page or website dedicated to travel to the location of your choice. This image should include at least one photograph, multiple layers, and text. The size of the image should 1920 × 1080 pixels.

References

"Blending Mode." n.d. Adobe Photoshop User Guide. https://helpx.adobe.com/photoshop/using/blending-modes.html. Accessed November 30, 2024.

Eskilson, Stephen. 2019. *Graphic Design: A New History*. 3rd ed. New Haven, CT: Yale University Press. https://worldcat.org/title/1091250235.

Meggs, Philip B. 1998. *A History of Graphic Design*. 3rd ed. New York: John Wiley & Sons. https://worldcat.org/title/37594815.

Taylor, Philip. 2013. *Munitions of the Mind: A History of Propaganda*. 3rd ed. Manchester: Manchester University Press. https://worldcat.org/title/1394872298.

6   Audio recording

Good audio quality is an essential factor in any media project that incorporates sound, whether it's for music production, podcasting, or to accompany a video. Fortunately, recording high-quality audio is achievable for even the non-audio professional. With the right equipment and techniques, you can create an environment ideal for recording good-quality audio.

This chapter delves into the essential aspects and evolution of audio recording. We'll begin by exploring the definition of high-quality audio and its significance. Next, we'll cover establishing an optimal recording environment and selecting and using the perfect equipment for your project. We'll also explore various recording techniques tailored to different audio types. Finally, we'll touch upon the legal considerations surrounding sound capture.

The evolution of audio recording

These days we probably spend more time listening to recorded sounds than live sounds. However, the ability to record sounds is a relatively recent invention as this technology has only been around for the past 150 years. During this relatively short time period, audio technology has evolved significantly, leading to the development of various recording formats and techniques.

In 1877, Thomas Edison stunned the world by playing the first recorded sound on his invention, the phonograph, a machine that could record sound by etching the vibrations onto a cylinder wrapped in foil. The user would turn a crank to rotate the cylinder and speak to record the sound. Playback was achieved by cranking the phonograph in reverse (Dyer and Martin 2010, pp. 195–199).

Edison was not the only inventor working on audio-recording devices. In 1886 a deaf educator and inventor named Alexander Graham Bell invented the graphophone which was similar to Edison's phonograph but had a few significant improvements. Bell developed a cylinder of wax that was more durable and offered a longer recording time over Edison's foil-covered cylinder. The device also created "a much more faithful recording" of the sounds. Bell acknowledged Edison's influence in a creative manner. The first recording Bell's graphophone played stated: "I am a graphophone, and my mother was a phonograph" (Grosvenor and Wesson 2016).

DOI: 10.4324/9781003462200-6

Figure 6.1 Thomas Edison and his phonograph

The next major innovation in sound recording and playback machines can be attributed to Emile Berliner who introduced the gramophone record in 1890. Its significance is that it used a flat disc instead of a cylinder to record sound. These discs were made from hard rubber and then finished with shellac which became the precursor to the vinyl records that were released in the 1940s and are still popular today ("The Gramophone" n.d.).

World War II drove audio technology in unexpected ways. Fritz Pfleumer was a German-Austrian engineer who invented magnetized tape for recording purposes which later evolved into a reel-to-reel tape recorder called the Magnetophon. During Adolf Hitler's ascent to power, Germany's Nazi Party explored the potential of tape recording for their own agenda. As a result, the research and development of this recording technique took on a secretive and covert nature, operating underground. Hitler was particularly fond of the reel-to-reel machine as it allowed him to "perform" in one location when he was actually at another because the pre-recorded speeches sounded indistinguishable from live recordings (Schwartz 2019). After the war, reel-to-reel recording machines made their way to the U.S. where it became a standard device for recording longer, higher-fidelity, and multi-track recordings.

While reel-to-reel tape had the support of audiophiles who appreciated its superior recording capabilities, it was "difficult to handle" (Millard 2005, p. 316). This weakness prompted the development of plastic cartridges called cassettes that could house the long tapes. Car manufacturers embraced the cassette and began incorporating cassette players into new automobiles. In 1963, the Phillips company introduced the compact cassette and encouraged other companies to license its use which helped it grow in popularity. Although the quality of the audio from cassettes were less superior to audio on a vinyl record, cassettes were much more portable and provided a satisfactory medium for less discriminating listeners. Their small size also lent themselves to attractive packaging. With the invention of the boom box and Walkman in the 1980s, compact cassettes secured their position as the best format for music on the go rendering other formats of cassettes, like the bulkier eight-track, obsolete.

In the 1970s many companies were experimenting with converting sound waves into pulsating electric currents that could be measured as binary code of digits. But it took a while for the industry to figure out how to store the digital information once the sound was translated to binary code. In 1982, the companies Sony and Philips introduced a solution: a compact disc (CD) system in which a laser beam read binary code from a disc's mirrored like surface. These new CDs sounded different and took some getting used to. Gone were the hisses and pops that were once associated with cassette tapes and vinyl records. Some audio engineers accustomed to the older formats "hated the way it sounded" (Lynskey 2015). But consumers adapted, accepting this new format for its convenience, portability, and sound quality. Digital recordings offered another significant benefit over analog forms; it could be duplicated without any degradation.

In the mid-1990s, another leap in audio recording and playback technology emerged with the advent of the MP3 format. MP3, short for MPEG-1 Audio Layer III, is a digital audio coding format that uses a form of lossy data compression, a method of compression that discards data that, in the case of audio, is not noticed by the listener. Developed by the Moving Picture Experts Group (MPEG), it revolutionized the music industry by allowing high-quality audio files to be compressed to roughly one-tenth of their original size, without a proportional reduction in audio quality. This compression made it feasible to store large music libraries on personal computers and portable devices, and to share music files over the internet, which was a driving factor in the digital music revolution. Apple embraced the MP3 format, introducing the iPod in 2001, "a breakthrough MP3 music player that packs up to 1,000 CD-quality songs into an ultra-portable, 6.5 ounce design that fits in your pocket" ("Apple Presents iPod" 2001). The MP3 format's impact on the music industry and on music consumption habits cannot be overstated, with its influence still visible in today's streaming-dominated landscape.

Why good-quality audio is important

When you listen to your favorite podcast or YouTube channel, do you notice how great the audio sounds? Maybe not. What you are more likely to notice is when the audio sounds bad. Poor-quality audio can make your message difficult to understand. It will also make your project sound unprofessional and will generally be unpleasant to listen to.

Poor-quality audio has many other negative consequences. It causes our brains to work harder to process information and reduces our productivity ("Poor Audio Quality Affects Work Productivity, Finds a Study" 2023). An audio signal devoid of noise greatly reduces cognitive load and enables learners to focus on the content rather than being distracted by poor-quality or noisy audio conditions. But, it's not just when we are trying to learn or work that poor-quality audio can be bothersome. Even when watching videos for entertainment, individuals are more likely to accept low-quality visuals in a video than they are to tolerate subpar audio quality (Chandler and Sweller 1991).

Good-quality audio ensures a pleasant listening experience for your audience. It also allows you to communicate your ideas more effectively by enabling listeners to better understand what you are saying. Good-quality audio is a crucial ingredient for getting viewers to deem a video "great" and keep them watching (Knott n.d.). The bottom line is that when audio is not good, viewers and listeners notice. They may not be able to articulate why it's not good but they will not like it, and they will want it to stop.

What makes good-quality audio

If you haven't been trained in the field, you may not be aware of the qualities of a recording that make it sound professional. To achieve great-sounding audio, the standards you should strive to achieve are low distortion, low signal-to-noise, wide frequency response, uninhibited dynamic range, and sonic complexity.

Low distortion

Distortion is an unwanted change in the sound due to technical factors, such as equipment limitations or choosing improper settings on the recording device. A highly distorted vocal recording can significantly reduce the clarity of speech. Low distortion means that the recorded audio sounds much like the original source.

Low signal-to-noise

Signal-to-noise refers to the ratio of audio signal to unwanted noise present in a recording. A high signal-to-noise means that the recorded sound is more prominent than the background noise. It also ensures that you capture all the details, even those quiet moments in between words.

Wide frequency

Frequency refers to the range of audible sounds that are reproduced accurately by your recording setup. A wide frequency ensures that all frequencies across the audible range (from the very low to the extremely high) are reproduced accurately and with clarity. It also helps to ensure that the audio sounds natural and not distorted due to an inability of the recording equipment to capture certain frequencies.

Full dynamic range

Dynamic range is a measure of the difference between the loudest and quietest sound. A wide dynamic range is important because it allows for more nuance and subtlety in the audio. Without a wide dynamic range, recordings can sound flat or dull.

Sonic complexity

If you are recording music, you should also consider the sonic complexity of your recording. Sonic complexity is a less tangible quality that refers to how well a recording captures the multiple layers and frequencies present in music. A recording with interesting sonic complexity provides the listener with the feeling that they are part of the music or recording, giving the listener the impression that there is no dimensional wall between them and the sound. It is with them right there in their room.

Audio-recording techniques

If you're not a trained audio engineer, it might be intimidating to start recording audio. Fortunately, most of us will not be expected create recordings suitable for playing through giant speakers in a stadium. The sounds most of us would need to record would more than likely be played on a computer and listened to with headphones or through built-in computer speakers. Nevertheless, we still want to capture excellent quality audio, and there are a few different ways we can go about doing it.

Recording audio directly into your computer or smartphone

Recording audio directly into your computer or smartphone is not an ideal method of sound recording due to potential interference from internal sounds like buzzing or whirring of the hard drive, resulting in poor quality. Computers and smartphones are designed for hundreds of other tasks besides recording audio. Therefore, their sound-capturing capabilities cannot match those of dedicated audio-recording devices.

If you must record audio into your computer, at the very least, you should use a USB microphone so that the built-in computer microphone is overridden by the sound captured by the external USB microphone. You should also position the microphone away from the computer and wear headphones while recording to avoid any feedback loops.

To record audio on your computer, you'll need software that can receive audio input, allow you to hit the "record" button, and save your recorded file. Luckily, both MACs and PCs come with free programs that can do just that. For MAC users, GarageBand is already installed on every device and can serve this purpose seamlessly. On the other hand, modern PCs are equipped with

Microsoft's Sound Recorder application. If you're looking for a more comprehensive solution with advanced controls and editing capabilities, consider installing Audacity. Although it's known as a sound editor, it can also be used for recording. Plus, it's a free and open-source program that works on both MAC and PC.

Recording audio on a video camera

A video camera has the capability to capture both audio and video, making it a valuable tool for recording sound. However, to achieve optimal results, it is recommended to use an external microphone connected to the camera. The built-in microphones in a video camera are designed to capture sound from the entire environment, which may result in picking up excessive background noise. Fortunately, video cameras are compatible with various types of microphones which allows you to put a microphone close to your sound source while recording on your video camera. Keep in mind that once you have recorded the audio using a video camera, you will need to extract the audio file from the camera's memory card and transfer it to your computer for editing.

Recording audio with an external recorder

If you're serious about recording quality audio for podcasts or videos, it's best to invest in an external recorder. An external recorder is a device that has one and only one function, and that is to record audio onto a memory card. These types of recorders usually have built-in microphones, but they also allow you to plug in external microphones as an alternative. External recorders are designed to capture audio with a higher quality than most computers and smartphones can. They generally offer more features like adjustable gain levels and limiting which will help maintain better sound quality when recording. When you finish recording your audio on an external recorder, you will need to transfer the audio files from the memory card in the recorder onto your computer.

There are several different types of portable audio recorders you can use which vary in features, price, and size. Audio voice recorders are inexpensive devices that are designed to capture speech. Most can accept an external microphone. However, the frequencies they are designed to record on are limited to the frequencies of human speech and they only record one track of audio, often in mono.

Audio field recorders are more expensive but offer additional recording capabilities. Some of the more popular models are made by Zoom or Tascam. These devices allow you to record multiple tracks simultaneously with more expensive models offering more potential tracks. You can plug a variety of microphones into these devices as well as headphones so that you can monitor and adjust your recording levels as you record it. Field recorders typically

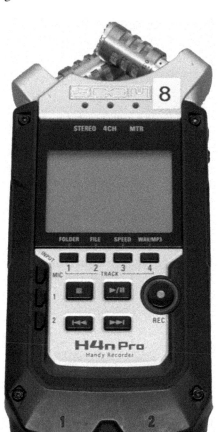

Figure 6.2 Zoom audio recording device

give you much higher sound quality than a video camera and offer far superior sound quality to recordings made on a computer or smartphone.

Microphones

When it comes to capturing audio, the most important piece of equipment is your microphone. A microphone is a transducer, a device that changes one form of energy into another. Its function is to convert sound waves into electrical signals which mirror the pattern of the sound waves, thereby creating an electrical "replica" of the sound.

Categories of microphones

There are three main categories of microphones, dynamic, condenser, and ribbon, which all use different mechanisms to convert the sound waves into electrical signals with the basic principle remaining the same. Understanding how a microphone works as well as the pros and cons of the different types can help you make informed decisions about the best type to use for your specific audio recording needs.

Dynamic microphones

Dynamic microphones are widely used in audio recording due to their affordability and versatility. Also known as "moving coil mics," they function by having a diaphragm connected to a suspended coil of wire within a magnetic field. As the sound wave causes the diaphragm and coil to move, an electrical current is generated. This mechanism facilitates efficient conversion of sound into electrical signals.

Dynamic microphones are known for being rugged and relatively resistant to moisture, making them great for outdoor recording. They have the ability to capture loud sounds, like drums or a powerful vocal performance because they have a large dynamic range and sound pressure level. Another advantage of dynamic mics is that they do not require external power. However, they do have downsides, the biggest being that they are less sensitive than other types of microphones.

Condenser microphones

Condenser microphones, also known as capacitor microphones, use a different mechanism for converting sound waves into electrical signals. They consist of two parallel plates which form a capacitor with an electric charge between them. One plate is a flexible diaphragm while the other is a rigid backplate. When sound waves hit the diaphragm, it vibrates and causes changes in the distance between the plates, resulting in varying electrical signals.

Condenser microphones are generally more sensitive than dynamic microphones, which makes them ideal for capturing subtle nuances in sound. They also have a wider frequency response range, meaning they can capture a broader range of sounds. However, because of this sensitivity, condenser microphones pick up a lot of background noise as well. Therefore, these types of microphones are best used in a quiet environment or with sound-dampening material around them. Condenser microphones are also more delicate and sensitive to handling and moisture, so they are better suited for indoor recording. Unlike dynamic microphones, they do require an external power supply.

Ribbon microphones

Ribbon microphones use a thin strip of metal (usually aluminum) suspended in a magnetic field as their diaphragm. When sound waves hit the ribbon, it vibrates and generates an electrical current that mirrors the sound wave.

Similar to dynamic microphones, ribbon mics are also less sensitive than condenser microphones and require no external power source. However, they have a unique warm sound that is highly sought after in the audio industry.

Due to their delicate nature, ribbon microphones are usually used in controlled studio environments. They are great for capturing vocals or acoustic instruments with a warmer and more natural sound. But, because of their delicate design, they must be treated with care and should never be exposed to high sound pressure levels or extreme temperatures.

Polar patterns

Another crucial factor to consider when choosing a microphone is its polar pattern, which refers to the directionality of the microphone's sensitivity. Microphones can have different polar patterns, including omnidirectional, cardioid, supercardioid, and figure-8. Each pattern has its unique characteristics and is best suited for specific recording situations.

Omnidirectional microphones

Omnidirectional microphones have a 360-degree sensitivity, meaning they pick up sound equally from all directions. This type of polar pattern is best suited for recording ambient sounds or group vocals as it captures the entire surrounding environment.

Cardioid microphones

Cardioid microphones have a heart-shaped pickup pattern and are more sensitive to sounds coming from the front while rejecting sounds from the sides and back. This makes them ideal for capturing solo vocals, instruments, or dialogue in a noisy environment.

Supercardioid microphones

Supercardioid microphones have a narrower pickup pattern than cardioid mics, making them even more focused on sound coming from the front. They excel at recording individual instruments, such as acoustic guitar or piano without picking up unwanted noise from other instruments in the room.

Figure-8 microphones

Figure-8 microphones have a bidirectional pickup pattern, meaning they are sensitive to sounds coming from the front and back but reject sounds from the sides. They are commonly used for recording duets or interviews, where two sound sources are opposite each other.

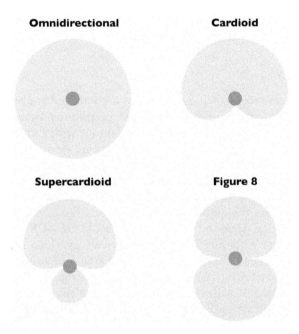

Figure 6.3 Microphone polar patterns

USB vs. XLR microphones

USB vs. XLR refers to the type of connection a microphone has. USB microphones are designed to plug directly into your computer or other digital recording device, making them convenient and easy to use. They also usually have built-in preamps and converters, which means they do not require additional equipment. XLR microphones, on the other hand, will only plug into an external audio recorder, but they provide better sound quality and offer flexibility for customization.

When deciding between USB and XLR microphones, consider your recording needs, budget, and technical knowledge before making a choice. USB microphones are a popular choice for beginners or those on a budget. They are also simple to set up and use, making them convenient for recording podcasts, voiceovers or basic music demos, and they provide a higher quality recording than the built-in microphone on a computer. On the other hand, XLR microphones offer better sound quality and flexibility in terms of adjusting levels and adding effects.

Selecting an appropriate microphone for your recording needs

When selecting a microphone for your audio-recording needs, you should weigh several factors such as the type of sound you want to capture, the environment in which you will be recording, and the hardware you will be using to convert the audio signal to digital.

In studio podcasting

Many podcasters record their audio within a controlled studio environment oftentimes interviewing subjects via phone or through video conferencing software. In this situation, a condenser microphone with a cardioid polar pattern would likely be a good choice as it can capture clear vocal recordings in studio settings. Since the speaker is typically not moving around and generally speaking from one direction, the cardioid polar pattern would help minimize undesirable room acoustics and background noise and focus on capturing the sound coming from the speaker's voice.

The more critical decision is whether you should use a USB or XLR microphone. If you are recording in-studio interviews with two or more microphones, you will need an audio interface or a field recorder with multiple inputs, and these devices typically require XLR microphones. While you can use a splitter to record with two USB microphones simultaneously into your computer, your software will treat it as one source. If you have the budget and plan to record on an audio field recorder, then an XLR microphone would be preferable.

On-location outdoor recording

On-location recording refers to recording outside of a controlled studio environment, such as in nature, at a live event, or in someone's home. If you are outdoors, a dynamic microphone is usually the best choice when you are recording a speaker or a musician, as these types of microphones are less sensitive to temperature changes and wind. If your goal is to capture the entire soundscape, an omnidirectional polar pattern would be a good choice. But if you are trying to record an interview, a microphone with cardioid or supercardioid would do a better job at blocking out the sounds in the environment. In this scenario, XLR microphones are often the preferred choice as they provide better sound quality and can be used with audio field recorders that are designed for outdoor recordings.

Recording vocals or instruments

In a studio setting, there is no one-size-fits-all microphone solution as it ultimately depends on the specific sound you are trying to achieve. In general, condenser microphones tend to capture more detail and higher frequencies, making them a popular choice for recording vocals or acoustic instruments. However, dynamic microphones can also be suitable for recording certain vocal styles or louder instruments such as electric guitar or drums. Typically, each instrument will require its own microphone, therefore you would need several XLR microphones plugged into an audio interface in order to record multiple tracks.

Demonstration videos

When recording audio for demonstration videos where your subject is moving around, a lavalier (lav) mic is a good option. Lav mics are small, lightweight microphones that clip onto the subject's clothing and can capture their voice clearly without picking up background noise. Lav mics can be wired or wireless, with wireless options providing more freedom of movement for the subject. These types of microphones are typically condenser and have an omnidirectional polar pattern because they are usually pinned to subjects' clothing and are not right in front of their mouths.

Film scene

In the film industry, production sound mixers use boom and shotgun microphones for recording audio on set. These microphones are typically highly directional condenser mics that are attached to a boom pole or stand and can be moved around to pick up sound from a variety of angles. You have probably seen them if you have watched any behind-the-scenes footage of professional film or television production. Boom poles are long, extendable rods that can be lowered over the actors' heads and positioned close to their mouths so that the diaphragm can pick up sound accurately. The job of the boom operator is to hold the boom mic as close as possible to the actor while keeping the mic out of the frame. Shotgun microphones are very similar to boom mics in that they have a highly directional pattern. In fact, many sound engineers use them interchangeably with booms. The difference is that shotgun microphones are mounted on stands and can't be moved around like a boom mic. Shotgun mics with supercardiod polar patterns are commonly used to record individual voices as they have a long, narrow pick-up pattern that capture sound from the direction they are pointed while avoiding the sounds coming from the sides, so you want to make sure they are facing the right direction when you set them up. Both of these types of microphones are typically XLR microphones as they allow for more precise control over levels and can be easily connected to an audio field recorder or interface.

Strategies for capturing good-quality audio

Now that you have a deeper grasp of the various microphone options and recording devices, let's delve into some additional techniques that will assist you in capturing high-quality audio.

Recording at an appropriate sample and bit depth

The sampling and bit depth are settings you can adjust on your audio-recording device. A standard sample rate for audio recording is 48kHz and a common bit depth is 24 bits. This ensures that your audio is translated into a digital format with enough precision to accurately describe any human audible sound. Sometimes such a high sampling rate and bit depth are not needed. For example, if you are recording a voiceover for a podcast or video, you can usually record good-quality audio at 16kHz with a bit depth of 8 as human speech is fairly low frequency. But if you are recording music, it is recommended to record at 48kHz for higher-quality and more detailed sound. Keep in mind that recording at a higher frequency results in larger file sizes, so it is important to balance the desired frequency range with practical storage considerations.

Careful mic placement

Choosing the right microphone and understanding its polar pattern is crucial for recording high-quality audio. But where you place your microphones can also have a significant impact on the sound quality. Experimenting with mic placement can help you achieve the desired sound for your recording. For example, placing a dynamic mic close to an instrument or vocalist can result in a more intimate and focused sound, while placing it further away can create a wider and more ambient sound.

In general, you want the microphone close enough to the source of sound you are recording so that you don't have any background noise interfering with the signal but far enough away that you avoid the proximity effect. The proximity effect refers to the amplification of lower frequencies to a greater extent than mid and high frequencies, resulting in a boomy or low-end heavy tone in a person's voice. For table microphones, you can usually avoid this effect by placing the microphone about an arm's length away from your speaker.

The angle at which the sound source is positioned in relation to the microphone can also have a dramatic effect on the quality of the audio that is captured. If you are using a directional microphone and the mic is placed "off axis," meaning it is not directly aligned with the sound source, it can result in the rejection of certain frequencies or even the entire sound coming from your target's mouth. This can have a significant impact on the tone and intelligibility of what they are saying or singing, potentially affecting the overall quality of the audio recording or performance.

Reducing background noise

Background noise can be a major culprit of poor audio quality. It is critical that you are aware of and account for any potential acoustic interference in your recording space as it can be a problem in both indoor and outdoor spaces. Wind and room tone are the major culprits in creating background noise, but there are various accessories and strategies you can use to diminish their effect on your audio recording.

Using a microphone stand is an effective technique for minimizing background noise. By setting up the microphone on a stand, you can significantly reduce vibration. When you hold the microphone in your hand, it may inadvertently capture the sound of your fingers moving across its surface while recording. With a microphone stand, you can enjoy a hands-free recording experience, ensuring optimal clarity and quality.

Adding a pop shield to your microphone is another device that can help reduce background noise. A pop shield is a foam or metal guard that fits over the end of the microphone and prevents loud pops from entering the recording.

When recording outdoors, wind can be a major source of noise. The best way to combat wind noise is with a windshield or blimp for your microphone. Many microphones come with built-in foam windscreens that can help reduce wind noise as well. If possible, try to select a location that isn't exposed to direct winds. In addition, have your subject face away from any gusts.

You may assume that recording indoors will solve any noise problems. Unfortunately, it is almost impossible to find a room that is completely silent. Common background noise-making culprits include buzzing lights, air conditioning, fans, refrigerators, etc. The surfaces of the walls can also contribute to the background noise. Room reflections can be caused by hard, reflective surfaces like walls and windows. These surfaces can create an echo effect in your recording space, making the audio muddy or unintelligible. There are a number of methods you can use to dampen the sound in a room to help reduce the background noise. Soft materials such as drapes, carpets, rugs, and furniture can help absorb sound waves in a room.

It's always a good idea to check out a space prior to scheduling a recording session. Go to the room or the outdoor space where you plan to record and listen to the sound of the room. Pay attention to any mechanical noise like air conditioners, fans, or other equipment that can be heard. If the interference is too loud and you can't get rid of it, you may want to move your recording session elsewhere.

After finalizing your recording spot, take a moment to record the ambient sound of your environment. This recorded sample will prove valuable during the editing process. Advanced audio-editing software can utilize this sample as a reference for eliminating unwanted frequencies from your main audio tracks.

Watching your levels

Any recording device and most recording software (if you are recording directly into your computer) will display the levels of the audio you are recording. Watch the levels readout as you capture your audio. They should peak between about –6 and –4dB. The levels display is color coded. The upper green range is typically the ideal level while yellow and red are too loud.

Distortion occurs when your audio signal is too loud and exceeds the maximum input level of the microphone or other equipment you are using.

Distortion results from either clipping or overloading. Clipping occurs when the input signal is too strong and causes the top of the waveform to get clipped off, resulting in an unpleasant, distorted sound. Overloading occurs when the input level is too high and it can cause a buzzing noise as well as distortion.

If you are recording multiple sound sources simultaneously such as speaking and live music, you run the risk of one of the sources being drowned out. This is why it is important to check the audio levels before recording. You want to make sure that each sound source is balanced with one another in order to get a crisp and clear mix without any one element overpowering the other.

Monitoring your audio

It is good practice to monitor your audio while recording to ensure that everything is being captured correctly. This means using headphones to listen to the audio as it is being recorded. Even when you have your technical settings perfectly dialed in, you may want to make some minor adjustments to the recording set up to improve the overall tone of the recording. Headphones also help minimize feedback and echo, especially when you are recording into your computer as they prevent the sound coming out of your computer from getting picked up by the microphone.

Listening to the tone

The tone of the audio is really a finer point when considering the overall quality of the audio. Your goal should be to capture audio that is clear and not too bassy or tinny. A bassy tone is when your audio is very bottom heavy and can be the result of too much low-end frequency or the proximity effect. A tinny tone can be caused by a lack of mid-range frequencies. Your microphone selection, placement, and environment will all affect the tone of your recordings. Therefore, it is wise to spend time listening to your recordings and making adjustments as needed.

Legal issues when recording audio

Any time you record audio, you should be aware of the legal issues associated with doing so. Depending on where you live, certain restrictions apply when it comes to recording audio without permission from the person or people being recorded. In the United States, it is generally legal to record audio without permission as long as the recording is made in a public space or you have been given consent from the person you are recording. However, if you plan on using that audio for commercial purposes (like a podcast or video) then you should always get written permission from the person being recorded. Likewise, if you record someone performing copyrighted material, you will also need written permission from the copyright holder. This is to protect against any potential legal issues that may arise from using copyrighted material without proper consent.

"Microphones are like paintbrushes" by audio engineer Carl Nappa

Microphones are like paintbrushes—they are not one size fits all. If you are painting a wall—you need a big brush. But if you are painting something more detailed, you will want to use a smaller, finer brush. The same philosophy applies to choosing a microphone. When you need to record a broad range of sounds, use a microphone that's up for the task. But if your goal is to record a small detail, you will need a much more sensitive and directional mic.

Study questions

1) List three different categories of microphones and describe the situations in which each type is used.
2) What is the difference between clipping and overloading when it comes to audio distortion?
3) How can you check the levels of your audio recordings?
4) What are the legal considerations for recording audio and using existing audio in your work?
5) Describe three methods of dampening sound in a room to reduce background noise.

Exercises

1) Research different types of microphones and take notes on their uses.
2) Experiment with setting audio levels and listen for distortion when the signal is too loud.
3) Record a sample audio clip in a public space and listen back to see how the background noise changes depending on where you set up your microphone.
4) Read up on your local copyright laws to understand what audio you can and cannot use.
5) Research different methods for soundproofing a space and practice dampening the sound in a room of your choice. Record some audio clips before and after the dampening process to hear how much background noise has been reduced.

References

"Apple Presents iPod." 2001. Apple.
Chandler, Paul, and John Sweller. 1991. "Cognitive Load Theory and the Format of Instruction." *Cognition and Instruction* 8 (4): 293–332. https://doi.org/10.1207/s1532690xci0804_2.

Dyer, Frank Lewis, and Thomas Commerford Martin. 2010. *Edison: His Life and Inventions.* Waiheke Island: The Floating Press.

Grosvenor, Edwin S, and Morgan Wesson. 2016. *Alexander Graham Bell.* Newbury: New Word City.

Knott, Ryan. n.d. "Why People Stop Watching Your Videos (And How to Avoid It!)." Techsmith. https://www.techsmith.com/blog/why-people-stop-watching-videos/.

Lynskey, Dorian. 2015. "How the Compact Disc Lost Its Shine." *The Guardian,* May 28.

Millard, Andre. 2005. *America on Record: A History of Recorded Sound.* 2nd ed. Cambridge: Cambridge University Press.

"Poor Audio Quality Affects Work Productivity, Finds a Study." 2023. *The Economic Times.* https://economictimes.indiatimes.com/news/how-to/poor-audio-quality-affects-work-productivity-finds-a-study/articleshow/97477949.cms?from=mdr.

Schwartz, Gideon. 2019. *Hi-Fi: The History of High-End Audio Design.* London: Phaidon Press. https://worldcat.org/title/1099690502.

"The Gramophone." n.d. The Library of Congress. https://www.loc.gov/collections/emile-berliner/articles-and-essays/gramophone/.

7 Editing and sharing audio

Audio editing is the process of manipulating and combining audio files to create a composition that can be exported in various formats. Whether it's for podcasting, music production, audio books, or sound effect design, audio editing is essential for creating professional-quality audio projects.

In this chapter, we'll start by looking at the history of audio editing and how it has evolved over the past several decades. Next, we will address the properties of sound: duration, volume, and frequency and how they are represented. We will also discuss the difference between mono and stereo audio. Then we will get into the basics of audio editing and how you can use different software programs and techniques to accomplish common audio-editing tasks such as trimming, fading, and normalizing. Next, we'll explore some tips on choosing the right audio-file types and settings to ensure your project sounds great when it's finished. Finally, we will examine web-based platforms that allow you to share your audio files whether it's via downloads, streaming or as a podcast.

Evolution of audio editing

The origins of audio editing have close ties to the developing film industry in the early part of the 20th century. During the era of early silent films, live music was frequently performed in theaters to accompany the visuals. However, in the 1920s, a significant breakthrough occurred with the introduction of sound-on-disc technology. This innovative development, called the Vitaphone, enabled "the synchronization of recorded music and dialog with the film, achieved through a turntable connected to a film projector via an interlocking mechanism" ("Sound-on-Disc" n.d.). This groundbreaking advancement revolutionized the cinematic experience, enhancing both the auditory and visual components of films.

The Vitaphone had a number of limitations. Any theater that wanted to show the film would have to own the device which was a costly endeavor. Another downside was that the sound was recorded directly on the disc, therefore it could not be edited after it was recorded. For these reasons, it was only a matter of years before the Vitaphone was obsolete and replaced by sound on film. This new

DOI: 10.4324/9781003462200-7

technique of recording sound directly onto film strips eliminated the need for accompanying records, making the process of recording and playing films more efficient and streamlined. It also enabled the ability to edit sound, although, since the sound was married to the film, the audio could not be edited independently.

The emergence of reel-to-reel tape recording in the 1940s marked a significant milestone in audio editing. This new technology allowed for editing and manipulation of sound recordings. Early analog tape supported two-track recording, but it eventually evolved into eight by the mid-1950s. Multi-track recording allowed for separate recordings of dialogue, music, and sound effects to be combined into one final mix. This was a huge advancement in audio editing as it allowed for greater control and flexibility in manipulating different elements of an audio project. It also signaled the beginnings of analog audio editing albeit in a quite primitive form. Editing audio involved cutting and splicing together pieces of the tape which was a tedious and time-consuming process that required great skill and precision. It was also a destructive process as the original tape would be physically altered. With this early form of editing, the editor's capabilities were limited. If the audio engineer wanted to add any type of enhancement or distortion to the recorded audio, it had to be accomplished by physically manipulating the playback device and rerecording the sound. Some audio engineers and musicians became quite famous for these types of distortion effects.

Figure 7.1 Four track recorder used by The Beatles in the 1960s [Josephenus P. Riley / CC BY 2.0 (via Wikimedia Commons)]

Everything changed with the advent of digital audio technology in the late 1970s. It was at this time when the first digital audio workstation (DAW) (a software application running on a computer that could record and edit) was introduced. This technology allowed for greater manipulation and editing of sound with more ease and precision than ever before. It also eliminated the need for physical cutting and splicing, making the process non-destructive to the original recording. Additionally, DAWs incorporated more complex features such as non-linear editing, which allows for working in a non-sequential manner. Initially DAWs could only be run on expensive mainframe computers but by the mid-1980s, advancements in personal computer technology allowed for DAW software to be run on standard desktop computers, and it was a game-changing development.

Today, audio-editing software has become even more advanced and accessible than ever before. With a variety of user-friendly and even free and web-based options available, anyone can try their hand at audio editing and creating professional-quality audio projects.

The properties and representation of sound

Before you can edit sound digitally, you need to understand how it is represented on the computer. Because sound is invisible, we need a means to describe the quality of the sound over time. This is the purpose of a waveform: a visual representation of an audio signal or sound that appears in your audio editing software. When sound is produced, it creates pressure changes in the air which are captured and converted into electrical signals by the microphone. These electrical signals are then translated into a digital form, which is represented by the waveform we see in audio-editing software. A waveform can provide valuable information about a sound, such as its loudness, pitch, and duration. Different sounds will produce distinct waveforms, allowing audio engineers to visually analyze and manipulate the audio.

A waveform is plotted on an x–y axis. The horizontal axis represents time which is measured in seconds. The simplest property to "read" from a waveform is the sound's duration or the length of time a sound lasts as it is the length of the sound wave.

The height of the waves in the waveform is the amplitude. A higher amplitude means a higher sound volume. Conversely, in areas where the waveform is non-existent, the audio is silent. The amplitude (or the volume) is measured in decibels (dB). An audio level of 0 decibels (dB) is the maximum level, and a quieter level is measured as a negative number such as –15dB. The ideal level for a voice is about –12dB which means it should be a little higher or lower than –12db as you listen back.

The density of a waveform is a representation of a sound's frequency. A sound with a wide wavelength (or low density) corresponds to a very low frequency, resulting in a low-pitched sound. Conversely, a waveform with more oscillations within a given timeframe indicates a higher frequency and a higher pitch, as the pitch of a sound increases with its frequency. Frequency

High Frequency Sound

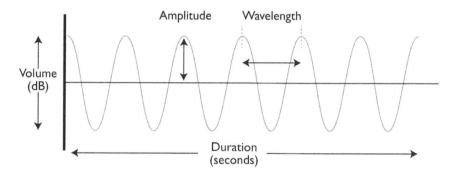

Low Frequency Sound

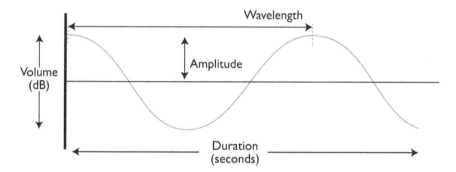

Figure 7.2 Representation of high frequency vs. low frequency sound

is measured in Hertz (Hz) and represents the number of waves present in one second. The range of sounds audible to humans spans from 20 Hz (very low pitch) to 20,000 Hz (very high pitch). Human speech typically falls in the range of 100–300 Hz.

Understanding these characteristics of your sound wave can help you when you start editing your audio files. Just by looking at the sound wave, you should get a sense of where there is no sound, what parts of the file are louder than others, where there are areas of higher or lower pitched sounds, and how long a sound lasts. Different types of sound have characteristic waveforms. For example, music often has a more complex, dynamic, and repetitive waveform with frequent changes in amplitude and frequency. On the other hand, speech or dialogue typically has a less complex and more erratic waveform.

Sampled sound

Sound is produced by vibrations that travel through the air and are perceived by our ears. To work with sound on a computer and incorporate it into a digital media project, it is necessary to "capture" it and convert it into a digital form. In the digital realm, sound is captured and stored as samples. A sample is essentially a recording of the pressure resulting from the vibrations at a specific moment in time. To accurately represent the changes in vibrations over time, samples must be taken frequently and described appropriately. These two factors, known as the sample rate and the bit depth, are characteristics that impact the quality of the captured sound. As we discussed in Chapter 6, these settings can be adjusted on your recording device.

The sampling rate refers to the number of samples of the vibrations that are taken every second. A higher sampling rate results in more samples taken within a specific time frame, leading to a more precise description of sound. The most commonly used sampling rates in music and audio production are 48 kHz, equivalent to 48000 samples per second. This particular rate is prevalent because it ensures that you will capture the highest frequency sounds that a human can hear. Capturing a complete sound vibration requires at least two samples and the highest frequency audible to humans is 20 kHz, therefore a sampling rate that is more than double ensures its accurate reproduction. During the CD era, the standard frequency for audio recording was 44.1 kHz; however, now that the medium has fallen out of favor, the audio industry has adopted the standard used for film audio recording which is 48 kHz.

Another factor that affects the quality of the audio we capture is the bit depth. The bit depth indicates how many bits (1s and 0s) are dedicated to describing each sample. We discussed this concept in an earlier chapter pertaining to the bit depth of a pixel-based image. The higher the bit depth, the more accurately a sound can be reproduced because we are using more bits to describe it. A bit depth of 24 bits (16.7 million possible levels) is the most used bit depth for audio production.

Mono vs. stereo

Audio is either mono (monophonic) or stereo (stereophonic). Mono audio has only one track while stereo audio has two tracks, a left and a right channel. In a stereo track, each channel can contain completely different sounds. Stereo audio is typically used in music production or sound design to create a more immersive and realistic experience for the listener.

When you record audio, it is important to consider whether you will be using mono or stereo. For instance, if you are recording a podcast, you may want to use just one microphone and record in mono. Once you bring it into your editing software, you can duplicate the track so that the audio comes out evenly on both sides of the headphones. On the other hand, if you are working with music production or sound design, you may want to record in stereo so that you can create a more immersive sound coming from different sources.

Different types of audio recorders record in mono vs. stereo. Basic voice recorders record in mono and field recorders record audio in stereo. There is a reason why these two devices work differently. The voice recorder is designed to record an individual's voice. Therefore, it makes sense to record it in mono.

You have one voice, so you only need one channel. A field recorder captures audio in stereo. This is because it's often needed to pick up the sound in an entire room. In recordings like these, there is typically more than one voice so it makes sense to record in stereo.

You can tell if your audio is mono or stereo by looking at the waveform in your audio-editing program. Mono waveforms have one channel, which means that all the sound is represented on one line. Stereo waveforms have two channels—left and right. Even if you capture your audio in mono, you will still want to distribute it as a stereo sound. That means that the same audio will come out of each channel; that is, your listener will hear the same sounds in the right and the left speaker.

Audio-file formats

There are numerous file formats available for storing audio files. In audio production, some of the most prevalent formats include WAV, AIFF, FLAC, MP3, and AAC. These formats can be categorized as either compressed or uncompressed with respect to how they store information. Among the compressed formats, there are both lossy and lossless varieties.

Uncompressed audio-file formats

WAV (Waveform Audio File) is an uncompressed format developed by Microsoft that stores data exactly as it was captured. It also holds its time code which is helpful when syncing audio to video footage. Since WAV files are the highest-quality audio, their file sizes can be large and difficult to manage and share.

AIFF (Audio Interchange File Format) is another uncompressed file format that was originated by Apple. Similar to WAV files, they preserve the entirety of the original sound, resulting in larger file sizes compared to MP3s. But unlike WAVs, they don't hold time codes, so they're not as useful for editing and mixing. They are primarily used by professionals in the music industry for master recordings.

Compressed audio-file formats

When it comes to audio compression, there are two primary types: lossy and lossless. These are terms that we discussed earlier with respect to bitmap images. *Lossy compression* reduces the size of the audio file by eliminating certain parts of the data that are deemed "less important." This is typically done through data algorithms that analyze and deduce which parts of the sound can be removed without significantly affecting the overall audio quality. On the other hand, *lossless compression* retains every single bit of data from the original file while still reducing the file size. Algorithms determine how to write the data in the file in a more efficient way so that the overall file size is smaller. Audio files with lossless compression tend to be larger than their lossy counterparts.

Lossless compressed formats

FLAC (Free Lossless Audio Codec) is a highly efficient and widely used compressed audio format. It ensures that every intricate detail of an audio recording is preserved, allowing for a listening experience that remains faithful to the original source. By utilizing advanced algorithms, FLAC reduces the file size by approximately half, without compromising the quality or richness of the sound. This makes it an ideal choice for audiophiles and music enthusiasts who seek the perfect balance between storage efficiency and audio fidelity. It's also open source.

Lossy compressed formats

MP3 (MPEG-1 Audio Layer 3) is the most commonly used audio format. MP3 files are compressed to dramatically reduce their file size, making it easy to store and share them. Saving a WAV file as an MP3 typically reduces the file to one-tenth of its original size. The introduction of the MP3 format in the late 1990s sparked a music sharing revolution. To this day, the MP3 format is popular due to its compatibility with a wide range of devices and platforms and its high degree of compression.

AAC (Advanced Audio Coding) is an audio format that offers higher sound quality than MP3s at the same bitrate. This makes it a good option for digital music distribution since it provides better audio quality compared to MP3s but still has a small file size.

Selecting an appropriate audio-file format

When choosing an audio format, always consider the purpose of your audio file. If you are working with high-quality audio or plan on editing and manipulating the sound, an uncompressed format such as WAV or AIFF is recommended. However, if you are sharing your audio online or need to save space on your device, a compressed format may be more suitable.

MP3 files are still the most widely used compressed audio format, but they do come with some limitations. The compression process eliminates some of the audio data, which can result in a loss of sound quality. Additionally, MP3 files have a lower bit depth and sampling rate compared to other formats such as WAV or AIFF. This means that when you are editing an MP3 file, there is less information available to work with, which may affect the final quality of your audio. When possible, it is best to use an uncompressed audio format for editing and then convert to a compressed format for distribution.

Audio editing

One of the most important skills in digital audio production is being able to edit an audio file. Audio editing involves manipulating and modifying recorded sounds to achieve a desired result. This includes tasks such as cutting, copying, pasting, and rearranging audio clips. It also involves adjusting volume levels, adding effects, and removing unwanted noise.

Audio-editing software

Audio-editing software, otherwise known as a digital audio workstation (DAW), is a tool that allows you to manipulate and modify digital audio. These software programs provide a range of functions, including recording, mixing, editing, and mastering audio tracks. They support a wide array of audio-file formats and facilitate multi-track and non-destructive editing, which allows you to make changes to an audio file without altering the original. Many DAWs also come with various built-in effects, filters, and tools for noise reduction, equalization, compression, and more, providing you with everything you need to fine-tune your audio to perfection.

There are many different audio-editing software options available, each with its own unique features and abilities. Most of them run on a desktop computer and (unless specified below) run on either a MAC or a PC. Some of the most popular and widely used ones include:

- **Audacity**: A free and open-source audio editor that is suitable for both beginners and advanced users. It offers a wide range of tools and effects for editing as well as support for multiple audio-file formats.
- **Pro Tools**: A professional-grade DAW used in many music and film production studios. It offers advanced features such as multi-track editing, MIDI (musical instrument digital interface) support, and high-quality effects and plugins.
- **Adobe Audition**: Part of the Adobe Creative Cloud, Audition is a powerful DAW that offers a seamless integration with other Adobe software. It has a user-friendly interface and provides extensive editing capabilities, making it a popular choice among video editors and podcasters.
- **GarageBand**: A beginner-friendly DAW that is widely available on MAC computers and iOS devices. It offers a range of pre-made loops, effects, and virtual instruments to help users create professional-sounding audio tracks without any prior experience.
- **Logic Pro X**: Another MAC-only DAW that is geared towards professional music production. It offers a vast array of editing and mixing tools, as well as a large library of virtual instruments and effects to choose from.
- **Sound Forge**: A less-expensive Windows only audio editing program, Sound Forge offers a robust set of editing tools for creating and manipulating high-quality audio files.

In addition to desktop-based software that you must purchase, there are also a number of freely available and subscription-based audio-editing programs that run inside of a web browser. These online tools offer the convenience of being accessible from any computer with an internet connection and can be used without needing to download or install any software. Some popular options include:

- **TwistedWave**: A user-friendly browser-based audio editor that offers basic editing features such as cutting, trimming, and fading audio clips.
- **AudioMass**: An intuitive browser-based audio editor that supports recording and extensive editing of audio tracks.
- **Soundation**: A web-based music production studio that offers both free and paid subscription options. It includes features such as multi-track editing, virtual instruments, and a wide range of audio effects.

Common audio-editing techniques

When it comes to audio editing, there are several techniques that are commonly used to achieve specific results. You will find almost all of these features in any DAW you choose.

- **Trimming**: The act of removing unwanted parts of an audio clip by cutting them out.
- **Fading**: Gradually reducing the volume at the beginning or end of an audio clip to create a smooth transition.
- **Crossfading**: Overlapping two audio clips and gradually fading out one while simultaneously fading in the other, creating a seamless transition between them.
- **Layering (or multi-tracking)**: Combining multiple audio clips or tracks to create a fuller, more complex sound.
- **Equalization (EQ)**: Adjusting the frequency balance of an audio clip to enhance or reduce specific frequencies.
- **Compression**: Reducing the dynamic range of an audio signal by compressing the loudest parts and amplifying the softer parts. This technique is often used to even out volume levels and make audio sound more consistent.
- **Limiting**: Taking the softer information and make it louder and the louder info and making the softer.
- **Normalizing**: Adjusting the overall volume level of an audio clip to a target value to achieve a more consistent sound.
- **Noise reduction**: Using software tools to remove unwanted background noise or hum from an audio recording.
- **Pitch correction**: The process of correcting off-key notes in a vocal performance by adjusting the pitch digitally.
- **Looping**: Repeating a section of audio to create a continuous sound or beat.

- **Time-stretching**: Altering the speed of an audio clip without changing its pitch, allowing you to create slow-motion or fast-forward effects.
- **Modulation effects**: Adding effects like artificial reverb and delays.

Obtaining audio files from other sources

In the previous chapter we discussed best practices for recording audio. The audio clips that you capture are often the raw materials that you will be working with in your audio-editing software. However, there may be times when you need to obtain additional audio files to use in your project.

Sound effects and music clips

There are many sources for obtaining sound effects to use in your audio projects. Of course, you can create your own sound effects by just experimenting with everyday objects in your home. I've actually spoken with a sound designer who creates some of her best sound effects by recording her cats. Once you record these sounds and import them into audio-editing software, you can manipulate them to sound completely different. What once sounded like a screeching cat can be altered in the software to sound like a car screech or a swipe of a laser.

If creating your own sounds seems like too much work, you can obtain sound effects from various websites. Some of these websites also offer music clips to download and integrate into your audio project.

- **SoundDogs.com**—offers loads of sound effects. You can download low-quality sounds for free for non-commercial use.
- **Zapsplat.com**—has a huge collection of free sounds effects and royalty free music.
- **FreeSoundEffects.com**—is exactly what its name says. The sounds you can download from this site are free for personal or educational use.
- **Freemusicarchive.org**—is a superior source for royalty free music.

Before integrating any sound or music clip into a project, make sure to check the terms of use and licensing requirements. Some sites may require attribution or have limitations on commercial use.

If you would like to use a music clip from a specific artist or album in your project, you will need to obtain permission from the artist which may not be feasible if the artist is very popular. A better option is to search websites designed to connect independent recording artists with creators who want to use their music in their projects such as MusicBed or Epidemic Sound. These recording artists often request nominal fees or attribution in return for use of their music.

You can also have original music recorded for a project, by hiring a freelance composer or musician through online platforms such as Upwork, Fiverr, or SoundBetter. These platforms allow you to browse profiles and listen to samples of work from various composers and musicians and choose one that best fits your needs and budget, and then figure out a plan to work together.

Exporting and sharing your audio files

Once you finish editing your audio project, you are ready to export it and share it. The final audio format you choose will depend on the intended use of your project. If you plan on sharing your final piece through the web, you will most likely export your composition as an MP3 file. This is because it will be played back through the speakers of a computer or mobile device which would make it difficult to hear differences in quality between compressed and uncompressed formats. If your project requires high-quality audio, exporting as a WAV file (or another uncompressed format) may be more appropriate.

There are several different ways in which you can share an audio file. If your intention is to allow users to download your audio file, you will need to upload it onto a website. Nowadays, cloud storage services like Dropbox or Google Drive make it easy to store and share large audio files. You can upload your file and generate a shareable link which you can then send to your recipients via email or social media. Alternatively, if you own a website and want to place links to your audio files within your site, that is easy to do as well. Most website-building platforms offer tools to integrate audio files within the page content. Another method for sharing audio files (if you don't want to host them on your own website) is to use a hosting service specifically designed for audio such as SoundCloud or Bandcamp. These platforms allow you to upload and share your audio files with a wider audience, but you can also grab the URLs of your pages containing your audio files from these sites and share them via email or on social media.

If your goal is to share your audio in the form of a podcast that you want to make publicly available, you will need to host it on a website from which you must create an RSS feed. Many web platforms will provide you with this tool. Then you will submit your RSS feed to various podcast directories and wait for it to be approved. To publish additional episodes, you will simply add the new audio files to your site in a similar manner and they will automatically be available on these channels.

If you aim to share your original music compositions on streaming services, there are a couple of options available. One is to submit your music directly to popular platforms such as Spotify, Apple Music, and Pandora. Another option is to work with aggregators like CD Baby. These aggregators assist artists who may not have a vast music collection in getting their music onto multiple streaming platforms, as there are sometimes thresholds disqualifying less experienced musicians from being able to submit directly to the popular platforms.

Legal issues when incorporating audio into your projects

Understanding copyright law is critical when using music in your audio projects. In essence, copyright law protects the creators of original works of authorship, including music, by granting them exclusive rights to copy, distribute, and perform their works. Any use of copyrighted music without express permission from the copyright owner constitutes an infringement, potentially leading to legal action. However, there are certain exceptions under the "fair use" doctrine for educational, research, or personal use. When working with music or other copyrighted materials in your audio projects, always ensure that you have the necessary permissions or that your use falls under the fair use exceptions. Remember, ignorance of copyright law is not a defense against infringement. Be aware, respect creators' rights, and always use music responsibly in your audio projects.

"A passing bus is no longer a problem" by professional audio engineer John Krivit

The capabilities of audio-editing software have come a long way. Years ago, if a noisy bus drove by while you were recording, you would need to re-record because the audio would be unusable. Fortunately, advanced editing tools have changed this paradigm. With modern audio-editing software, you can zoom into the audio spectrogram and pluck that disturbance right out.

Study questions

1) What are the most common audio-file formats? Which are lossy compressed, lossless compressed, and which ones are uncompressed?
2) What are some techniques used in audio editing to improve the quality and consistency of sound?
3) Where can you obtain audio files for your project? How do you ensure that you have the proper rights and permissions to use them?
4) What is the recommended format for exporting an audio file if it will be shared through the web? What other methods exist for sharing audio files?
5) If you want to make your audio available as a podcast, what steps do you need to take in order to distribute it through major podcasting directories?

Exercises

1) Create a short audio project using editing software of your choice. Experiment with different effects and techniques to improve the sound quality.

2) Research copyright law in your country and write a brief report on how it applies to the use of music in audio projects.
3) Practice exporting and sharing an audio file by creating a Dropbox or Google Drive account and uploading your project file. Share the file with a friend or family member and ask for their feedback.
4) Interview a podcaster and find out how he or she edits and updates her latest podcast content.
5) Research different freelance composer and musician platforms, such as Upwork or SoundBetter, and identify at least three that you would be interested in working with on your fantasy podcast.

Reference

"Sound-on-Disc." n.d. MoMA. https://www.moma.org/collection/terms/sound-on-disc.

8   Shooting video

Shooting high-quality video is an art that harnesses both technical skills and creative vision. It's more than just hitting the "record" button; it's about understanding the intricate interplay of light, composition, movement, and sound to effectively tell your story. In the past decade video has exploded online, creating a demand for people who can effectively communicate with this medium.

This chapter focuses on the art of video production. We will begin by exploring the evolution of video production and the convergence of film and video. Next, we will cover why video production knowhow is important and where and how these skills are needed. Finally, we will discuss what equipment you need for a video shoot, how to best prepare, and some additional strategies you should use to ensure your shoot is successful.

The evolution of video

The first type of video to exist was analog. Analog video refers to the original process by which the electronic signals, representing captured light, were displayed as moving images. These signals were continuous in nature, meaning they varied continuously with the image but displayed at such a rapid rate that the viewer only saw the image and not the streams of light. The origins of analog video date back to the late 19th and early 20th centuries when pioneers in the field were exploring ways to transform images into electronic signals for transmission and display.

The birth of television, a significant milestone in this journey, utilized analog video signals to deliver moving images. Eccentric Scottish engineer John Logie Baird was among the first to demonstrate this technology. In 1925 he scanned an object and projected "a recognizable image, complete with shades of grey" ("The Story of BBC Television – John Logie Baird" n.d.) .The BBC adopted his technology and soon Baird was running television programming for the station. Baird's innovation was followed closely by an American, Philo Farnsworth, and a Russian-American, Vladimir Zworykin, who pioneered electric televisions (Eboch 2015, p. 18).

DOI: 10.4324/9781003462200-8

By the 1950s, analog video had become a ubiquitous medium used in television broadcasting. Shortly thereafter, the first videotape recorder was created that captured the images from television cameras by writing the camera's electrical signal onto magnetic videotape. Initially, analog video was stored in a variety of formats, but the most popular was videotape, a magnetic tape used for storing video as well as sound. In the early days, two-inch quadruplex videotape was utilized in television studios. However, it was the invention of the VHS (Video Home System) in the 1970s, and its competitor Betamax, that revolutionized analog video storage, enabling consumers to record and play back TV broadcasts or films as "videocassette recorders became sufficiently inexpensive to be purchased by millions of families for use in the home" ("Videocassette Recorder" 2023). These tape-based systems stored analog signals as magnetic patterns on a ribbon of videotape, encased within a plastic cassette that the user would slide in and out of the machine. As a somewhat ephemeral medium, the quality of analog video storage could degrade over time, with repeated viewings leading to a loss of both picture and sound quality.

The invention of digital video heralded a new era in the world of video production. In contrast to its analog counterpart, digital video translates images and sounds into binary format (zeros and ones). This technological leap was facilitated by the advancements in computers and the digitization of data in the latter half of the 20th century. The first digital video systems were developed in the 1970s but came to prominence in the 1980s. The primary advantage of digital over analog video lies in its resistance to quality degradation. Digital signals can be copied and manipulated without any loss of quality, making them ideal for editing and distribution. Furthermore, digital video files can be stored on computers, DVDs, and later flash drives and cloud storage, and played over the internet, vastly expanding the possibilities for video production and consumption.

Before the era of digital video, film and video were two distinctly different mediums. Video production was confined to traditional television sets, while film was reserved for the big screen. Shooting on film and shooting on analog video were two inherently distinct experiences, both in process and result. Film cameras create a series of negatives that had to be processed

Figure 8.1 VHS player, © Raimond Spekking / CC BY-SA 4.0 (via Wikimedia Commons)

to result in an editable film strip. Analog video cameras captured moving images by scanning an electron beam across a phosphor storing the signals on tape. Shooting on film was much more expensive than analog video, but it could produce moving images with a greater range of color values.

When digital video cameras emerged in the 1990s, they revolutionized the industry. Being able to instantly see what was recorded and easily edit footage on a computer brought a new level of efficiency and creativity to video production. Early digital video cameras offered nowhere near the quality of film, but eventually they improved. And as technology continued to evolve, cameras also got smaller and more affordable, allowing for greater accessibility and flexibility in shooting locations.

By the early 2000s, feature filmmakers took notice, recognizing the capabilities of digital cameras, and began shooting major motion pictures in a digital format. The 2002 release of *Star Wars: Episode II – Attack of the Clones* was one of the first major Hollywood films to be shot almost entirely with digital cameras. Before commencing the shoot, director George Lucas insisted that "the resolution of the imagery needed to at least match—preferably exceed—the quality of standard 35mm film" (Seastrom 2022). He succeeded in getting Sony to develop cinema-quality digital cameras that could shoot at 24 frames per second, the same as 35mm film cameras. This marked a significant shift in the industry, blurring the lines between film and video production.

The convergence of film and digital video has ushered in a novel era in the sphere of video production. This amalgamation has blurred the lines between professional cinematographers and independent filmmakers, offering affordable, high-quality digital alternatives to traditional film cameras. Today, we see a blend of filmic techniques and digital workflows, where filmmakers leverage the tangible texture and richness of film, and the flexibility and efficiency of digital video. This convergence not only opens up huge creative possibilities but also democratizes the field of video production, making it accessible to a wider audience. With the rise of consumer-level video cameras and user-friendly editing software, the barrier to entry has been significantly lowered. It's now easier than ever for anyone with a camera and a creative vision to produce high-quality videos.

The explosion of online video

With the rise in internet bandwidth and the widespread popularity of platforms like YouTube, integration of video on social media channels like Facebook and Instagram, and the emergence of video-first platforms like TikTok, video content is flooding the internet. "In 2021, a million minutes of video content [was expected to] cross the internet every second" (Mowat 2018). In 2022, video comprised of 82% of all internet traffic, and approximately 89% of US internet users watched online videos. And these numbers will more than likely continue to rise as the number of internet users worldwide is increasing by 10% every year (Lukan 2023).

The video we view online serves various purposes. While entertainment is still a significant driver, other video genres are gaining traction. From product demos to educational and instructional content to video advertisements, the internet has become a platform for businesses and organizations to reach their target audience.

Product demonstrations and reviews

Video is an excellent tool for showcasing a product's features and demonstrating its usage. It brings products to life, emulating the experience of holding it in your hands and playing around with it. A video demonstration provides tangible proof of the effectiveness of your product. A customer-created video product review integrated with "vendor-generated product descriptions [has been shown to] powerfully affect consumers' perceptions about the product" (Xu et al. 2015). Companies recognize the power of video to help sell product and are increasingly incorporating them on product pages.

Product demonstration and review videos can be multi-functioning marketing content. Videos hosted on YouTube and incorporated into product pages may show up in the platform's search engine results pages, providing more visibility for the product. Additionally, these videos are shareable on social media, which allows them to reach a wider audience. When done strategically, videos on YouTube can attract new customers, leading them to the product website.

Education and instructional videos

Video has become an integral part of education. When schools and universities moved online due to the pandemic, video lectures became ubiquitous. The general population became accustomed to this type of learning and have increasingly turned to online video for instruction. "During a March 2020 survey, 22 percent of U.S. respondents stated that they had watched more online instructional videos due to social distancing and self-quarantining practices" ("Share of Adults Who Watch More Online Instructional Videos Due to Social Distancing during the Coronavirus Pandemic in the United States as of March 26, 2020" 2022).

Companies and organizations frequently use instructional videos for employee training. They also create instructional content as a means to educate potential customers while promoting their own products, services, and affiliates. An effective online instructor can build trust as well as a following that can lead to sales.

Brand storytelling

Video is an ideal medium for communicating a brand's story, message, or mission. Powerful visuals, combined with emotive audio and music, can yield a moving narrative that connects with viewers on a deeper level than just text or images alone. This can greatly contribute to brand awareness and customer loyalty.

Videos that are designed for brand storytelling can be delivered in a variety of formats. Shorter, montage-style non-narrative videos are often used on company's website home pages. They can also be shared by third-party media outlets on social media or in their publications (like an online magazine). Longer, more cinematic videos are often used for product launches and similar events and shared via live streaming services, like Facebook Live or YouTube Live.

Social media marketing

Social networking use is one of the most popular activities on the internet. "In 2022, 4.59 billion people were using social media worldwide, a number that is projected to increase to almost 6 billion in 2027" ("Number of Social Media Users Worldwide from 2017 to 2027" 2023). It's no surprise that social media platforms have become an integral part of marketing strategies, and video is at the forefront.

Oftentimes videos shared on social media feature the people and processes behind the scenes at a business or organization which can strengthen a consumer's connection to it. The meteoric rise of the Dollar Shave Club illustrates the power of video content shared on social media for successful brand marketing. In 2012, Dollar Shave Club shared a video of the founder, Michael Dubin, giving a tour of the company's warehouse while espousing the benefits of their blades in a raw and charismatic manner. While the blades were technically no different from any other razor blades on the market, the video went viral, and attracted a loyal following. The success of the Dollar Shave Club is just one example of how social media "video has proven to be an incredibly powerful way of affecting behavior" (Mowat, 2018).

Nowhere is this phenomenon more evident than in the rise of influencer marketing, which leverages video to showcase products and promote brands. Social media influencers with significant followings have the power to sway consumer behavior, and businesses are harnessing this by collaborating with them in sponsored content videos.

Advertising

Video advertising has become increasingly pervasive and will continue to increase substantially in future years. In fact, video advertising is projected to grow ten-fold between 2022 and 2030 (Licensors et al. 2023). Advertisers have found that "video advertising costs less than traditional advertising in terms of brand building and information dissemination" (Xiao et al. 2023). They have also found that it "helps to positively impact business marketing and sales" (Licensors et al. 2023).

Video advertising comes in several different forms online. On YouTube, pre-roll ads are shown before a video is played, and mid-roll ads are displayed in the middle of longer videos. Social media platforms like Facebook also offer in-feed video advertising options that play as users scroll through their feed. Video ads (typically without audio) can also be found within the content of a website or displayed as banner ads on various websites.

One of the reasons why video advertisements are so effective is because they can be highly targeted, reaching specific demographics and interests with precision. They also have the advantage of being able to convey a message or story in a visually captivating way, making them more memorable for viewers.

Video equipment essentials

The democratization of video production has been largely facilitated by the decreasing cost and increasing accessibility of video equipment. A few decades ago, professional-grade video cameras were prohibitively expensive, restricting access to broadcast companies and affluent filmmakers. However, today, the landscape has significantly changed. High-quality video cameras, capable of shooting excellent videos, are available at a fraction of the price, making them accessible to hobbyists, independent filmmakers, and small businesses. Moreover, the advent of smartphones with powerful cameras and editing apps has put video production capabilities in the pockets of virtually every individual. Nevertheless, the question for an aspiring filmmaker often arises: what equipment do I need to create a professional-looking and sounding video?

Video cameras and additional lenses

Your camera is the most crucial piece of equipment for shooting video. While smartphones and basic consumer video cameras may work for some projects, others will dictate the use of a higher-quality camera that will allow for more control over some of the technical aspects of your videos. Before deciding what type of a video camera or cameras you need for your video shoot, you should be aware of how the video you are creating will be used. The purpose of the video as well as where it will be deployed will determine the resolution, aspect ratio, frame rate, and other technical specifications you should consider when selecting a camera.

Understanding the capabilities of the different types of video cameras will help you decide whether to shoot a video on your iPhone or a professional video camera. These capabilities include the image quality, sensor size, possible frame rates, and the camera's image stabilization ability. The image quality refers to the resolution of your video camera and is measured in pixels. The higher the number, the better the quality. Most professional-grade cameras shoot at least in 4K resolution which refers to the number of pixels (4000) on the horizontal axis of the frame. This is also the image quality available in the newer iPhone cameras. Some professional video cameras can now shoot in 8K which provides an incredibly high level of detail, capturing over 33 million pixels per frame. A camera's sensor functions by capturing light and transforming it into an electrical signal, which is subsequently processed to generate a digital image. It affects the image quality by determining how much light can enter the camera's sensor to capture an image. A larger sensor will produce a cleaner, more detailed image. Between version 12 and 13, Apple increased the iPhone's sensor size from 12 megapixels to 48 resulting in a more "defined and sharper" picture (Savvides 2022). Professional video cameras also boast the ability to shoot at higher frame rates than the cinematic standard 24 fps which is useful if you need to capture very fast movement with precise detail. Another advantage of pricier professional video cameras over their smartphone counterparts is their sophisticated image stabilization capabilities. They are much better at capturing sharp images when the camera or the subject is moving.

With all this said, in many cases a smartphone can be a viable substitute for a professional digital video camera. In fact, several feature films that were deemed to have "high cinematic quality" were recently shot entirely on an iPhone (Prakoso 2024). However, before you commit to shooting your project with an iPhone, you should consider some additional limitations. First, you may run out of storage space. Professional video cameras store footage on SD cards, so it is possible to swap out a full card for an empty one in the middle of your project. With an iPhone, you will need to periodically transfer your footage to a hard drive or a computer which can be time-consuming and may disrupt the filming process. Second, professional video cameras generally have copious settings that allow you to achieve cinematic effects. New iPhones offer shooting modes such as "Cinematic" and "Action," but they are "not a perfect simulation [of the capabilities of a professional video camera] by any means" (Edwards 2022). Another limitation is the microphone. An iPhone has a built-in mic, but it will not likely be close to your subjects you are filming. And it does not have multiple ports to plug in external mics, so you will need to also have an audio field recorder. Finally, you may want to shoot with multiple iPhones simultaneously. This can save time during the editing phase, by allowing for multiple angles and viewpoints to be included in the final product. It's also a useful backup in case one camera fails.

In addition to the camera itself, supplemental lenses can profoundly enhance the quality and impact of your video production and dramatically alter the appearance of your footage, allowing for a variety of artistic effects. Wide-angle lenses, for example, provide a broader field of view than standard lenses, making them ideal for capturing landscape shots or tight interior spaces. Telephoto lenses, on the other hand, magnify distant subjects and are often used for wildlife videography or sporting events. One of the significant advantages of professional video cameras is their ability to swap lenses, giving you an extensive range of creative possibilities that usually surpass what a smartphone camera can offer and elevate the overall quality of your work.

Microphones, recording devices, and headphones

As we have discussed in previous chapters, the sound quality of your video can have a radical impact on how it is received. While most cameras come with built-in microphones, they are usually not the best solution for recording high-quality audio. This is because microphones mounted on the camera are typically not close enough to the sound source. Additional microphones and sound recording devices are often required on a video shoot.

In a previous chapter, we covered the types and strengths and weaknesses different types of microphones, but choosing microphones for video production presents some additional challenges. The tricky aspect of recording sound in video production is that while you want your microphones to be close to your subject, you do not want your microphone to be part of the scene. For interviews or dialogue-heavy scenes, a lavalier microphone, which can be clipped onto the subject's clothing and be fairly discreet can provide clear and crisp audio. Shotgun microphones are also a popular choice for recording dialogue, as they can be placed slightly off-scene and capture sound from a speaker while minimizing background noise. A boom microphone, held by a boom operator or mounted on a stand, is another option for capturing clear audio in larger spaces. But for a small production, finding a boom operator is not always possible.

While it is possible to plug external microphones into a supplemental port on a professional video camera, you will get better sounding audio if you plug the microphones into an audio field recorder. The only downside to capturing your audio on an external recorder separately from your video is that the audio and video will need to be synced together. This is very simple to do though. Have you ever seen a production assistant run in and clap a clapboard prior to the start of a scene? The purpose of this action is to identify the scene that is being shot to assist in the editing process. In addition, the clap creates a distinct spike in the audio track that you can align with the visual action of the clapboard closing within your editing software. You don't need to have an official clapboard to take advantage of this technique. You can do something similar by holding up some notes on a piece of paper in front of the camera and clapping your hands.

A recently added feature to some video-editing programs is the ability to automatically sync the audio and video as long as you have recorded some type of audio with the video. The software can match the lower-quality sound from the video camera to the high-quality sound from the field recorder and merge the media together so that you hear the higher-quality audio with the video clip.

High-quality, over-the-ear headphones are another crucial piece of equipment to have on a video shoot. They allow you to monitor audio levels accurately and detect any unwanted sounds or disturbances in the recording environment. When plugged into your recording device, they provide real-time feedback about what the microphone is capturing, which is critical as audio issues often go unnoticed without this direct auditory input. With the aid of headphones, you can catch and rectify any audio problems on the spot, ensuring you don't face the disappointing and possibly costly scenario of discovering such issues during post-production.

Lighting equipment

Lighting can make or break a scene, so it's important to have the necessary tools to properly light your video shoot. While natural lighting may suffice for some outdoor shoots, indoor scenes often require artificial lighting to achieve the desired look and feel. At a minimum, you should bring three lights to your shoot. Lights used in video production are mounted on adjustable stands and can be manipulated to create different moods in a scene by changing their position, intensity, or color temperature. Furthermore, having a few light modifiers, such as reflectors and diffusers, can help you shape and direct the light more precisely.

Tripods, sliders, and other camera supports

Keeping your camera stable and resulting footage smooth will yield a more professional look. This is where camera supports such as tripods and sliders come in handy. Tripods are essential for stationary shots, while sliders can be used to achieve smooth tracking or panning shots. For handheld shots, consider using a stabilizer or gimbal to reduce shakiness and create more fluid movements. Monopods can also be used for on-the-go filming, providing a bit more stability than handheld shots.

Other accessories

In addition to essential equipment such as cameras, lenses, microphones, and lighting tools, there are various other accessories that can be useful during video production. These include spare camera and microphone batteries along with associated chargers to facilitate continuous filming without interruptions. Additional memory cards are also essential to avoid running out of storage space, especially when shooting in high resolution. It's also beneficial to have laptops and portable hard drives for backing up footage and freeing up space on memory cards. Extension cords and power strips are necessary to supply power to all equipment on location, and sandbags are particularly helpful for outdoor shoots to maintain tripod and light stand stability in windy conditions.

Video preproduction

A successful video shoot starts with pre-planning, otherwise known as the preproduction phase. Since a video shoot can require the assistance of others, space availability, lighting requirements, acquisition of props, etc. it's essential to prepare for every aspect of the production in advance to avoid wasting time and money. It is during this preparatory stage that all the groundwork is laid, from developing the concept, writing the script, creating storyboards to scouting locations and casting characters and assembling the crew. A thorough preproduction process ensures that every aspect of the shoot is meticulously planned, reducing the chances of unforeseen challenges, and facilitating a more streamlined and efficient production phase. It's crucial to allocate sufficient time and resources for this stage, as the quality of preproduction directly influences the outcome of the shoot, impacting the overall quality and effectiveness of the video.

The type of preparation that is required for a video shoot depends on the type of video you are creating. If you are just shooting yourself, for example, you do not have the same time constraints and pressure that you might have if you have other people involved with your project. Nevertheless, strategic preproduction will make your process smoother and will produce better outcomes.

Prepare your script

The purpose of a script is to help you clarify your ideas, coordinate the production team, and assess the resources needed. "The techniques and processes of good script writing are a study in themselves," especially when it comes to writing for scripted television shows and feature films, but even smaller-scale productions benefit from a well-written script (Millerson 2001). The form of the script can vary significantly depending on the type of video you are producing. For example, a scripted sequence may be used for commercials or corporate videos, while a documentary-style film may have more of an outline structure and the script may take shape after filming has commenced. The script should convey the program's main purpose and include character dialog, describe locations, costumes, and props, and suggest framing and camera angles. Sharing the script with everyone involved in the shoot beforehand allows for better preparation and a smoother production phase.

It may feel like overkill to create a script for a video that you are going to shoot and edit yourself. However, having a script can significantly improve the quality of your video. Have you ever watched a YouTube video where the person in the video rambles on and on? It can be painful to watch. Writing a script in advance helps you organize your thoughts and ensure that all important points are addressed in the video. Additionally, it serves as a reference during editing, making it easier to determine which shots should be included in the final cut. While you may not need to prepare a verbatim script, it's a good idea to have your points written out so you don't go too far off on a tangent. An audience will more likely engage with well-prepared and succinct video than a less-organized one. We will discuss scriptwriting in greater detail in a subsequent chapter.

Create a storyboard

A storyboard is a visual representation of the shots and sequences in your video. It's essentially a comic-book version of your script, showing each shot and how they will be connected to tell a story. Storyboards are helpful for both the preproduction and production phases, as they provide a reference point for everyone involved in the shoot. Creating a storyboard allows you to experiment with different shots and sequences without having to actually stage and film those shots, allowing for a more creative and dynamic final product. It also forces you to consider how to best communicate your message through the lens of your camera as different types of shots serve different purposes.

Some of the most common shots used in film and video that would be drawn in a storyboard include:

- Wide Shot: A shot that captures the entire scene within the frame. This type of shot is useful for establishing location or showing a group of people.
- Medium Shot: A shot that gets closer to your subject showing body language and gestures. It should be used when you want to show more of the person and less of the setting.
- Close-Up: A shot focused on a specific element, person, or object within the scene. It can be used to show details and emotions or create an intimate connection with the subject. Extreme close-ups can bring a level of intensity to a scene.
- Over-the-Shoulder Shot: A shot that is taken from behind one character and facing another. This type of shot is used to show interactions between characters or provide a different perspective on a scene.
- POV (point-of-view) Shot: A shot that shows the viewer what a character is seeing, creating an immersive experience for the audience.

There are many other types of shots used by filmmakers. The point here is that how you shoot the scene can communicate just as much (if not more) than the shot itself.

Create a shot list

Prior to your shoot, you should have a detailed shot list based on the planning you did in your storyboard. A shot list is a comprehensive document that outlines the specific actions and elements to be included in a particular shot or scene of a film. It serves as a blueprint, detailing the precise composition and components required to bring that shot to life on screen. A shot list should include information such as shot number, shot description, camera movement, desired emotion or tone, actors/subjects involved, and any necessary equipment or props. It's also helpful to include a storyboard or sketches of each shot to provide a visual reference for the production team.

Creating a shot list is important for several reasons. The process of creating a shot list allows you to visualize how each shot will look and plan accordingly for any necessary equipment or props. It helps to ensure that all necessary shots are captured, avoiding the need for reshoots or missed footage. When working with a larger production team, the shot list provides a reference for the filmmaker and crew during the production phase, allowing everyone to work efficiently.

Careful planning of these shots may appear excessive for a tutorial video on YouTube. However, it's crucial to have a general idea of what you want to showcase and how, even in these scenarios. While you might believe that only one shot is necessary, for example, if you are demonstrating a process, incorporating close-ups can significantly enhance the informative value of your demo. When editing the video, strategically cut to the close-ups throughout the demonstration. Compiling a list of all the required close-ups before filming will ensure that you capture all necessary footage.

Optimize your shoot

Once you have created your shot list, you may notice that shots at different points within your video will be shot in a similar way. To be more efficient, you should capture these shots at the same time to improve your efficiently. Just because shots are listed in order, you do not need to follow that order when shooting.

Scout locations

Identifying the ideal location for your video shoot can have a dramatic impact on the quality of your video. From natural lighting to background noise, various factors can impact the look, feel, and sound of your footage. Reviewing potential locations ahead of time will help you determine if these locations meet your requirements.

When scouting locations, consider factors such as accessibility (for both filming equipment and crew), lighting options (natural vs. artificial), background noise levels, availability during filming dates, and any necessary permits or permissions. Additionally, if you are shooting in a public space, it's important to consider how you will handle any interruptions or unexpected bystanders.

When shooting an interview or a demonstration, it's critical to find a spot with a clean and uncluttered background so that it does not compete with the primary action in the video. Additionally, look for a room that is long and deep. This is important because it allows you to position your subject at various distances from the camera, creating more depth within the frame. By doing so, you can achieve a striking contrast between the subject and the background, effectively blurring the background and making the subject stand out more prominently.

When capturing indoor shots, seek out well-lit rooms with ample natural light streaming in through windows for a more authentic look. Steer clear of spaces illuminated by overhead fluorescent lights or any lighting positioned directly above the subject, as they can cast unattractive shadows.

It's incredibly important to locate a quiet space for your video shoot. This means avoiding rooms near elevators, busy streets, air vents, ringing phones, nearby people, or areas with constant background noise. To evaluate the acoustic properties of a room, experiment by closing your eyes for 30 seconds and attentively listening for any disruptions in sound. Be sure to not only consider the noise level during your initial visit, but also take into account any potential activities or events that may occur on the day and time of your shoot.

Assemble your team

The success of any video production largely depends on the collaboration and coordination of everyone involved. When you are involved with shooting a larger-scale video, it's crucial to assemble a skilled and dedicated team that shares your vision for the video. Depending on the scope of your project, your team may include a director, cinematographer, sound technician, lighting specialist, makeup artist, and actors/subjects. If you don't have access to these roles individually, consider hiring a production company that can provide a full crew for your shoot. In addition to technical skills and experience, look for team members who are reliable, communicative, and able to work well under pressure. Good teamwork will not only make the production process smoother but also contribute to a higher-quality end product.

Prepare the actors or subjects

Before filming, your actors or subjects should be properly prepared for their roles in the video. This includes providing them with a clear understanding of their character or role, rehearsing any necessary lines or actions, and discussing the desired emotion or tone for each scene. Make sure to communicate any specific instructions or directions clearly and encourage open communication with your actors/subjects to ensure a successful shoot.

When filming a sit-down interview, directors often advise their subjects to respond to the questions being asked in full sentences. For example, a response of "My name is John Smith" is much better than "John Smith." When interview subjects speak in full sentences they better assist in driving the narrative of the story.

If you are shooting an interview or a product demonstration, provide dress guidance to your subjects. They should avoid wearing busy patterns and stripes that might cause distortion and distract a viewer's attention. Solid colors tend to work best. If you are shooting in front of a green screen, avoid using the color green in clothing or accessories. This is because a green screen is used to integrate a virtual background, and if the subject's clothing is too similar in color to the background, the software will not be able to detect the difference between the subject and the green screen. Consider having subjects dress in a company or organization's brand colors if you are shooting a video that is intended to support a brand. Paying attention to grooming can significantly improve the appearance of your subjects on film. Applying a light layer of foundation can reduce shine on faces, while a gentle touch of hairspray can help tame flyaway hairs. Additionally, make sure to provide your actors or subjects with any necessary props or costumes prior to filming. This will not only save time during the shoot but also ensure that the desired look and feel is achieved for each scene.

Prepare yourself for your video shoot

As the person behind the camera, it's important to also prepare yourself for a successful video shoot. This includes having all necessary equipment and back-ups ready in case of technical issues, as well as familiarizing yourself with the shooting location beforehand. Make sure to have a shot list and storyboard readily available for reference during filming.

Shooting can be stressful and exhausting, so you need to prepare yourself for optimal performance. Wear comfortable clothing that allows for movement and avoid any noisy jewelry or accessories. Dressing neutrally, such as in black or grey, can also help you blend into the background and not distract from the focus of the video. Closed-toe shoes are a must to prevent injuries when moving around heavy equipment. In addition to equipment and wardrobe preparation, make sure to take care of your own well-being before filming. Stay hydrated, get enough rest, and take regular breaks to avoid burnout or fatigue during the shoot.

Prepare your equipment

Nothing can derail a video shoot faster than technical difficulties. To avoid potential issues, prepare and test all of your equipment before filming. This includes checking the camera settings, audio levels, lighting equipment, and any other necessary tools or accessories to make sure they are in good working order. It's also a good idea to have backup equipment on hand in case of any malfunctions or failures. This can include extra batteries, memory cards, and even an additional camera if possible.

No matter what type of camera you use, make sure you have enough storage space to capture the entire shoot. Running out of storage mid-shoot can be a frustrating and time-consuming setback. Most cameras store media on memory cards, usually SD (secure digital) cards. When you insert an SD card into the camera, you are presented with an option to format it. Formatting the SD card erases everything on the card and therefore maximizes its storage capacity. But this takes time to do. Plus, you will need to transfer any footage from the SD card to a hard drive before you format it. Therefore, commencing your video shoot with several formatted SD cards will make your process much more efficient.

You don't want your camera to die in the middle of filming an important scene. Charge all your camera batteries beforehand and bring extras with you as backups. You also want to bring a charger so that you can be charging camera batteries while you are shooting to ensure you always have one ready.

Dust particles on your lens can ruin an otherwise perfect shot. Before heading to the shoot location, make sure to clean your lenses thoroughly and check for any dust or debris that may affect the quality of your footage.

Always double check the settings on your camera and audio recorder prior to your shoot. Most video cameras will allow you to shoot at various resolutions. For the most part, you will usually want to set your video resolution to 1920 × 1080 pixels or higher. Ideally, you'll set the resolution to 4K (3840 × 2160 pixels) or higher if needed. These settings are controlled by the built-in menu on the camera. Choosing appropriate settings on your audio recorder is also very important. Always make sure that you are recording in the proper mode and format. It's a terrible feeling to realize that you have captured all of your media at the wrong setting.

Video production

Proper preparation for a video shoot is crucial; however, you still need to actually film something. The techniques you use to capture your footage can have a big impact on its overall quality.

Set up your lights

Before you arrive at your shooting location, you should have a good sense of what the lighting will be like in the space and have planned your lighting needs accordingly. If you are shooting outside, you may not need any lights at all. In sunny conditions, a reflector is a great tool to reflect hard light and soften it before it hits the subject.

If you are shooting indoors, you will likely need to use supplemental lights. A common configuration that works well in many cases is known as the three-point lighting setup. This arrangement consists of three lights: a key light, a fill light, and a backlight. The key is the main source of light for your scene and should be the brightest. It's typically positioned to one side of the subject, slightly above eye level, to create shadows and add dimension. Fill lights are used to reduce the harshness of shadows caused by key lights and soften the overall lighting in a scene. They are usually placed on the opposite side of the key light and are less intense. Backlighting is used to separate the subject from the background and create a sense of depth. It's usually positioned behind or above the subject, with a soft light source to avoid harsh shadows.

Stabilize your shots

Many beginner film producers shoot their videos by simply holding their cameras. This leads to shaky footage and can be very distracting for the viewer. Always use a tripod or other stabilization device to keep your shots steady. If you must shoot without a tripod, you can use the "human tripod" method where you hold your camera with both hands, keep your elbows close to your body, lean against a non-moving surface, and try to limit any unnecessary movements.

3 POINT LIGHTING

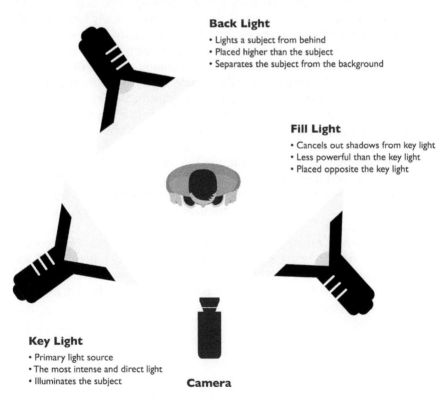

Back Light
• Lights a subject from behind
• Placed higher than the subject
• Separates the subject from the background

Fill Light
• Cancels out shadows from key light
• Less powerful than the key light
• Placed opposite the key light

Key Light
• Primary light source
• The most intense and direct light
• Illuminates the subject

Camera

Figure 8.2 Three-point lighting setup

Frame your shots

During your shoot, you should use your storyboard and shot list to remind you of what shots you need and their type. But as you are shooting, you should also be thinking about framing your shots in a way that is visually appealing and does not detract from the story being told. This involves considering the placement of your subject and any other elements in the frame, as well as the composition and balance of the shot.

There are several common framing mistakes that beginning filmmakers tend to make and you should try to avoid. Always make sure that the horizon line is straight. If it's not, it can make the shot look crooked and be disorienting. When shooting people, watch your headroom. Headroom refers to the space between the top of someone's head and the top of the frame. Too much headroom can make a shot feel unbalanced, while too little can make the subject look squished. Strive for consistency in framing. For example, when two close-ups are shot at significantly dissimilar angles, they can look inconsistent when edited together.

A helpful guideline for composing visually pleasing and balanced shots is to use the rule of thirds. We discussed this framing strategy in Chapter 2 on photography, but the same rule applies when shooting video as well. Imagine your frame divided into three equal parts both horizontally and vertically, creating a grid with nine sections. The key elements of your shot should align with these lines or intersections to create a more dynamic composition. The rule of thirds should be considered when filming any type of shot where it is a close-up, wide, mid, or over-the-shoulder. When employing the rule of thirds, you may wonder where the open space in the frame should be. Generally, you want the open space to be on the side that's opposite of where the subject is facing or moving towards. This creates a sense of balance and direction in your shot.

Occasionally filmmakers will break the rule of thirds. When done well, it can create a powerful effect. For example, placing your subject in the direct center of the frame can convey a sense of power or importance. But as with all creative choices, it's important to understand the rules and break them with intention, rather than just doing so randomly.

Integrate camera movements when framing your shots when appropriate. This can add visual interest and help to guide the viewer's attention. Some common camera movements include panning, tilting, and tracking. Don't overdo it though. Adding random zooms and pans can distract from the action and leave your viewers queasy.

Log your shots

Keeping track of your shots during your video shoot will make your editing process much more efficient. This is often done in the form of a shot log which is usually the job of an assistant director during the shoot. Each page of the shot log sheet should include the date, page number, project name, and production company. Then for each clip, you should record the file name of the clip (which you should be able to see on the camera), the scene, the take number, a shot description, and any comments. Comments are a great opportunity to include information about mistakes, or whether or not the shot was good. Logging was traditionally done on paper; however, you can now use software to accomplish this task.

Capture additional footage

Have you ever noticed how a photographer will take hundreds of photos at an event but maybe only print or showcase just a few? Photographers understand that the more shots you take, the greater the likelihood that you'll get a good one. The same philosophy holds true when shooting video. After narrative films are completed, they often use only one tenth of the footage that was shot. The percentage of footage used in a final documentary film is even lower. It's much better to shoot more footage than you think you need. So, while it's important to stick to your shot list and storyboard, don't be afraid to capture additional footage on the day of filming. This could include alternative angles, B-roll shots, or even spontaneous behind-the-scenes moments that add authenticity and emotion to your video. Additionally, capturing extra footage can provide options during the editing process and make your final product more dynamic. However, be cautious not to go overboard and end up with so much footage that it makes the editing process overwhelming.

Legal issues when shooting video

When shooting a video, it's important to protect yourself from legal trouble. It's always best to obtain permission to shoot at any location and get releases from anyone who will be appearing in your video. If you plan to sell or distribute your video, these releases and licenses will be necessary for legal purposes. It's also important to be aware of any laws or regulations regarding filming in public spaces, as well as privacy concerns when recording individuals without their consent.

"Prep for your shoot like you are preparing for a performance" by cinematographer and professor June Kyu Park

It's not a good sign if what you are doing on set is your first time. Filmmaking, like an intricate orchestral performance, requires numerous rehearsals. Test and learn all your gear before the shoot. Thoroughly study materials, whether it's a script, storyboard, or interview question-naire, beforehand. On the day of shooting, you are supposed to be in cruise control, yet still prepared for unexpected changes, as they are inevitable.

Study questions

1) What are some common types of shots in video production? What purpose do they serve?
2) How can the rule of thirds help with framing shots?
3) Why is it important to capture extra footage during a video shoot?
4) What factors should you consider when choosing a location for shooting your video?
5) How can having a variety of shots enhance the overall quality of a video?

Exercises

1) Practice framing different types of shots using the rule of thirds.
2) Experiment with different camera movements to see how they can add interest to a shot. Explain why you added the camera movement when shooting the particular shot.
3) Write a short script for a 30-second commercial. Then, create a shot list and storyboard for it, including both planned shots and potential additional footage. Consider the types of shots you will need to tell your story effectively.
4) Research different video resolutions and their typical uses. How does the resolution affect the quality and file size of your footage?
5) Watch a movie or TV show and pay attention to the different camera movements and how they enhance the storytelling. Try to identify any shots that break the rule of thirds and analyze why it was effective in that particular scene. Additionally, take note of any behind-the-scenes footage or B-roll shots that may have been included in the final product. How did these additional shots add to the overall impact of the video? What insights can you gather for your own video production process?

References

Eboch, M M. 2015. *History of Television*. Essential Library of Cultural History. Min-neapolis, MN: Essential Library.

Edwards, Josh. 2022. "5 Steps to Shooting Pro Quality Video on Iphone." Rocketyard. https://eshop.macsales.com/blog/83821-5-steps-to-shooting-pro-quality-video-on-iphone/.

Licensors, I. T. S., Disclaim, S., Express, A. L. L., Implied, O. R., Limitation, I. W., Warranties, A. N. Y., Availability, F. O. R., Or, M., and For, F. (2023). *Global Digital Video Advertising Market Size to Exceed USD*.

Lukan, E. (2023). *50 Video Statistics You Can't Ignore in 2024.* Synthesia. https://www.synthesia.io/post/video-statistics

Millerson, Gerald. 2001. *Video Production Handbook.* 3rd ed. London: Focal Press. https://worldcat.org/title/474797943.

Mowat, Jon. 2018. *Video Marketing Strategy: Harness the Power of Online Video to Drive Brand Growth.* London: Kogan Page. https://worldcat.org/title/986718414.

"Number of Social Media Users Worldwide from 2017 to 2027." 2023. Statista. https://www.statista.com/statistics/278414/number-of-worldwide-social-network-users/.

Prakoso, Chris. 2024. "13 Movies That Were Shot with an iPhone." Moblivious. https://moblivious.com/apple/movies-shot-with-an-iphone/.

Savvides, Lexy. 2022. "iPhone 14 Pro Cameras vs. 13 Pro: All the Ways They're Different." CNET. 2022. https://www.cnet.com/tech/mobile/iphone-14-pro-cameras-vs-13-pro-all-the-ways-theyre-different/.

Seastrom, Lucas. 2022. "Clones at 20 | 4 Ways Star Wars: Attack of the Clones Helped Change Filmmaking." Starwars. https://www.starwars.com/news/clones-at-20-4-ways-star-wars-attack-of-the-clones-helped-change-filmmaking.

"Share of Adults Who Watch More Online Instructional Videos due to Social Distancing during the Coronavirus Pandemic in the United States as of March 26, 2020." 2022. Statista. https://www.statista.com/statistics/1108533/online-instruction-video-usage-during-coronavirus-usa/.

"The Story of BBC Television – John Logie Baird." n.d. BBC. https://www.bbc.com/historyofthebbc/research/story-of-bbc-television/john-logie-baird.

"Videocassette Recorder." 2023. Britannica. https://www.britannica.com/technology/videocassette-recorder#ref162378.

Xiao, L., Li, X., and Zhang, Y. (2023). Exploring the Factors Influencing Consumer Engagement Behavior Regarding Short-Form Video Advertising: A Big Data Perspective. *Journal of Retailing and Consumer Services,* 70, 103170.

Xu, P., Chen, L., and Santhanam, R. (2015). Will Video Be the Next Generation of E-Commerce Product Reviews? Presentation Format and the Role of Product Type. *Decision Support Systems,* 73, 85–96.

9 Editing and sharing video

Video editing is a transformative process in video production, turning raw footage into a captivating final product. In this chapter, we will explore the evolution and fundamentals of video editing, beginning with crucial pre-editing tasks such as transferring and logging your footage. Next, we'll examine the essential video-editing tasks that you can accomplish with modern non-linear editing software like Adobe Premiere and Final Cut Pro. Lastly, we'll discuss the exporting, saving, and sharing of your video project.

What is video editing?

Video editing is the process of piecing together different elements from various video clips, rearranging, removing and adjusting them as needed, applying color corrections and filters, and integrating transitions between clips with the goal of creating a cohesive final product. Video editing is considered a post-production process meaning that it is done after the video content is shot.

If you have done a good job of capturing all the shots that you outlined in your shot list, it may seem like your job as an editor should be relatively easy. You simply need to start by extracting the clips that match the scenes in your storyboard and assemble them all together. With that said, there are a number of stylistic decisions you will need to make during the editing process that contribute to the overall feel of the finished piece. These decisions range from choosing the right music and sound effects to setting a pace and applying color correction and visual effects. The choices you make in each of these areas contribute to the story that you are telling and, ultimately, the success of your video.

In this chapter we will cover the evolution of video editing. Next, we will dive into the technical aspects of video editing, including how to prepare your footage, what software to use, and what types of tasks you might need to do in the program. From there, we will explore the creative side of video editing and discuss various techniques that can be used to enhance the overall quality of your final product. Finally, we will touch on exporting and sharing your finished video project.

DOI: 10.4324/9781003462200-9

The evolution of video editing

In the early days of motion pictures, film editing was accomplished by physically cutting and splicing film together. It was a destructive process since the source footage had to be cut apart to create a final product. Editing film in this way took time and precision since cuts and splices had to be done by hand.

The advent of videotape revolutionized the video-editing process, introducing the technique of tape-to-tape editing. Editors connected two videotape machines to assemble completed videos by playing segments from source tapes while recording onto the final tape, continually swapping out the source tape and locating the desired clips. This video-editing method is referred to as "linear video editing" because the editor worked in a sequential manner, recording various pieces from different tapes to build the final composition.

In the late 1980s, personal computers became more affordable and powerful, ushering in a new era of video editing. Video content could now be digitized and stored on hard drives, and the emergence of video-editing programs enabled editors to manipulate the files in a non-sequential manner. Editors simply located the clip and placed it anywhere along a timeline. It could be moved around, trimmed, stretched, and removed which was not possible in tape-to-tape editing. This revolutionary technique, known as non-linear editing, granted editors flexibility and enhanced their efficiency in the editing process. Initially, non-linear digital editing systems were expensive and limited by the storage capacity of the computer hard drive. In 1989, when the first version of Avid Media Composer was released, editors could only create short-form videos and commercials. However, a few years later, engineers at Disney figured out how to edit from external hard drives which opened

Figure 9.1 Ampex AVR 3: professional quadruplex video recorder, Circa 1975 [J. Thurion / CC BY-SA 3.0 (via Wikimedia Commons)]

the possibility of editing much longer content ("The History of Non-Linear Editing" n.d.).

In the early days of non-linear video editing, even though the video-editing system manipulated digital content on the computer, the form of the final video was published to videotape. Over time, though, non-linear video-editing systems evolved to support the publishing of video content onto DVDs. These days, video-editing programs offer a vast array of export formats and even the option to directly publish videos to the web.

Pre-editing tasks

Transferring video files onto your external hard drive

Before you can begin editing, you will need to transfer all your files to a hard drive. If your footage was captured on a camera that saves files to a memory card, simply connect the card to your computer and transfer the files to a hard drive. If you recorded the footage on an iPhone, there are several ways to transfer video files. You can connect your phone to your computer and sync the files, use AirDrop, or upload the files to the Cloud using an app like Dropbox and then sync them to your computer before moving them to an external hard drive.

Video files are often large, which is why most video editors opt to store their footage on external hard drives. By utilizing external drives for your video projects, you not only free up valuable internal storage on your computer, benefiting central processing unit (CPU) processing, but also gain the convenience of easy mobility between computers and the peace of mind that comes with having a reliable backup for your files.

Logging your footage

Before jumping into the actual editing process, you should have a good understanding of the footage you are working with. This includes knowing what has been shot, how it was shot, and how you want to put it together. If you did not log your footage while shooting, you should do this prior to commencing your edit. You simply need to watch and label each video clip according to its content. This meticulously categorized log serves as a roadmap when constructing the final video, essentially minimizing the time you would otherwise spend searching for specific clips or sequences during the editing process. It also allows you to quickly identify and isolate the most compelling or relevant segments of your footage, thus streamlining the editing workflow.

Organizing your media

On most video projects you will shoot much more footage than what you will actually use in your final project, so before you start editing, you should preview your footage and decide what you will likely want to use and what you don't. It's much easier to edit with a pared-down selection of clips. Next, you can import your selected clips into your software and begin organizing them into "bins" which are essentially folders within your editing project. For example, you may want to have a bin for interviews, one for b-roll footage, and another for music or sound effects. This organization will make it easier to find and access specific clips as you begin editing your project. Most editing software will also allow you to attach notes and other meta data to your clips to help you locate the clip as you edit. Once you have a basic understanding of the footage you are working with, and you have organized it and tagged it, you are ready to start editing.

Video-editing software

Numerous video-editing software options are available, each offering unique features and capabilities. Among the popular professional-level packages are Adobe Premiere, Final Cut Pro, and Avid Media Composer. Additionally, there are several free and affordable video-editing programs, such as DaVinci Resolve, Lightworks, Shotcut, and iMovie, which impress with their functionality. When selecting video-editing software, consider your experience level, the type of videos you plan to create, and your budget. It is always wise to conduct research and try out different programs before committing to one.

Avid Media Composer

Avid Media Composer was a pioneer in the non-linear video-editing industry, and it is still a major player in the field. It is considered a professional-level program and is often used for television shows, commercials, and even feature films. The company boasts on their website that "AVID is no stranger to the Academy Awards," as many Oscar-winning films were edited with AVID Media Composer ("Award-Winning Moment for Avid and the Art of Editing" 2023). What makes AVID Media Composer stand apart from other non-linear video-editing systems is its powerful tools for organizing and managing large projects, as well as advanced color-correction and audio-mixing capabilities. The program is known for giving editors the most control over their projects. However, it may have too steep of a learning curve for beginners. Avid Media Composer has the advantage of being able to work with both PC and MAC systems.

Final Cut Pro

Final Cut Pro is another widely used professional-level video-editing program, known for being a bit more intuitive to learn and use. It is owned by Apple and only runs on a MAC. Once a beloved software by the editing community, it ignited "vitriolic and satirical commentary across the Web" when Final Cut X was released in 2011. This version was so reviled that it inspired an online petition from users to restore previous versions (Idelson 2011). Some editors abandoned the program and started using Premiere. Since 2011, Apple has changed course and brought back many of the features and even reverted the name back to Final Cut Pro.

Despite its tumultuous history, Final Cut remains a dominant professional-level video-editing program. It offers a user-friendly interface and powerful features such as multicam editing, advanced color grading, and 360-degree video support. Final Cut Pro also has the advantage of being able to handle larger projects with ease and offers a convenient process for collaboration with other editors, but it only runs on a MAC.

Adobe Premiere

Adobe Premiere is one of the most popular and robust video-editing software options used by professionals. While it was once seen as more of a consumer-level program, it is now used increasingly in professional environments. Many major motion pictures have been edited with Adobe Premiere. It has an extensive range of features including multi-camera editing, motion graphics, and advanced color-correction tools. Adobe Premiere is also integrated with other Adobe Creative Cloud programs such as After Effects, Photoshop, and Audition for a seamless workflow. It also runs on both a MAC and a PC.

Figure 9.2 Non-linear video editing

DaVinci Resolve

Initially designed as a color-grading tool, DaVinci Resolve has evolved into a comprehensive professional video-editing software. It stands on par with Adobe Premiere but is renowned for its reliability and superior color grading capabilities. One of its major advantages is the availability of a free version with robust features. Additionally, the Studio version, offering more advanced features, is reasonably priced.

Lightworks

Lightworks, similar to DaVinci Resolve, is available in both free and pro versions. With its user-friendly and intuitive interface, it is particularly suitable for beginners. Lightworks also offers a wide range of features found in more expensive programs, including advanced color-correction tools and support for up to 4K resolution footage. Furthermore, it is compatible with MAC, PC, and even computers running the open-source Linux operating system.

Shotcut

Shotcut is another free, open-source video-editing software with an easy-to-use interface and a wide range of features such as advanced audio-editing tools and effects. It supports many file formats and resolutions, making it a versatile choice for various projects. Like Lightworks, it runs on a MAC, PC, and the Linux OS.

iMovie

iMovie is Apple's free video-editing software, available for all MAC users. It is an excellent entry-level option for video editing and perfect for beginners. It has a user-friendly interface and offers basic editing features such as trimming, transitions, and audio adjustments.

Sourcing video

Typically, the video you are editing is material that you have shot or footage that has been supplied to you. However, there may be times where you want to use footage that is not your own. To source video, you can check out to stock-footage websites such as Storyblock, Pexels, or Pixabay which offer a vast library of videos for purchase. Additionally, many of the aforementioned stock-image databases offer video footage as well. These sites provide a range of quality videos for personal or commercial use.

When sourcing video from external sources, it is essential to check the licensing terms and conditions to ensure that you have permission to use the footage for your project. Some websites may require attribution or have restrictions on how the footage can be used. It is always best to read and understand the terms before using any video in your project.

Video-editing tasks

Once you have chosen your video-editing software and organized your footage, it's time to start the editing process. The steps you will take to edit a video will be similar regardless of the software you choose. These tasks include setting up your project file, importing footage, assembling clips, trimming, adding transitions, laying in audio, adjusting the levels, color balancing, adding titles, and exporting your final project.

Setting up your project file

A project file in a video-editing program is the file that contains pointers to all of your imported media and edits. When you create your project file, you will need to select appropriate settings such as video resolution, aspect ratio, and frame rate which should be dictated by the final use of your edited video. Keep your project file in a folder with, or adjacent to, your media that you import so that all files pertaining to the project are in one place.

Importing and organizing your media

After setting up your project file, the next step is to import and organize your raw footage, audio files, and graphics within the project file. Every video-editing software has a repository in which imported media are stored. In Adobe Premiere, for example, this area is called the Project Panel. Some programs also allow you to preview and scrub through clips before importing them. You can also attach notes and markers to the media while they are in this repository.

It's essential to maintain an organized workflow by creating bins or folders within the project for different types of media, such as clips, sounds, and graphics. This organization simplifies your editing process, making it easier to locate and manage the assets as you construct your narrative. For efficiency, it's advisable to label each file with clear, descriptive names and consider categorizing them by the scene, shot type, or take number. Having a meticulous and structured project file can significantly streamline your video-editing workflow.

A principle of non-linear video editing that is important to understand is that any modification you make to your media inside of the program does not impact your source material. The clips you are working with a merely pointers to the original file. Therefore, you can experiment with different edits without fear of modifying your original files.

Assembling clips on the timeline

The timeline is where you will arrange and assemble your video into sequences. The timeline is comprised of layered tracks for audio and video components. You can drag and drop media onto the timeline in any order you choose. Typically editors assemble the footage of the characters or subjects speaking onto the timeline first. Then, they will lay B-roll shots (shots that support the primary footage or convey different visual information) over the talking-head footage. This process can vary widely depending on the editor's style and the project goals.

Trimming and cutting clips

In most cases, the video clip you want to use has excess footage at the beginning or the end. It is advisable to trim off the unwanted portions of a clip before dragging or inserting it onto the timeline. Fortunately, in non-linear video-editing programs, trimming is not destructive. You can grab back frames that you have trimmed off if you decide you want them back, even when the clips is on the timeline. Typically, after you get the clips on the timeline, you will likely want to make more precise trims. This is where tools like the razor and the ripple trim tools are most helpful to cut or trim your footage in precise points. Additionally, most programs have keyboard shortcuts that allow you to perform trim edits quickly. Memorizing these shortcuts can significantly speed up an editor's workflow.

Adding and balancing audio

Oftentimes, audio is attached to your video clip, so when you import your video footage into your project, the audio track will come with it. If you record your audio on a dedicated audio recorder, you will need to sync it to your video and have it replace the audio that is attached to the video. In addition to the audio that is associated with the video, oftentimes editors integrate other types of audio into a video project. These can include background music, sound effects, or voice-overs. These supplemental sounds would be layered over the primary audio in different tracks on the timeline.

To avoid a cacophony of unintelligible sounds in a video, editors take great care in balancing out the various audio tracks. In general, the primary audio track (the sound of people speaking) should be the loudest, peaking at –12dB to –6dB. Music is typically lower in volume but still audible and adds emotional cues to the telling of a story. It should peak around –18dB to –24 dB. Sound effects are the quietest of the three but still important in creating a realistic and immersive video experience. Sound effects are even lower in volume level than music, typically –30dB to –40dB and provide subtle ambiance that can make a scene more believable or add elements of humor or fright. You can adjust the gain (the strength of the audio signal level) and the volume of your audio tracks in the video-editing software.

Adding still images

Still images can play a major role in a video project. They can be used as title cards, informational slides, visual aids, or even to enhance the narrative. Still images are often used when video footage is unavailable. Oftentimes editors will add visual interest to a still by panning and zooming into the image. This technique, known as the "Ken Burns effect," because he uses it so frequently in his documentaries, can make an otherwise static image more dynamic and engaging.

If you want to add still images to your video, you can import them just as you would a video clip or audio file. Then you just drag them onto the time-line in the desired location. By default, your video-editing program will hold the still image on the timeline for a given amount of time (five seconds is typi-cal). But you can easily change this setting or increase or reduce the amount of time any static image is held. If you plan on panning or zooming into the image, you will need to have sufficient resolution (more pixels than the video frame size) to ensure that the image will not become blurry or pixelated.

Applying and animating effects

Audio and video effects can enhance and/or correct issues with your cap-tured media. You can apply effects to both your video tracks as well as your audio tracks. Common effects that you may apply to your audio track include noise reduction and pitch corrections. For video, common effects include color modifications, scales, distortions, rotations, blurs, and filters. Effects can greatly enhance the final product but should be used sparingly as they can quickly become overwhelming or distracting.

Many video-editing software programs allow you to animate effects, mean-ing you can adjust the properties of an effect over time. For example, you can gradually add a blur to an image or increase the volume of a voice-over during a transition. This is known as keyframing, setting a starting level for a property, an ending level and specifying the type of motion between these two keyframes (e.g., ease in, ease out, linear, etc.)

Adding transitions

Transitions serve the purpose of seamlessly switching between clips, whether it's a cross-dissolve or a more intricate effect like a fade or a wipe. Certain transitions aid in establishing a cohesive flow such as a morph between clips when an "um" is removed from footage of a speaker. Beginning editors have a tendency to want to take advantage of the elaborate transitions that are avail-able in the software, but too many can become distracting and even cheapen your video.

Adding text

Text is a critical element in many types of video projects, but should be used only when necessary, effective, and stylistically appropriate. Text is commonly used for identifying subjects in a documentary (also known as a lower third), on screen titles and captions. Creative moving text can also add visual interest and is often used for opening title sequences and rolling credits. Video-editing software typically includes built-in templates for animated text, which can be customized with different fonts, graphics, and movement. Text should not dominate the video screen but instead act as a complement to the main content. The font style, size, and color should match the overall tone of the piece. Like static images, you can set the amount of time the text appears on the stage and apply effects to the text if you want it to move or fade in or out. More elaborate text-based animation sequences are usually done in a compositing program like Adobe AfterEffects and then integrated into a video-editing program.

Color balancing and color grading

Color balancing is an essential step in video editing to ensure that all clips have a consistent look across the entire project. Most video-editing programs come with built-in color correction tools that allow you to adjust brightness, contrast, saturation, and other color properties. This is especially important when working with footage from multiple cameras, as each camera may capture colors differently.

Color grading takes this a step further by allowing you to manipulate the colors in your video to achieve a certain look or feel. For example, you can make your video appear warmer or cooler depending on the mood you want to convey. You can also add filters to enhance specific colors in your video or even create a black-and-white effect. Both color balancing and grading should be used thoughtfully, as they can greatly affect the overall mood and tone of your video project.

Editing style and techniques

Editing plays an enormous role in telling a coherent story. When editors break the consistency and logic of the story, audiences can be confused or become disinterested. These issues may not be noticeable to the editor who is too close to the project, which is why having another set of eyes can be helpful in identifying and correcting these inconsistencies.

Editors are not just technicians who assemble shots together to tell a story. They are also artists who use timing, rhythm, and composition to create an emotional connection with the audience. The style in which a video is edited can have a dramatic impact on the way it is perceived. For example, fast cuts and a high-energy soundtrack may convey an intense action scene, while long takes and soft music can create a sense of tranquility in a nature documentary. Editors are sought out for their unique style and ability to evoke certain emotions through their editing techniques.

Understanding the different types of cuts and transitions available will help you choose which one is most effective for your video project. Some common editing techniques include jump cuts, which involve using two shots that are similar to create a seamless transition; cross-cutting, where the editor switches between two or more scenes to build tension or show parallel actions; and cutaways, which are brief shots of something else that are inserted into the main scene to provide additional context or add visual interest. Non-linear digital editing tools allow you the flexibility to experiment with different editing styles and techniques to find the best fit for your video project and engage viewers on a deeper level.

Exporting and sharing edited video

Once you've completed all your edits and are satisfied with the final product, it's time to export your video for sharing and viewing. The wide array of file formats and compression algorithms available can be overwhelming, but each one offers unique advantages. Before exporting, ensure you choose the appropriate file format based on your intended use and audience. Sometimes these settings are dictated by a client or by a platform that will host the video. Consider adjusting the resolution and bit rate to optimize playback quality and file size. This will ensure an optimal viewing experience while maintaining the desired level of file compression.

Video-file formats

MP4 (MPEG-4) is the most widely used video-file format. It is recognized as a universal format meaning it can be played on most devices and is an acceptable format to upload to video-sharing platforms. If you plan to embed your video on a webpage, then this is most likely the format you want to use. Although the MP4 format incorporates excellent compression, the resulting videos still maintain a high-quality look.

AVI (Audio Video Interleave) is a commonly used video-file format that boasts compatibility with both Windows and MAC operating systems. While it may not offer the same level of compression as MP4, it provides superior video quality and is ideal for TV viewing.

The MOV (QuickTime Movie) format, developed by Apple for their devices, is widely known. Unlike the MP4 format, MOV offers less compression and is limited to the Apple ecosystem. However, if you intend to upload a .MOV file to YouTube, there is no need to convert it to MP4 as MOV is supported on the platform.

WMV (Windows Media Video) is a Windows-based video format that offers high-quality playback and streaming. While it's not as widely used as MP4 or AVI, it does have its benefits such as the ability to display high-definition videos at smaller file sizes.

FLV (Flash Video) is a format created for Flash media players and offers high-quality streaming even at low bandwidths. It was specifically designed for video within Flash websites or online platforms that support Flash content.

Since Flash is not supported on mobile devices, this video-file format is used much less often.

Video compression

Video compression is the process of reducing the size of a video file while maintaining as much quality as possible. It is beneficial in that it allows for faster uploads and downloads, as well as saving storage space. However, excessive compression can result in a loss of visual quality. When videos are over-compressed they can look blurry and pixelated, therefore finding a balance between file size and quality is the goal.

There are various compression codecs (algorithms) available that use different techniques to achieve compression. For this reason, some are more or less suitable for different types of video content. Some use lossless compression which is appropriate for videos with detailed imagery whereas lossy compression might suffice for a basic social media video. Intra-frame compression is a type of compression that considers the pixels in each frame independently, making it suitable for videos with many changes between frames. Inter-frame is better suited for videos with many static or repetitive scenes, such as documentaries or interviews because it achieves compression by summarizing similarities of adjacent frames.

Common video compression codecs

H.264 (also known as MPEG-4 Part 10) is an inter-frame compression codec and currently the most widely used. It offers high-quality video at relatively small file sizes and has become the standard for web-streaming and sharing platforms like YouTube and Vimeo. It is typically used as a lossy compression codec, but it does have a lossless mode.

HEVC (High-Efficiency Video Coding), also known as H.265, is a newer video-compression format that offers even higher quality at smaller file sizes compared to H.264. However, it's not yet widely supported and may not be compatible with all devices.

MPEG-2 (Moving Pictures Experts Group) was the standard for DVD formats and is still commonly used for TV broadcasting and DVDs. It provides good quality at a lower compression rate, making it suitable for large screens. It, too, is a lossy compression codec.

VP9 is an open-source video compression format developed by Google and used primarily for web streaming on platforms like YouTube. It offers high-quality playback at smaller file sizes but may not be supported on older devices or browsers.

When deciding which compression algorithm to choose, consider the intended use and audience of your video as well as the compatibility with different devices and browsers. Experimenting with different formats and compression codecs can help you find the best balance between quality and file size for maximum impact. Fortunately, non-linear video-editing software allows you to have full control over these aspects of your final product, ensuring that your video is optimized for its purpose.

Sharing your video

In the early 2010s, DVDs were the prevailing method for sharing videos. However, with the rise of online video platforms and streaming services and the continued growth of available bandwidth, sharing videos online has become increasingly easy and efficient. Large video files can be easily uploaded, downloaded, and streamed with relatively minimal buffering or lag. This increased bandwidth not only enhances the viewer experience but also provides vast opportunities for content creators and marketers to reach wider audiences, engage users interactively, and deliver impactful visual narratives.

Video-sharing platforms

Platforms like YouTube, Vimeo, and social media sites have democratized content distribution, allowing creators to reach a global audience with a simple upload. Not only does this enhance visibility, but it also offers instant feedback and engagement from viewers. Virality is now a component of video sharing, where content can spread exponentially if it resonates with the audience. These platforms offer a range of features such as the ability to upload and store videos, customize privacy settings, track views and engagement, and even monetize your videos through ads or subscriptions.

YouTube is the second largest search engine in the world (Ertemel and Ammoura 2021). People go to YouTube looking to be entertained or seeking answers to their questions and "many times YouTube is the internet's best source for answers to queries" (Manjoo 2023). Therefore, sharing your videos on YouTube can help you build an audience, gain exposure, and even generate revenue through ads or sponsorships. To reach a wider audience on YouTube, consider optimizing your video title, description, and tags with relevant keywords and using eye-catching thumbnail images to attract viewers.

Vimeo is another popular video-sharing platform known for its high-quality playback and customization options. Unlike YouTube, which has more of a social media aspect to it, Vimeo is geared towards professionals and creatives. It offers various subscription plans for individuals and businesses, allowing for more control over the display of the video content.

Before uploading your final project to a video-sharing platform, check their specific requirements for file formats, compression, and resolution. This will ensure that your video is optimized for the platform and can be viewed by a wide audience. You may also need to consider any copyright or licensing issues if using copyrighted material, music, or images in your video.

Integrating your videos on a website

In addition to sharing your project on video-sharing platforms, you may also want to integrate your videos on your own website or blog. This can help increase engagement and keep visitors on your site for longer. There are two ways you can integrate video content on a webpage: embedding and hosting.

Embedding involves using a code snippet provided by the video-sharing platform to display your video on your website. This allows for easy playback and customization options, but the video is still hosted on the external platform. On YouTube, you can extract the embed code from any video (even ones that are not yours) and paste the HTML into your website code. Actually, some website platforms make it even easier, allowing you to simply supply the video URL in order for it to display the video within the page. The only issue is that if that video is deleted from YouTube, it will no longer play within your page.

Hosting, on the other hand, involves uploading your video directly to your website or blog. This gives you more control over the content and eliminates any third-party platform risks. However, hosting your own videos can take up a lot of storage space and a little more technical know-how. In order to display a self-hosted video file on your webpage, you will need to use the HTML5 video tags to reference the video and ensure that the video-file format is MP4. Some website-building platforms will make this easier for you, providing an upload tool through which you can locate your video, upload it, and place it on your webpage. When integrating videos on a website, make sure to properly optimize them for web viewing by compressing the file size and choosing a suitable resolution. You may also want to consider using closed captions or subtitles for accessibility purposes. This can all be done easily via the export settings in your video-editing software.

Sharing your videos on social media

Social media has become a powerful tool for video sharing and marketing. Platforms like Facebook, Instagram, and Twitter (now X) have all integrated video into their services, making it easier to reach a wider audience with your content. Videos on social media can be shared directly from platforms like YouTube or Vimeo, but you may also want to create native videos specifically for each platform.

Different social media platforms have varying requirements for video length, aspect ratio, and file size. For example, Facebook recommends reframing videos to a 4:5 proportion. ("Best Practices for Optimizing Your Video on Facebook" 2021). This is because most users view videos on their phones in portrait mode, and the 4:5 aspect ratio takes up more screen space. Instagram reels should be between 1.91:1 and 9:16 and can be up to 90 seconds long. ("Instagram Help" 2022) X (formerly Twitter) has a limit

VIDEO ASPECT RATIOS

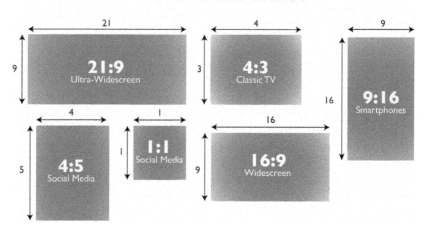

Figure 9.3 Common video aspect ratios

of 140 seconds for video post, but no recommended aspect ratio ("X Help Center" n.d.).

Oftentimes the videos shared on social media are smaller parts of longer-form content. Fortunately, video-editing programs are making it easier to extract videos for these platforms. For example, the reframe utility in Adobe Premiere will create a duplicate sequence with different aspect ratios, making it easier to export videos in multiple dimensions.

When sharing videos on social media, always consider the platform and its audience. Use relevant hashtags, write engaging captions, and keep your videos short and impactful. Viewers often scroll through their social media feeds with their audio muted, therefore providing subtitles or text overlays can help increase engagement and ensure your message is received. Social media is also a great place to interact with your audience through comments and likes, so make sure to actively engage with them to build a community around your content.

Ethical and legal issues also need to be taken into consideration when sharing video content. Subjects in your videos should be aware of how you plan to distribute your video. This should be addressed in the release they sign prior to shooting. When using video footage you did not shoot into your final composition, be mindful of fair use and copyright laws. Always use royalty-free material or obtain permission from the original creator. Additionally, be aware of any sensitive or controversial content in your video that may have legal implications. This can include confidential information, or content that may infringe on someone's privacy rights. When in doubt, don't use the footage or consult a legal professional before sharing your video publicly.

> **"Making good editing decisions" by professional video editor Bryce Bagwill**
>
> I think the key to making good editing decisions starts with the editor being sensitive to the right things to make the project feel like it should. This can be different across different genres for sure but if you understand where you are trying to take the audience (toward humor, drama, etc.) then you must focus on all the little things (often not part of any script) within a sea of options that will add up to the audience having the experience you want them to have.

Study questions

1) What considerations should you make when preparing your video for sharing on a specific video-sharing platform?
2) What are the two ways to integrate video content on a website?
3) Why is it important to consider ethical and legal factors when sharing video content?
4) Explain how you can gain a following by uploading videos to YouTube.
5) What are some of the common tasks involved in video editing?

Exercises

1) Create a list of popular video-sharing platforms and their specific requirements for file formats, compression, and resolution.
2) Locate a website that has a YouTube video embedded on it. View the Page source and locate the embed code.
3) Choose a social media platform and create a native video specifically for that platform.
4) Write a release form (based on examples you find online) for subjects featured in your video, outlining how the video will be used and distributed.
5) Practice editing a short video using tools such as Adobe Premiere or iMovie.

References

"Award-Winning Moment for Avid and the Art of Editing." 2023. AVID. https://www.avid.com/resource-center/avidoscars-com.

"Best Practies for Optimizing Your Video on Facebook." 2021. Facebook. https://creators.facebook.com/10-video-best-practices/?locale=en_US.

Ertemel, Adnan Veysel, and Ahmed Ammoura. 2021. "Is YouTube a Search Engine or a Social Network? Analyzing Evaluative Inconsistencies." *Business and Economics Research Journal* 12 (4): 871–81.

Idelson, Karen. 2011. "Final Cut Pro Update Draws Backlash." V*ariety*. https://
variety.com/2011/digital/news/final-cut-pro-update-draws-backlash-1118
039277/.
"Instagram Help." 2022. Instagram. https://help.instagram.com/27209583980060
62/?helpref=uf_share.
Manjoo, Farhad. 2023. "There's Already a Better Search Engine Than Google. It's
YouTube." *The New York Times*, February 27.
"The History of Non-Linear Editing." n.d. Simon Says. https://www.simonsaysai.
com/blog/the-history-of-non-linear-editing.
"X Help Center." n.d. X (formerly Twitter). https://help.twitter.com/en/using-
x/x-videos.

10 Animation and motion graphics

Animation has been a popular form of media for decades. While the term "animation" may bring to mind entertaining cartoons, it is important to recognize that animations serve as a valuable medium for communication, setting moods, and enhancing understanding. Motion graphics, which are a type of animation, often involve moving type with graphics rather than characters and are typically non-narrative. Traditional animation, on the other hand, is frequently employed to tell stories. The methods of creating animation and motion graphics vary greatly, ranging from computer-generated imagery to the use of physical props captured digitally. The end uses of animation and motion graphics are diverse, encompassing films, television programs, video games, advertising, educational videos, and data visualizations.

In this chapter, we will explore the evolution of animation and motion graphics. We will learn the different ways in which animation is made as well as the pros, cons, and unique characteristics of each method. Subsequently, we will explore how animations are used for different purposes. Finally, we will explore various techniques and tools used to create animation and motion graphics.

What is animation?

Animation is a captivating process that brings still sequential images to life by displaying them rapidly. It cleverly exploits the limitations of our eyes, as they struggle to differentiate between these swiftly displayed images, resulting in the illusion of seamless movement. To achieve this illusion, it is crucial for the images to be displayed rapidly, with a minimum rate of ten images per second in order to deceive the eye. Each individual image in an animation must possess subtle variations from the others, achieved by manipulating elements such as position, size, shape, color, and rotation of objects. This thoughtful orchestration of visual elements is what breathes life into the art of animation.

The images that make up an animation can be made in many different ways. A simple way to make an animation is to hand draw a series of images, photograph or scan them, and then import them into a video-editing program

DOI: 10.4324/9781003462200-10

holding each image for 1/12th of a second and then export a finished animation as a video file. But hand-drawn animation is just one of many ways in which animation can be made. Today, with the help of computers and software programs, animations can be created through a variety of methods. Computer-generated images, 3D characters and environments, photographs that have been manipulated in some way—all of these can be used to create animations. But even traditional animation practices benefit from the integration of the computer.

Evolution of animation

While one might assume that the origins of animation would be attributed to an artist or a filmmaker, it was actually the research of a 19th-century physician who inspired early experimentations with the medium. British physician Peter Roget published a paper entitled "The Persistence of Vision with Regard to Moving Objects" in 1824 in which he explained that "the eye's retina retains an image briefly after it has disappeared, which means that if images are flashed in rapid succession, they appear to the human brain as one continuous image" (Cavalier 2011).

This discovery inspired the development of many optical toys that took advantage of this phenomenon, the most notable being the "daedalus," translated from Latin as "the wheel of the devil" invented by mathematician William Horner in 1834. The invention of this device, which was later improved upon and later referred to as a "zoetrope" is widely acknowledged as a pivotal moment for modern animation. The zoetrope was a rotating cylinder featuring 12 painted images on a sleeve inside. When the cylinder spun rapidly and the images inside were viewed from the outside through slits in the cylinder, each image appeared to be interconnected. This fundamental concept of combining multiple still images to produce the illusion of motion served as the cornerstone for the art of animation.

Moving forward in the timeline of motion studies that laid the foundation for modern animation and motion graphics, it is imperative to discuss the work of Eadweard Muybridge. A pivotal figure in the development of motion pictures, Muybridge is famously known for his groundbreaking series of photographs titled "The Horse in Motion" in 1878. His work meticulously chronicled sequential phases of motion, utilizing an array of cameras to capture split-second intervals, thereby providing a detailed look at the previously unobservable subtleties of movement. This research not only disproved long-standing misconceptions about animal locomotion but also established foundational principles that would greatly influence the trajectory of animation and motion graphics. Muybridge's ability to dissect motion into individual frames directly informed the techniques used in the following century to create the fluid movement integral to animation, thus immortalizing his contribution to the visual arts and storytelling.

In the late 1800s, Frenchman Émile Reynaud evolved the field of animation by combining sequential drawings with early film technology. The device he patented, called the Théâtre Optique, utilized hand-drawn strips of images on a roll of gelatin that were viewed with the help of a projection system. In the last decade of the century, Reynaud screened his animations around Paris. This revolutionary technique of creating animations on a flexible medium (celluloid film stock) allowed for longer and more complex animations and paved the way for the next generation of animators.

The introduction of moving pictures in the late 19th century triggered a race to develop groundbreaking technologies that would allow artists to bring their worlds and stories to life. In 1906, French illusionist and director Georges Méliès created *A Trip to the Moon*, considered by many as one of the first science-fiction films ever made. "He was the first to crudely move objects around" to create a stop-motion animation, which was a technique he "accidentally discovered" (Cavalier 2011). Nevertheless, Méliès established a new standard of visual storytelling that would continue to be built upon in the coming decades.

The first decade of the 20th century saw an increase in interest in animation techniques, delineating a time when the "history of animation really became distinguishable from the history of the cinema" (Cavalier 2011). Several artists around the world were experimenting with the medium, creating the "first instances of drawn and stop-motion animation" (Furniss 2016). By the end of the decade, studios were forming with a specific focus on creating 2D animations and stop-motion productions.

Character animation, the act of bringing a character to life through movement and performance, became a major focus in the 1920s, thanks to artists like Winsor McCay. McCay's short film *Gertie the Dinosaur* was one of the first animations to feature a character with personality and emotions. This was an incredibly complex work of animation for its time, involving over 10,000 hand-drawn images. McCay also pioneered the use of celluloid (or cels) in the production of drawn animation "where the area of the cartoon [that remained] immobile is drawn onto [a background] cel, while the corresponding moving area within the frame [is] drawn on a cel that is overlaid" (Callahan 1988). This technique (known as cel animation) would speed up production times and be adopted by animation studios.

The 1930s saw the rise of animated feature films. Up until then, animations had primarily been shorts and used as filler material between the main attractions. But this all changed once Walt Disney Studios released the first animated feature *Snow White and the Seven Dwarfs* in 1937. This film was a "huge success" and a game-changer for the animation industry (Furniss 2016). It utilized advanced techniques such as multiplane camera movements (moving the camera to create the illusion of depth), Technicolor, and a new distinct animation style that brought the characters to life which captivated audiences around the world. The success of this film prompted Disney to

Figure 10.1 Poster for animated film, "Gertie the Dinosaur"

continue producing feature-length films and build a team of animators who would pioneer revolutionary techniques and a new distinct animation style.

In their 1981 book *The Illusion of Life*, Disney animators Ollie Johnston and Frank Thomas introduced the 12 principles of animation to help traditional animators create worlds and characters that more convincingly upheld the laws of physics. The pair were part of Disney's "Nine Old Men," the core group of animators who were instrumental in creating Disney's animation style. These 12 principles have now become widely recognized as a theoretical bedrock for all artists working on animated video production.

The 12 principles include:

- **Squash and Stretch** refers to the concept that objects alter their shape in response to external forces. For instance, when a ball collides with the ground, it momentarily flattens while still retaining its overall volume. This phenomenon showcases the dynamic nature of objects and their ability to adapt to various circumstances.

- **Anticipation** refers to the preparatory movement preceding the main action. It is crucial for a character to bend its knees before jumping, as it would appear unnatural otherwise. This subtle yet essential motion adds realism and fluidity to the overall performance.
- **Staging** involves utilizing motion to direct the viewer's gaze and emphasize key elements within a scene. For example, a character's movement can lead the audience's eyes to a specific object or action, helping to convey important information.
- **Straight Ahead Action and Pose-to-Pose** are two different techniques that yield a different visual style for an animation. Straight Ahead Action involves drawing frame by frame, resulting in a spontaneous and chaotic appearance. On the other hand, Pose-to-Pose animation involves establishing keyframes at the most extreme poses and then filling in the frames in between. This technique creates a more planned and deliberate feel.
- **Follow Through and Overlapping Action** is when a person or any moving object comes to a stop and certain parts may continue moving in the same direction because of the forward momentum force. This phenomenon is commonly observed when an object's motion ceases, but the residual energy causes some components to exhibit a delayed stopping effect.
- **Ease In and Ease Out** illustrates the principle of gradual acceleration and deceleration. When an object is in motion, it doesn't immediately reach its maximum speed. Instead, it gradually accelerates, a phenomenon known as "Ease Out." Similarly, when an object comes to a stop, it initially slows down, which is referred to as "Ease In."
- **Arcs** tend to create a more natural-looking animation, because, in nature, most movement doesn't happen in a straight line.
- A **secondary action** is used to support or emphasize the main action in a scene. For instance, when a character runs, their hair should sway from side to side. This additional movement adds depth and realism to the overall scene.
- **Timing** is a crucial aspect that determines the placement of each action frame on a timeline. Unrealistic timing can make your animation unbelievable. For instance, if you animate an object falling from the sky too slowly, it will appear to defy the laws of gravity, which can be distracting for the viewer. It is important to strike the right balance in timing to ensure a seamless and convincing animation.
- **Exaggeration**, in the context of storytelling, involves amplifying a character's traits and behaviors to evoke a comedic or dramatic effect. It can prevent animations from appearing dull and lifeless when they are overly precise and realistic.
- **Solid Drawing** is crucial to achieving a precise three-dimensional impression in animation. An animator must skillfully portray form and anatomy, effectively conveying weight and volume, and master the interplay of light and shadows.
- **Appeal** involves designing characters that are interesting by emphasizing their most defining feature. The key is to strike a balance between simplicity and adding just the right amount of detail.

While Disney was the dominant force in American animation for many years in the mid-part of the 20th century, it wasn't long before others took notice. Existing movie studios such as Warner Brothers and MGM started up their own animation divisions. Some of the famous animators to emerge during this era included Tex Avery, Chuck Jones, and Friz Freleng who are best known for their work at Warner Bros., creating iconic characters such as Bugs Bunny, Daffy Duck, and Porky Pig. These artists "reinvented animation by taking the developments that had been made in character animation and pushing them to the limits with a zany, exaggerated and extreme style" (Cavalier 2011).

The invention of television in the mid-1950s provided a new vehicle for animated content. One of the biggest names in animation to emerge during this time was Hanna-Barbera Productions. Founded by William Hanna and Joseph Barbera, the studio produced popular cartoons such as *Tom and Jerry*, *The Flintstones*, and *Scooby-Doo*. They employed limited animation techniques, which emphasized cost-saving and quick production methods, but, nevertheless, "managed to maintain a funny and memorable watchability due to the writing, characters, and catchy tunes" (Cavalier 2011).

The 1960s and 1970s ushered in an era of experimentation in animation. The counterculture movement and the rise of psychedelic art influenced

Figure 10.2 Animator working on a stop motion animation [Coentor / CC BY-SA 3.0 (via Wikimedia Commons)]

many animators, leading to a surge in avant-garde animated films. One prime example is Ralph Bakshi, who is best known for his controversial, ground-breaking, and first X-rated animated film *Fritz the Cat*. Stop-motion animation also gained popularity during this time, with the works of Tim Burton and Will Vinton gaining critical acclaim and inspiring future generations of animators.

As technology advanced in the 1980s, traditional hand-drawn animation began to give way to computer-generated imagery (CGI). The introduction of CGI revolutionized animation, allowing for more complex and realistic animated sequences. In 1995, Pixar released the first fully 3D animated film, *Toy Story*. This film was trailblazing, and it set the stage for the next few decades of animated films. By 2004, Disney closed its 2D animation studio and started to prioritize 3D animation. Animation technology has improved so much over the years. Now animators are able to create incredibly detailed 3D environments, characters, and effects with relative ease. These days 3D animation can look incredibly realistic, so much so that it can be seamlessly blended into live footage. Faster computer and gaming system processing power now facilitates the rendering of 3D animated content in real time.

Evolution of motion graphics

As the art of animation evolved, so did the discipline of motion graphics. Motion graphics, a branch of animation, incorporates typography, illustrations, and graphic images to effectively convey messages and stories. While several early filmmakers and animators are credited with early experimental forms of motion graphics, it did not become a discipline until the middle of the 20th century, and it took shape in some of the title sequences of classic films.

Saul Bass is considered one of the early pioneers in the world of motion graphics and is particularly known for his contributions to the development of feature-film-title sequences. His designs were simple, concise, yet impactful, effectively capturing the essence of the movies they represented. The slicing black and white lines throughout the *Psycho* (1960) title sequence established just the right tension for the movie. Notable for his collaborations with legendary directors such as Alfred Hitchcock and Otto Preminger, Bass created timeless title sequences for films like *Vertigo*, *Psycho*, and *The Seven Year Itch* and inspired a generation of motion graphic artists.

Bass's contribution to the field of motion graphics cannot be overstated. "He created the visual identity for some of Hollywood's most iconic films of the 1950s and 1960s" (Hooper 2023). Yet, he was also responsible for creating the logos for some of the largest corporations in the world, such as United Airlines, Quaker Oats, and AT&T. It's only natural that the field of motion graphics would eventually expand into other areas such as advertising and marketing.

The latter part of the 20th century witnessed a surge in the application of motion graphics beyond film, permeating the advertising and marketing industries. The rise of television as a dominant media outlet provided an unprecedented platform for advertisers who adopted motion graphics to craft compelling narratives and build brand identities. Pioneering this visual evolution, television commercials, and network branding segments began to feature dynamic animated sequences that captured viewers' attention, often conveying messages within seconds. As software capabilities advanced, so did the complexity and quality of motion graphics, enabling marketers to blend live-action footage with animated elements to create a seamless and sophisticated viewer experience. This period laid the groundwork for motion graphics to become an integral component of visual communication, shaping the way brands and products are promoted to consumers.

Forms of animation

There are several different methods you can use to make an animation. Each method offers its own unique set of challenges and opportunities, allowing animators to bring their creative visions to life in diverse and captivating ways.

Drawn animation

Probably the easiest form of animation to understand is traditional 2D drawn animation. A flip book serves as a perfect exemplification of this technique.

Figure 10.3 Motion capture in progress [Raíssa Ruschel / CC BY 2.0 (via Wikimedia Commons)]

By creating sequential drawings on each page and flipping through the book, the images are displayed in a rapid sequence and the illusion of movement is created.

As you can probably imagine, drawn animation is quite labor intensive because you need to create at least 12 drawings for every second of animation in order to achieve a smooth, fluid motion. Despite this challenge, many animators continue to use this method as it is inexpensive and very accessible. One way animators speed up their drawing process is to work on a light table. They place their drawings on the light table and then draw the next image on top of the previous one. The previous drawing gives them a point of reference as to where the next drawing should be.

Cel Animation

Cel animation is similar to drawn animation, but it involves drawing the characters and background separately on a transparent sheet of plastic called a "cel." This allows for more flexibility and ease in re-using the same backgrounds or characters in different scenes. Sometimes numerous sheets are layered on top of each other as more than one character or object is moving. Cel animation was often used in traditional hand-drawn animation before the advent of computer-generated imagery.

Cel animators figured out another way to make the animation process go a bit faster. A more experienced animator would plan out the movement of the characters and establish key poses at certain moments in time called keyframes. Then, a less experienced animator would draw in all the in-between frames.

In both drawn and cel animation, the physical images must be captured by a camera. Each image would be laid flat on a shooting stand with the camera mounted on top. The animator would take a picture of each image to build the animated sequence. When animation was shot on traditional film cameras (which were designed to play at 24 frames per second), the animator typically "shot in twos" meaning that each image was captured twice on two sequential frames of film. So, instead of one image being held for 1/24th of a second, each image was held for 1/12th of a second. Shooting in twos saved the animator quite a bit of work and the playback was fast enough to fool the eye into seeing the animated movement. Animators who still work in these traditional mediums (drawn and cell animation) no longer need to shoot in twos because they can capture their images onto a digital camera and just hold each image 1/12th of a second in their video-editing program.

Stop-motion animation

Stop-motion animation is a meticulous and time-consuming process that offers a unique charm and tactility not replicated by digital methods. By photographing real-world objects in small increments and sequential poses, animators can create fantastical animations frame by frame. This technique can utilize a variety of materials, including clay figures, puppets, or even everyday objects. The result is a distinctive style of animation that carries with it a physicality and depth with an organic, hand-crafted feel.

There are several different types of stop-motion animation:

- **Claymation** is a form of stop-motion animation using clay figures and probably what most people imagine when they think of stop-motion animation.
- **Object-Motion** is a technique employed to bring non-malleable objects to life by moving them around in a scene.
- **Cut-out animation** uses flat paper elements (drawings, letters, etc.) that are moved around on a surface and filmed one frame at a time.
- **Pixilation** is the art of moving humans and objects around in a scene in small increments and taking pictures at every interval. Using this method you can create the illusion of movement; for example, people gliding along the floor and objects moving in ways not possible in reality.
- **Time lapse** is a technique that involves taking pictures of a scene over time and then putting them together in sequence as if the camera were rolling. This sort of animation can be used to show natural phenomena like clouds moving by, or more complex animations such as babies developing from cells.
- **Puppet Animation**: Puppet animation uses a mechanical or computer-controlled puppet that is moved frame by frame.
- **Silhouette Animation** involves backlighting cutouts of various objects and characters to bring them to life.

2D computer animation

2D computer animation is the process of creating moving images from two-dimensional graphics with the help of software. It is a modern form of animation that offers more speed and flexibility compared to traditional methods. This technique has become a popular method of creating a great deal of animation that we see on television due to the software's ability to efficiently integrate sound effects, music, and text.

2D computer animation mimics cel animation techniques yet makes the process much faster and easier. For example, layers operate like cellulose in that they can be stacked, and objects can be moved independently of one another. Onion skinning in 2D animation software mimics the experience of drawing on top of the previous drawing on a light table. You can see the details of the previous frame while you are drawing the current frame. 2D animation software also integrates the concept of keyframing and tweening. You can position an object or character in one location in one frame and another position in another frame and tell the computer to create all the frames in between. When you create an animation in a 2D animation software, you don't have to use a camera to transfer your drawings into the computer, you simply render out your frames to generate a movie.

2D computer animation is relatively fast to produce when compared to traditional animation methods. However, it still takes a considerable amount of time. Many popular shows and cartoons are created through 2D animation software. 2D animation software is also often used to create motion graphics. However, despite its sophisticated toolset and time saving shortcuts, 2D computer animation still mandates a significant amount of drawing aptitude and a good comprehension of animation and design principles.

2.5D computer animation

2.5D animation, also known as pseudo-3D animation, is a combination of 2D and 3D techniques. This type of computer animation is done within a 2D animation software and takes advantage of its features to create an illusion of depth. Techniques such as layering, scaling, shadowing, and camera movements are used to create the effect of 3D. 2.5D animation originated in the 1980s within video games as a way to provide depth and realism without the need for 3D graphics. However, it has since been adopted for other end uses such as cartoons and motion graphics.

3D computer animation

3D computer animation is the most advanced form of animation, offering a level of detail and realism that cannot be achieved through other methods. It utilizes three-dimensional digital models and environments to create lifelike animations with textures, lighting effects, and camera movements. This type of animation is often used in feature films, television shows, and video games.

You can easily tell the difference between 2D and 3D animations by looking at the final piece. Disney classics like *Snow White* and *Cinderella* are examples of 2D animation, while the more contemporary films such as *Toy Story* and *Frozen* are examples of 3D animation. In 2D animation, everything happens on a flat surface using the x and y axes. While talented 2D animators can create the illusion of depth, the characters and objects are still limited to a two-dimensional plane. 3D animation, on the other hand, takes place in a three-dimensional space, objects and cameras can move along the X, Y and Z planes.

The main distinction between 2D and 3D animation lies in the production process. 2D animation is created entirely in a two-dimensional space. A sequence of drawings are created, and by slightly altering each drawing, a progression is created that, when played rapidly, creates the illusion of movement. The process of creating 3D computer animation is quite different. Instead of drawing each frame, the animator creates 3D objects and then manipulates their position, size, rotation, etc. Once the animator is done building the models, assigning colors and textures to the objects, and choreographing the movement then the computer generates the animation. 3D animation gets even more complex when characters are involved. Three-dimensional characters can have elaborate shapes and clothing and move in many different ways which adds another dimension to the production process.

The various tasks required to produce a 3D animation are quite distinct: modeling, surface definition, animating, and rendering, so much so that on larger productions these tasks (and even micro tasks within these groups) are often delegated to different members of the team. For example, some 3D artists may specialize in modeling, while others may specialize in character animation or rendering.

Modeling

The process of 3D modeling involves creating three-dimensional objects using a combination of tools provided in the software. These models can range from simple geometric shapes to intricate characters or landscapes. There are various methods for 3D modeling, including sculpting with virtual clay, constructing objects using 3D primitives like spheres and cylinders, or scanning real-world objects into the computer using a 3D scanner. The versatility of 3D modeling allows for endless possibilities in creating virtual representations of physical objects.

The tools an animator uses to create the 3D model are chosen based on the type of model the animator needs to build. If the animator needed to build a model of an orange, for example, then the easiest method would be to use a sphere primitive. If, on the other hand, an animator needed to build a banana model, then she might be able to start with a cylinder shape, but then she would need to bend and distort it and add on a stem. Sometimes animators need to build models from precise dimensions. Most 3D animation modeling components will allow an animator to use exact measurements when building objects when dimensional accuracy is critical.

The surfaces of 3D models within a 3D animation program are made up of polygons which are constructed using points or vertices. A polygon requires at least three vertices to form a surface or face, but it can have more. The lines between vertices are called edges. If you use more polygons to define a surface, the model will be smoother in appearance and therefore take a longer time to render. A 3D modeler must weigh the benefit of higher resolution against render time.

Rigging

In character animation, once a 3D model is created, it undergoes the vital process of rigging to infuse it with life. Rigging involves attaching a digital skeleton to the model, enabling animators to manipulate and move it realistically. This intricate process often entails creating joints and controls that ensure seamless movement of every part of the model. "The best riggers continuously visualize the extremes of movement the character will eventually exhibit" and design the skeleton and joints accordingly (Van Horn 2018).

Surface definition

After constructing a 3D model, the animator's next step is to define its surface. The surface, which represents the outer appearance of the object, plays a crucial role in the final animation. This involves assigning various attributes such as colors, textures, reflections, transparency, and bump maps. For instance, if the animator is creating an orange, she might opt for a bumpy, orange surface to accurately depict the fruit's exterior.

Composition

The composition is the process of arranging all the elements in a scene. This includes positioning models, setting camera angles, and moving lights to create atmosphere and shadow effects. The animator may also choose to add particles, such as smoke or steam, for a more realistic effect. The most important element that the animator sets in the scene is the camera because the perspective of the final animation is dictated by the location of the camera.

Animation

The animation phase is the process of actually moving the models in a scene. During this phase, the animator will adjust position, orientation, and scale of the objects in relation to each other. The animator will use techniques such as inverse kinematics (the process of determining joint angles based on the joint angles of the connected appendages) and forward dynamics (determining the movement endpoint of an object based on the capabilities if its joints) as well as a variety of tools, such as keyframes and motion paths, to make the movements realistic. Keyframes are used to set start and end points of motion, while motion paths are used to create curved paths between those keyframes. Animators can also use physics simulations to generate realistic motion like pieces of cloth moving in the wind.

Sometimes a 3D animator will even apply motion to the camera to create zooming or panning effects. Imagine if an animator applied movement to a virtual camera that moved along the path of a roller coaster. The resulting animation rendered from the perspective of that camera would make the viewer feel as if he were riding on a roller coaster.

When character animation is involved, the animator can manipulate the various character body parts by setting keyframes on the controls that she has integrated within the 3D model. It's like working with a very complex marionette. Another method for generating character movement is called motion capture. Motion capture involves recording a live actor's motions and movements using markers and video. When this movement data is applied directly to the model. The result of motion capture is incredibly realistic looking movement since the movement data is coming from real life.

Rendering

During the rendering phase of 3D animation, the computer generates a sequence of images based on the actions defined in the timeline. This final rendering showcases all the properties of the 3D models, surfaces, composition, and motion through the lens of a virtual camera placed within the scene. Rendering can be both resource-intensive and time-consuming as it involves generating 30 images for every second of animation. Nonetheless, it is an essential step in producing the final animation. The final animation that is generated is typically in the form of a video file.

Uses of animation

Animation is a versatile art form that extends beyond cartoons and finds applications across diverse industries. Sectors such as advertising, education, architecture, as well as web, app, and game development, all harness the power of animation to captivate audiences and convey their messages effectively.

Entertainment

One of the most common uses of animation is for entertainment purposes. Animated feature films such as *Toy Story*, *Shrek*, and *Frozen* have not only

Figure 10.4 Motioion graphics are continuously displayed on the exterior of the Sphere in Las Vegas, USA

earned millions at the box office but also garnered critical acclaim for their groundbreaking visuals and storytelling techniques. Both 2D and 3D animation is widely used in TV shows both geared for children and adults such as *The Simpsons, Family Guy*, and *South Park*.

Advertising

Animated content can be used by advertisers to reach a large audience in an engaging and fun way. Animated content tends to be brighter and more colorful than video footage, so it can be an effective way to catch a viewer's attention. Animated commercials are made using all forms of animation, from stop motion such as the creative Lunchable ads and the classic California Raisins, to the playful 2D animated ads from Oreo and Gatorade, to the realistic looking 3D animated ads featuring a mighty polar bear from Coca-Cola.

Education

Animation has emerged as a formidable tool for educators. Through animations, complex concepts can be demonstrated in an easily comprehensible manner, captivating students' attention. Animated videos enable students to explore and visualize subjects that would otherwise be inaccessible due to size or cost constraints. From showcasing cellular processes that are invisible to the naked eye to illustrating the grandeur of planetary motion, animation has proven its educational prowess. Moreover, beyond the confines of the classroom, animations are frequently employed in litigation to elucidate intricate evidence and concepts for jurors.

Architecture

For architects designing buildings, 3D animation is an invaluable tool for visualizing a space. It enables the creation of precise representations that offer a glimpse into the future, aiding architects in making informed decisions during the initial planning phases. Moreover, 3D animation allows for immersive walkthroughs, granting clients and investors a preview of the building before construction commences.

Web, app, and game development

Animations can also be used to enhance the user experience in web applications and games. Animations can help guide the user through a website or app, teaching them how to use the application with gentle visual cues. Animations are also used heavily within video games, creating a sense of realism and immersion that make users feel as if they are truly in the game. Some games use animation strictly for visual stimulation or are simply eye candy that make the game more visually appealing. Regardless of the purpose, animation plays a crucial role in creating an enjoyable and interactive experience for users.

Uses of motion graphics

While still technically animations, motion graphics have a distinct niche and purpose in the realm of motion media. Motion graphics are typically used to convey information or data in a dynamic and visually appealing way, or to set a mood or tone for a video.

Title Sequences

Motion graphics have maintained their role as the go-to medium for title sequences in films and TV shows. From the iconic James Bond opening credits to the intricate titles of *Game of Thrones*, motion graphics have a unique look that can set the tone for an entire production. Motion-graphic title sequences are often very stylized and creative, showing off the production company's art.

The evolution and importance of compelling motion-graphics title sequences is demonstrated in the original 1960 and the 2001 version of the film *Ocean's Eleven*. In both the original (designed by Saul Bass) and the newer counterpart, neon elements (perfectly suited for the movie's Las Vegas setting) pop in to frame the actors' names. In both versions, the tightly choreographed movement of type and words allude to the elaborate coordination of actions the viewer is about to witness in the movie's heist plot. But the newer version features more detailed graphics and speedier transitions made only possible by the advancement of technology.

Branding

A logo communicates the essence of a brand, but with sound and motion, motion graphics can further enhance the brand image, and oftentimes they may be used within a company's promotional video or on the home page of a website.

Corporate branding is a relatively new phenomenon that caught on in the mid-part of the 20th century. When legendary American graphic designer Paul Rand designed the eye-catching IBM logo, he demonstrated that branding was an effective tool to set a company apart from the rest. Logos began to make their way into TV commercials, so adding motion to a logo was a logical next step. In the early 1980s, MTV took the idea of branding and motion to the extreme by showcasing their logo filled with ever-changing colors and patterns moving spastically on the screen. These branding interludes told the viewers what to expect from their unconventional channel: energy, variety, fun, and innovation.

Awareness campaigns

Motion graphics are frequently utilized in public service announcements and news stories to raise awareness about important issues. They make it easier for viewers to understand complex topics such as global warming, poverty, and disease because the designer can seamlessly integrate word and image. Unlike a static infographic, they also facilitate the display of change over time. Within these types of motion graphics, the integration of universally understood symbols can also be used to boost comprehension. Animation can make these pieces more engaging and captivating to the audience with creative use of color and movement, making it easier for an audience to remember and understand the message.

Explaining a concept

Like animation, motion graphics are a powerful visual tool to explain a concept or demonstrate how something works. While instructional 3D animations take advantage of the medium's ability to render realistic reproductions of the subject of interest, instructional motion graphics tend to be more diagrammatic. Pieces made for this purpose use symbols and illustrations, type, and motion to convey an understanding of a product or process in the simplest way. This technique can be especially effective when trying to explain a complex topic such as a new technology or scientific phenomenon.

Entertainment

With the prevalence of large screens within public spaces, motion graphics have taken center stage. They have become an expected element in events and integrated into a space's decor. Whether it's a background display during a concert or a central element in a hotel lobby, motion graphics add depth and excitement to the overall experience.

The production process

Throughout this chapter we have discussed many examples of animation and motion graphics from cartoons to title sequences to scientific 3D visualizations. Regardless of the type of animation being produced, the process can be very labor intensive, therefore starting with a clear plan in mind and a strategic process will help keep projects on time and within budget. For animation and motion graphics, pre-production encompasses several tasks such as creating a script, storyboard, and character designs. Production comes next and involves the actual creation of assets, animation, and sound. Postproduction is the final stage of production where editing and revisions take place before rendering the final product.

Scriptwriting

The first step in any animation or motion-graphics project is scriptwriting. The script outlines the story and dialogue or action of your animation. Although animation may be considered a visual medium, a well-written script is the backbone to an engaging and successful piece. It may include both vocal and non-vocal audio cues such as sound effects and music. It is the basis for all of the visuals and will define how the characters act, move, and interact with each other. If the pieces is more abstract, then the script may be more of an explanation of what is happening on the screen.

Scriptwriting plays a critical role in the production of any animated content, more so even than in the production of a live action film. When shooting live action, the filmmaker shoots much more footage than she will ultimately need, therefore the script provides guidance to the editor in postproduction. Animated content is much more time consuming to produce, therefore greater emphasis is often placed on the refinement of the script prior to production. For example, "Pixar Animation will spend at least three years refining story and visualization before animation begins" (Wells 2007, p. 15).

Storyboarding

Once a script is written, the next step is to create a storyboard. The storyboard will serve as a blueprint for the project and helps the animator map out each scene frame by frame. It is essentially a series of illustrations drawn within a frame the same proportion as the actual size of the film (typically 16:9) that will visually demonstrate the action within each scene and can help the production team better understand how the project will look.

In the early stages of animation, storyboards were crafted on paper and attached to boards, hence their name. This allowed the team to visualize the flow of the animation as a team. Nowadays, storyboards are created digitally using software like Adobe Illustrator or Photoshop or dedicated storyboard software such as Studiobinder or Storyboarder.

Audio recording

Before animation can commence, a scratch track must be recorded. A scratch track is a temporary version of the soundtrack which is recorded to help the animator keep their timing while they animate. This can be useful when creating a character lip-sync or when trying to match characters' movements with sound effects. In a motion-graphics piece, a preliminary soundtrack is helpful as well for establishing the appearance of various elements and the timing of the movement.

Animatic

An animatic is a quick, rough cut of all the scenes that will appear in the animation. It usually consists of drawings from the storyboard set to the scratch track and/or music. This is essentially a preview of what the finished animation will look like. It allows the production team to get a better sense of the timing and flow of the story before investing more time into the production process. Motion-graphics pieces also have animatics. They are created in a similar way, but with the addition of 3D or still images, text, and other elements to illustrate how the piece will look.

Design and timing

The next step is the design and timing phase. This is when the storyboards are sent to design departments and character sheets are developed. Character design involves illustrating any characters that appear in the animation, as well as their costumes and environments. The character sheets define how a character looks from a variety of angles with a variety of poses and expressions, so that all artists working on the project can deliver consistent work. At this point, the production team also wants to make sure that each character looks and moves differently with the goal of making them each unique. Additionally, the production team may also create 3D (or clay) models to help visualize what the characters will look like. During this process, the timing director takes the animatic and analyzes exactly what poses, drawings, and lip movements will be needed on what frames.

In a motion-graphics piece, there may not be characters per se; however, the environment or objects must also be designed. Figuring the look and feel and the timing of the overall pieces is a crucial step in the development of any motion-graphics piece.

Layout

The process of layout in animation is similar to the process of blocking camera shots for a cinematographer working on a live-action film. Here, the background layout artists decide on the camera angles, paths, lighting, and shading for the scene. When the layout drawings are done, they are integrated into a Leica reel (essentially a more refined animatic). Once this is done, the animation proper can commence.

Animation

Since the production of an animated television show or feature film can be such a time-consuming and tedious process, it's frequently tasked to an entire team of animators who have different areas of expertise. For example, one animator may be responsible for creating the movement of a specific character, while another may specialize in backgrounds and particle effects (like explosions).

As the various pieces come together, the director will review them and make sure that they are all in line with the original vision. The animation process is a collaborative effort between many departments, but ultimately it is the director's job to ensure that the story is cohesive and that all elements work together. Once the animation is complete, it is sent to the postproduction team where special effects, color correction, sound effects, character dialog, and music are added.

Animation and motion-graphics software

Software for traditional animation

If you are creating an animation using traditional methods like drawn, cel, or stop motion, your software needs are relatively straightforward. You just need a program that can compile a sequence of images into a finished movie. A free video-editing program will suffice, although you'll have more editing capabilities with a professional-level program like Adobe Premiere. By importing all the images into Adobe Premiere, setting a default timing for each image (e.g., 1/15th of a second), and arranging them on the timeline, you can easily render out your animation as a video file.

Alternatively, you can use a program through which you will capture and assemble all of the frames of your movie. One option is Dragonframe. Dragonframe is a program specifically designed for creating stop-motion animation, but you can use it to capture 2D drawn or cel animation as well. It offers some helpful features when you are building a stop-motion animation such as onion-skinning and frame-by-frame editing, as well as previsualization tools to help you plan out your shots before shooting them. It also has options for adding dialogue and sound effects, making it a versatile tool for all types of animation for bringing traditional animated content into the digital world ("Dragonframe" n.d.).

2D animation software

There are several robust 2D animation programs on the market, some of which are even free. However, probably the most popular 2D animation software used to make animated television shows is Toon Boom Harmony. Toon Boom Harmony is a professional animation program used by animators all over the world. Some of the popular shows created in Toon Boom include *The Simpsons* and *Family Guy* (Mak 2018). The reasons why the software has become an industry leader is due to its character-rigging capabilities as well as smart lip-syncing tools.

Another popular 2D animation program is Adobe Animate which is the new incarnation of Adobe Flash, a program used by animators and web designers for years. The reason why Adobe rebranded this program was to disassociate the program from the deprecated Flash player that was once heavily used on the web and to emphasize its sophisticated animation capabilities. Adobe Animate is a robust 2D animation program and popular choice for those who create 2D animated web content and even animated television shows like *Star Wars: Galaxy of Adventures* (Shukla 2019) and *Woody Woodpecker*

Shukla 2021). Animations created in Animate can still be integrated within a website, they just need to be saved in a native web format.

Another Adobe program that is used to create 2D animated content is Adobe After Effects. It differs from Adobe Animate in that it works primarily with pixel-based graphics as opposed to vector graphics. It can be used to produce 2D animation but its strength is in combining video footage with 2D and 3D graphics which is why it is used more for motion graphics than character animation.

3D animation software

When it comes to generating 3D animations, there are numerous options available, surpassing even those for 2D animation software. Among the most popular programs for 3D animation are Maya, 3DS Max, and Blender. Each of these programs possesses its own unique strengths and limitations. Interestingly, Maya and 3DS Max, both owned by AutoDesk, have contrasting origins and recommended applications. On the other hand, Blender stands out as a free and open-source alternative.

AutoDesk Maya was originally conceived as a versatile and powerful program specifically designed for creating 3D animated entertainment content. With its robust character animation and special-effects capabilities, Maya has become the go-to software for many professional animators and studios. It has played a significant role in the creation of numerous popular 3D animated films. Its extensive features and tools have made it a preferred choice for bringing imaginative worlds and captivating characters to life on the big screen. In fact, it is the current software of choice for Disney animators.

3DS Max is AutoDesk's 3D animation program with a very different strength. It's grew out of Autodesk's popular program AutoCAD which is the leading software used for drawing architectural plans and 3D object fabrication. Therefore, it should come as no surprise that the strength of 3DS Max is in creating 3D objects with specific dimensions and properties. The program is considered less of an entertainment software and more of an instructive, visualization program. It's great for creating 3D walkthroughs of buildings that are drawn in AutoCAD.

Blender is a program that is more akin to Maya. It's modeling tools allow the animator to build organic, amorphous objects, apply motion to those objects, and render out the animation. It is a free open source program and can be used for both personal at home learning or commercial projects. Since the program is open source, there is no tech support line you can call if you are struggling with the program. But there is a huge community of Blender users and developers online where you can go to get your questions answered.

Motion-graphics software

While 2D animation programs like Toon Boom Harmony and Adobe Animate can be used to create motion graphics, most often the program of choice is Adobe AfterEffects. This is due, in part, to the software's sophisticated video-compositing abilities. In many motion-graphics pieces, you can see video behind moving type or even interacting with it. Imagine, for example, words spinning into a black hole. That black hole may be video footage that is colorized and enhanced to look ominous and then laid behind the animated content to establish such a look.

Animated tools and techniques for the non-animator

Creating animated or motion-graphics pieces requires careful planning and production. However, it's important to note that you don't need formal training in the field to explore this creative medium. With the right tools and techniques, anyone can craft captivating animated content, even without being an expert animator.

Animated GIFS

The animated GIF is one of the simplest forms of animation, easily shareable and creatable by almost anyone. It consists of a series of images that can play once or loop continuously, creating captivating movement. However, animated GIFs have a few limitations. They are restricted to 256 colors and can quickly become large in file size due to the number of frames. Additionally, they do not support sound. Despite these limitations, they remain a delightful medium for creating eye-catching content on social media or within marketing emails.

There are a variety of tools you can use to create an animated GIF. Adobe Photoshop is a popular choice as it allows you to build the frames as layers—which you can lower in opacity to see the previous layer underneath (like onion skinning). When you are done building all the sequential layers, you convert them to frames and set the timing on each one. Alternatively, there are also many online tools you can use to create your GIFs. Sites like Giphy provide a great platform for quickly and easily making animated GIFs from existing images or video clips.

Drag and drop 2D animation

Drag and drop 2D animation programs significantly simplify the animation process, making it accessible to a broader audience, including those with minimal animation experience. These programs such as Animaker and Powtoon come with extensive libraries of characters, objects, and scenes, allowing users to rapidly compose and enact narratives without laborious frame-by-frame animation. Such software is invaluable for marketing and advertising professionals who leverage motion graphics to create engaging content that can quickly translate complex ideas into clear, visually appealing stories.

Animaker is a free 2D animation web-based software for beginners, with easy drag-and-drop functionality and a simple interface. One fun feature is that it will generate speech from the text you enter. In Animaker, you have the option to include background music, sound effects, and voice-overs to your content. You can select from the available sounds in the Animaker library or use your own audio files. After you build your animation, you can export your completed piece as an MP4 file or send it directly to YouTube.

Another easy-to-use web-based 2D animation program is called Powtoon. Like Animaker, it is also free and it allows users to create animated videos and presentations for various purposes such as marketing and training. Powtoon also has a drag-and-drop editor and a variety of pre-designed templates. Within the application there is also free clip art you can incorporate into your animation and additional resources behind a pay wall.

Drag and drop 3D animation

If you want to create 3D animations without the steep learning curve of specialized software, there are also drag-and-drop programs available that will generate 3D animations. One example is Daz Studio, which allows users to import characters and scenes from its library or other downloaded content. It provides a user-friendly approach to animating 3D characters, eliminating the need to grasp complex concepts like keyframes and rigging. Daz Studio also simplifies 3D rendering and supports the creation of both still images and animations. Similar to 2D drag-and-drop animation tools, Daz Studio is web-based and offers a free trial, but it is not entirely free.

"Why advertisers like animation" by professor and independent animator Michael Long

Good animation engages the audience, asking them to fill in details with their minds. This technique is what makes animation suitable for advertising and marketing, because it draws the viewer in by having them complete the picture.

"Animation's infinite possibilities" by Disney layout finaling supervisor Kristin Pratt

Animation (2D and CG) is perhaps the single most robust medium for storytelling. It lends itself to exaggerated world-building and characters, but it can also swing the pendulum towards hyper-realism when you think of its use in visual effects. The art of animation is infinite in its possibilities.

Study questions

1) Explain the differences between 2D and 3D computer animation.
2) How does the use of motion-graphics enhance marketing and advertising content?
3) What are some limitations of creating animated GIFs?
4) Explain how 3D computer animation is made.
5) Explain how the history of animation was affected by developments in the film industry.

Exercises

1) Create a simple animated GIF using Adobe Photoshop or an online tool like Giphy.
2) Use Animaker to create a 2D animation with speech generated from text or explore Daz Studio and try creating a basic 3D animation.
3) Research the use of motion graphics or animation on social media and write a short report on your findings.
4) Watch a classic animated film and take note of the techniques used to create movement and convey emotion through animation. Share your thoughts on how animation has evolved over time.
5) Interview a professional animator or motion graphics designer and ask them about their creative process, tools they use, and challenges they face in their work. Summarize your findings in a short report.

References

Callahan, David. 1988. "Cel Animation: Mass Production and Marginalization in the Animated Film Industry." *Film History* 2 (3): 223–28.

Cavalier, Stephen. 2011. *The World History of Animation*. Berkeley, CA: University of California Press. https://worldcat.org/title/668191570.

"Dragonframe." n.d. Dragonframe. https://www.dragonframe.com/dragonframe-software/

Furniss, Maureen. 2016. *A New History of Animation*. New York: Thames & Hudson. https://worldcat.org/title/940361738.

Hooper, Mark. 2023. "The Deadly Design of Saul Bass's 'Vertigo.'" Sotheby's. https://www.sothebys.com/en/articles/the-deadly-design-of-saul-basss-vertigo.

Horn, Erik Van. 2018. "3D Character Development Workshop: Rigging Fundamentals for Artists and Animators." Dulles, Virginia: Mercury Learning and Information Dulles, Virginia. https://worldcat.org/title/1036204148.

Mak, Philip. 2018. "Top Animation News: Simpsons and Family Guy Films, SIGGRAPH and More!" ToonBoom. https://www.toonboom.com/top-animation-news-simpsons-and-family-guy-films-siggraph-and-more.

Shukla, Ajay. 2019. "Star Wars: Galaxy of Adventures." Adobe Blog. https://blog.adobe.com/en/publish/2019/09/04/star-wars-galaxy-of-adventures.

Shukla, Ajay. 2021. "Celebrating 80 Years of Woody Woodpecker with Adobe Animate." Adobe Blog. https://blog.adobe.com/en/publish/2021/01/14/celebrating-80-years-of-woody-woodpecker-with-adobe-animate.

Wells, Paul. 2007. *Scriptwriting*. Basics Animation. Lausanne, Switzerland: AVA Publishing.

11 Building websites

The methods in which developers build websites have evolved significantly over the years. In the early days of the web, a site could only be made from HTML code and transferred to a web server via an FTP (file transfer protocol) program. These days, content management systems and website builders make website creation much simpler for those with little to no coding experience.

In this chapter we will discuss how the web has evolved, how websites are built using core web languages—HTML, CSS, and JavaScript—and how they come together to form an interactive experience. Next, we will discuss content management systems and how a popular blogging system (WordPress) became a leading website content management system. And finally, we will look at website builders like Wix and Weebly which use templates and drag-and-drop tools to allow users to create a website without having to know any HTML or other programming languages.

Origins of the World Wide Web

Oftentimes people confuse the World Wide Web and the internet, but these two technologies are not one and the same. The internet is an interconnected global network of computers. It was founded in 1969 as a government project, simply connecting two computers at UCLA and Stanford together. The network grew from there; however, there were some limitations to the system. While information could technically be shared between systems, navigating between computers with different protocols and architectures was often too cumbersome.

In 1989, Sir Tim Berners-Lee (a physicist working in the CERN lab in Geneva, Switzerland) came up with a way to access information over the network through hyperlinks—text that you could simply click on that would lead you to other pages of information. This is when the World Wide Web was born, and it revolutionized how people accessed and shared information over the internet. The World Wide Web is essentially an information retrieval system which uses hypertext links to connect documents located on different computers all over the world. The World Wide Web put a graphical user interface on the internet.

DOI: 10.4324/9781003462200-11

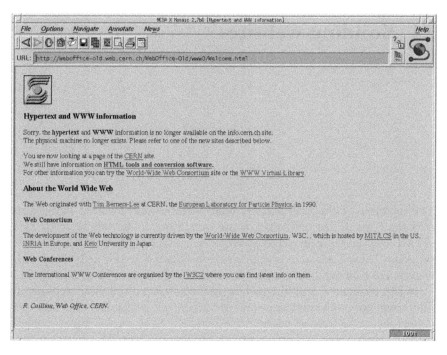

Figure 11.1 The Mosaic browser [Charles Severance / CC BY-SA 4.0 (via Wikimedia Commons)]

Shortly after Berners-Lee's breakthrough, the first web browser, called Mosaic, was created and made publicly available by a University of Illinois graduate student named Marc Andreesen. Mosaic (which later became Netscape Navigator) made the web publicly accessible. And because it was so easy to use, it opened up the web to a much larger audience.

The invention of the web, the arrival of the browser, and the government's removal of commerce restrictions over the internet throughout the mid to late 1990s all led to the birth of e-commerce. Websites such as Amazon, eBay, and others quickly became household names and platforms for many businesses to sell their products. This period of time became known as the dot-com boom due to the rapid growth of online businesses. For many companies who raced to sell goods online, it also led to a bust as the hype exceeded the reality that not every business could be successful selling online.

In the late 1990s, even companies and organizations that were not selling online often wanted some type of presence on the web. These early websites were fairly basic and, because they were akin to a simple brochure, often referred to as "brochureware." But even as simple and straight forward as they were, they still needed to be created by web programmers using a new markup language called HTML and transferred via a protocol called FTP. So, to be able to publish even the most basic website to the web, one needed some technical know-how.

In the early 2000s, blogging platforms started to become popular. Blogging was a way for individuals to easily publish content online without having any technical knowledge of web programming. WordPress (which was launched in 2003) quickly became the most popular platform people used to build blogs. Social media sites like MySpace were also created during this time, allowing users to easily build a profile page and share content with friends. These platforms were significant because they gave the non-technical user a voice on the web.

In 2007, the release of the first iPhone presented a new challenge for web developers. With the incorporation of web browsers on mobile devices, it became necessary for websites to be optimized for smaller screens. This led to the development of responsive web design, which allowed websites to adapt and display properly on different devices. Mobile devices also introduced the world to apps which are stand-alone programs that can be downloaded and installed on a hand-held device, and they quickly became a popular way for businesses to reach their customers.

Today the web is more interactive than ever before. Websites have become much more sophisticated and advanced, often including immersive experiences such as videos, animations, and other interactive elements. The methods in which you can build a website are also more diverse and accessible, allowing almost anyone to create a website. But, before we get to these tools and platforms, let's take a closer look at how websites are built.

Coding a website

Building a website from scratch requires that you have a working knowledge of HTML, CSS, and JavaScript. Technically, you can actually build a website in pure HTML, but it probably wouldn't look very pretty. HTML (Hyper-Text Markup Language) is the primary language used to create websites. It's a markup language that defines the structure and presents the content on a web page. HTML is comprised of "tags" that surround content and tell the browser how to display, format, and layout the page.

Writing HTML is quite simple. In fact, you can compose HTML in a basic text editor such as Notepad. There are also many freely available HTML editors that you can download and use. The benefit of using an HTML editor over a text editor is that it often includes features such as color coding and auto completion which can make HTML easier to read and write. The first step is to create an HTML document. This is done by opening up your text editor and adding some basic tags like the <html> and <body> tags. Next, you can start adding elements such as headers, paragraphs, images, and links to other sites or other pages on your website. Most websites are comprised of multiple pages, therefore you will need to create additional HTML documents for each page. In order for a browser to understand that your document should be interpreted as HTML, you need to save it as a .html file.

After the HTML documents are created, you can start using CSS to style and add visual unity across HTML documents. CSS (Cascading Style Sheets) is a language that is integrated within the HTML page. Using CSS, you can apply colors, backgrounds, fonts, borders, and other design elements to the HTML page. CSS is a newer innovation as it emerged a few years after the birth of the World Wide Web. CSS can be written within the same HTML document, or you can create a separate CSS file that contains all of your style information and refer to the CSS file in your HTML document.

Once the styling is complete, you may want to use JavaScript to create dynamic effects such as animations, automated forms, and slideshows. JavaScript is a scripting language that allows developers to create dynamic effects, such as animations, automated forms, and slideshows. It is also used for client-side validation, which ensures that the data submitted from a webpage is valid before it is sent to the server. Again, like CSS, you can write the JavaScript code within the HTML document, or you can create a separate JavaScript file that contains all of your code and link the JavaScript file to your HTML document.

One aspect to web development that has become critically important is a website's responsiveness. A website should be able to adjust its layout and design to the device that it is being viewed on. Making sure your site is responsive requires a working knowledge of media queries which can be easily added to your CSS file. A media query is a way of detecting information about the device requesting the website, specifically the dimensions of the device's screen

HTML

```
<HTML>
  <HEAD>
    <TITLE>
    My website
    </TITLE>
  <HEAD>
<BODY>
```

CSS

```
<style>
Body {
    color: #000000;
}
P {
    margin:0px;
}
</style>
```

JavaScript

```
<script type=
"text/javascript"
```

Content & Structure   **Presentation**   **Behavior**

Figure 11.2 HTML, CSS, and JavaScript

so that you can display elements on the page differently based on the device. An alternative method to using media queries to make your website responsive is to employ the free and open-source Bootstrap framework in your website. The Bootstrap framework is a collection of CSS and JavaScript files that you reference in your website header. Once they are included, you can specify the special Bootstrap syntax to trigger responsive behavior.

As you are building your website, you can preview your work by opening your HTML pages in a browser. If you have never built a website, you probably have never done this. But every browser incorporates this functionality. You can simply open an HTML page that lives on your computer by using the File -> Open command from any browser menu. In addition to being able to preview your site, browsers also offer developer tools that allow you to do more sophisticated testing.

Once you have written all the code for your website and are satisfied with how it looks, you must upload the HTML, CSS, and JavaScript files to a web server so that the world can see and experience your site. The program that is most often used to send files to a web server is called an FTP (file transfer protocol) program. An FTP program establishes a connection to the web server and then you drag and drop your web site files into the hosting space. Again there are many freely available FTP programs. Alternatively, most web-hosting companies provide a file-management feature where you can upload your files directly through a webpage.

Because HTML, CSS, and JavaScript are the key three ingredients web developers use to build websites, they are often referred to as the core web languages. Working with just these three languages, it is possible to create a website that is interactive, visually appealing, and easy to navigate. HTML, CSS, and JavaScript have evolved quite a bit over the years, broadening the capabilities of what each language can do. The latest standards and best practices for using core web languages are dictated by the nonprofit organization, W3C (the World Wide Web Consortium) that oversees standards on the web. They publish extensive references on their site (www.w3c.org) in addition to providing comprehensive training on their sister site, W3Schools (www.w3schools.org) which contains tutorials and references for HTML, CSS, and JavaScript.

Now that we have covered the basics of building a website, you may be wondering, how people will access the website you just created? In order for the world to see your website, you need to put your files on a web server, and you also need to register a domain name and point it to the location of your website on your web server. The service of providing web hosting, selling a domain name, and pointing that domain name to your website are often done by the same company which is known as a web host/domain registrant.

Setting up web hosting and acquiring a domain name

Web hosting is fairly straightforward. When you pay a company to host your website, you are essentially getting space on a web server on which you store your website files. A web server is simply a computer running web-server software with a continuous connection to the internet. Anyone can set up a web server and host their own website, but host companies offer the added benefit of very fast connection speeds to the internet so that your site is served up quickly. They also have backup servers to mitigate website downtime.

Almost any company that offers website hosting is also a domain registrant, meaning that you can buy your domain name through that company as well. Buying a domain name is actually a misnomer, because when you make this purchase, it is actually a lease. You pay for the rights to use the domain name for a set period of time. When that time period ends, you have the option to extend your lease or let it expire. At that point, anyone has the ability to purchase it. You will notice that you can purchase a domain name with a variety of extensions. .com (which stands for commercial) is probably the most common domain extension but there are a lot of other options available, for example, .org, .edu, .net, .mil, all of which are intended to reflect the purpose of the site.

After you purchase the domain name, you must point it to the server location of your website which is designated by an IP address. IP addresses are the physical addresses of web servers. Since they are a long string of numbers, they are difficult to remember. For this reason, the Domain Name System (or DNS) was created. A domain name is essentially an alias to an IP address. When someone types in your domain name, the DNS will look it up and direct the user to your website. When you point your domain name to an IP address, you are creating a record in the DNS.

The Domain Name System is made up of a network of databases that are constantly communicating with one another so that they all have the most accurate and up-to-date information. For example, if I register the domain name www.juliesburgershop.com and point it to the IP address of my web server, that pairing is shared throughout the entire domain name system so that everyone on the World Wide Web will be able to get to my website by typing in my domain name. The DNS also keeps track of who currently owns a domain. Therefore, while you own the domain name, no one will be able to purchase it through another company. Because the Domain Name System is a shared worldwide database, it technically does not matter which company you use to register your domain. Typically, however, it's a bit easier to point your domain name to your host if you buy them from the same company.

More complex web development

The process of building a website that I described earlier in this chapter is pretty rudimentary and not typically how websites are built anymore. Oftentimes, websites need to have more advanced capabilities such as being able to communicate with a database. Consider any e-commerce site. To keep track of inventory, orders, etc., the site must be able to read and write data from a database. But, in order to have a database-driven site, you must employ more complex web-development languages like ASP.net or PHP. A webpage written in a language like PHP still maintains the structural properties of an HTML page, it simply has special lines of code inside of it that are read and parsed out by the web server before displaying the resulting HTML page to the viewer that requested it.

One significant downside of coding a website from scratch is that it's not easy to maintain. Since all of the web content would exist within the code, making changes to a website requires editing code and transferring the modified files to a web server. This process can be tedious, especially if your website consists of hundreds of HTML documents. Prior to the advent of content management systems, if a website owner needed to make a change to their website copy, they would need to contact their developer to make these edits. There was simply no other way for a site owner to change the copy on their site. For this reason, many websites that were launched were never changed.

Content management systems

This lack of control over the content of one's website was the impetus for the development of content management systems. A content management system (CMS) is a platform that allows users to easily manage the content of a website. It has tools built in for managing, editing, and publishing content. When a site is built using the framework of a CMS, the web developer no longer creates every page from code. Instead, they set up and customize a website that the client can freely edit.

Building a website on a CMS is actually not very difficult. First, the CMS itself must be installed in the directory on the web server where the site resides. Fortunately, many web-hosting companies make installing a CMS easy by offering "one-click" installs to deploy the CMS. Once it's installed, the developer must configure the site according to the customer's needs. Some of these customizations can be done with the tools within the CMS, but oftentimes a developer will add custom HTML, CSS, and JavaScript to enhance the look and functionality of the site. After the developer is finished, she can give the client access via a user ID and password to access the back end so that they can login and make edits to content on their site. The back end is accessed via a login page within the site, for example: www.juliesburgershop.com/wp-admin.

Choosing a CMS

There are a few different content management systems available, each with their own strengths and weaknesses. Most CMSs are open-source, meaning they are developed and maintained by the community at large. Some popular open-source CMSs are WordPress, Drupal, and Joomla. Choosing a CMS should be based on the developer's familiarity with the CMS, client preference, type of site, and capabilities of the hosting environment.

WordPress

As I mentioned earlier, WordPress began as a blogging system in the early 2000s, but over the past two decades it has become the leading CMS, with it being the platform of choice for over 43% of all websites across the web ("About Word-Press" n.d.). One of its core strengths is its ease of use. Since it was designed to be a blogging tool (used by anyone and everyone), it really is user friendly. There is also an extensive library of plugins and themes that can be integrated into a WordPress site that extend a site's capabilities and change its look. A few well-known websites that are built on WordPress include Harvard University, NASA, and Rolling Stone ("WordPress Archive" n.d.).

Drupal

Drupal is another popular CMS that is free and open source. It is known for its modularity and flexibility. It's a more complex system than some of the other CMSs with powerful features, built-in security, and scalability. Drupal provides more control over the look and feel of a website but requires a bit more technical knowledge than WordPress to set up and maintain. Drupal is the platform of choice for many large organizations such as the BBC, NBC, and MTV UK ("About Drupal" n.d.).

Joomla

Joomla is yet another free, open source, and popular CMS used primarily by small businesses. It's similar to WordPress in terms of its ease of use and extensibility. Some of the advantages it offers over WordPress is that it has an integrated e-commerce system and reservation system which can make it an attractive platform for small businesses that need these services. Some highly trafficked websites that are built on the Joomla platform include the Guggenheim Museum, IKEA, Holiday Inn, and Linux (Raza 2019).

You may assume that understanding core web languages is not necessary if you are building your website on one of the aforementioned content management systems. That is not necessarily the case. WordPress, Drupal, and Joomla are all built with the core web languages as well as PHP, therefore familiarity with code can give you an edge when customizing a website.

Building a website on a platform

If you're not comfortable with coding, setting up a website on a CMS platform may seem overwhelming. Fortunately, there are several website builder platforms available which allow users to create a website without having to code. These platforms are typically subscription-based, bundling the hosting and content management tools into one monthly fee. They also facilitate the registration of your domain name and will take care of pointing your domain to your site on their platform.

Using one of these platforms is a great way for an individual to get their website up and running without having to learn web development. The downside of using one of these platforms is that you might be limited to their functionality and design templates. They also tend to be more expensive than setting up the website with your own hosting and installing a free CMS.

Some popular website builder platforms are Wix, Squarespace, and Weebly.

Wix

Wix is a cloud-based website builder platform that has been around for nearly two decades. It has hundreds of professionally designed responsive templates and an easy-to-use drag and drop website builder. With Wix, you can build your site for free, see if you like the platform, and then upgrade your plan and purchase a domain name to point to your site if you decide to make it your site's resting place.

Squarespace

Similar to Wix, Squarespace is a website builder platform with hundreds of templates and drag-and-drop tools. Squarespace is known for its modern, sophisticated design options and easy-to-setup e-commerce capabilities.

Weebly

Weebly is a popular website-building platform with an intuitive drag-and-drop editor. Weebly is known for its generous free plan—so if you are on a shoestring budget, it may be the platform for you. If you want to use your own domain name to point to your Weebly site, you will need to upgrade to a paid plan.

Principles of web design

There are plenty of great tools to help you build your website, but creating a site that is user friendly, understandable, and brand-appropriate requires an understanding of the principles of web design. Here are some basics to consider when designing a website regardless of the technology you use to build it.

Orientation

When the user arrives on the website, will they understand its purpose? Will they know what they can do on the site? Make sure that the goal and purpose of the website is clear and easy to find. You have a very limited amount of time to convince a user to stay on your site and explore.

Typography

Visitors to any website should be able to read and understand the content quickly. Ornate fonts can add character to a site but are often not easy to read. Limit decorative fonts that reflect the brand for headers and stick with basic sans serif fonts for larger areas of body copy to ensure legibility.

Choose your colors strategically

The colors you choose for your website should reflect the brand. Of course, you may want to add colors to your site beyond the ones in your logo, but these colors are a great starting point. It can be helpful to use online color palette builders to help you round out your color scheme. When you build a color palette, pick colors that layer well. Make sure that there is sufficient contrast among your chosen colors to layer elements on top of each other. Avoid trying to integrate too many colors. A more limited color palette will make your site feel more cohesive.

Consistency

A website should have a coherent look and feel throughout. Make sure the design elements are consistent across all of pages to reassure users that they are on the same site. Consistency in design and functionality also aids usability. For example, if links and buttons change color and style throughout the site, the user may question what is clickable and what is not.

Navigation

The navigation should be easy for users to understand and use. A user should never have to guess where to go on the website. Your users should be able to move in a logical fashion through the site without getting lost or confused. Using well-known navigation conventions and language takes advantage of users' existing knowledge and facilitates immediate understanding.

Establish visual hierarchy

Ensure that users can easily scan the page and identify what content is important by giving it visual prominence. The most important information should be the most apparent.

E-commerce sites

Building a website with e-commerce capabilities adds another level of complexity to the web-development process. Fortunately, you can readily add these features into a site if you are using a CMS or one of the aforementioned web platforms. It may just involve installing an additional module and/or paying for a higher level of service. In addition, if you are running an e-commerce site, you must make sure that your site is secure and that you can receive payments by connecting your website to a merchant account.

Adding e-commerce capabilities to a website that is built on a platform like Wix, Squarespace, or Weebly is relatively simple. You simply sign up for the e-commerce package when you purchase a subscription to the service or upgrade your plan to allow for e-commerce. Then, customize the look and feel of your store, add your products, and you are pretty much ready to start selling online. If you know that you want the focus of your site to be e-commerce, you may want to explore other website-building platforms that are specifically dedicated to creating e-commerce sites like BigCommerce and Shopify. These are both subscription-based services that may be a bit more expensive, but they also come with many features and support related to e-commerce.

If you are building a website on a CMS like WordPress, adding e-commerce capabilities is a bit more involved. The leading plugin to make a WordPress website an e-commerce site is WooCommerce. It's a free plugin that comes with some basic features, but it can be extended to meet the needs of just about any e-commerce site. Setting up an e-commerce site on WordPress requires a bit more technical know-how, but if you are already knowledgeable about the CMS or have an experienced developer to help, then it can be a great platform for creating a successful online store. Because, like WordPress, WooCommerce is free and open source, this is probably the least expensive route for building an e-commerce site. While there is a bit of a learning curve to working with WordPress and WooCommerce, because they are so popular, there are many resources as well as plugins to help you get started.

Another option you can use for building an e-commerce site is the freely available e-commerce application, Magento (now Adobe Commerce). Magento is a powerful open-source platform that offers great flexibility and can be used to build an extensive online store. It is like WordPress in that you can install the software within many different hosting environments. But it is different from WordPress in that it is designed specifically for e-commerce. Some of the most robust e-commerce stores online today are built on the Magento platform, including Ford, Vizio, Landrover, and Christian Louboutin (Yantsan 2023).

A critical component of any e-commerce site is being able to collect payments. This can be done by connecting your website to a merchant account such as PayPal or Stripe. A merchant account collects the funds from your customer, keeps a small percentage, and then transfers the remainder to your bank account. Different e-commerce platforms work with one or more of these merchants which is something you can research prior to setting up your online store. Once you have an account, you will need to set it up in your CMS or website platform. That connection facilitates the secure processing of payments from customers. Whether you build your e-commerce site in WordPress with WooCommerce or on a website platform, connecting your e-commerce site to a merchant account is relatively simple and straightforward.

Whenever you collect credit-card information on a website, it is critically important that the transaction be secure. This means that your website must be secured with an SSL (secure socket layer). Have you ever noticed that after typing a web address into your browser, the address changes from http:// to https:// and a lock appears in the address bar? That means the site is secure and enabling an SSL. Setting up a secure site has gotten much simpler, as typically an SSL now comes with a hosting package, you simply need to enable it. Without an SSL, customers will not be able to securely share their credit-card information and your e-commerce site will not work.

Driving traffic to your site

What is the point of building a website if no one will ever come to it? If you are using your website to monetize your business, you must drive traffic to your site. Fortunately, there are a number of ways to do this.

SEO

Search engine optimization (SEO) is a great way to generate organic traffic to your website as 80% of all web traffic originates as a search query (Duk, Bjelobrk, and Čarapina 2013). Incorporating keywords into the content, titles, and tags on your website will increase the chances that your site is among the top results when a search query is made, but there are no guarantees that your website will end up on the first page of Google when someone searches for a term related to your website. There are many different factors that go into how Google chooses to list the search results for any type of query. And although a lot of "experts" claim they know what algorithm Google uses to serve up search results, no one really knows except the engineers at Google. In addition, the algorithm changes frequently, so while your site may be listed as a first page result from a Google search one day, it could easily change positions the next day.

Nevertheless, there are some best practices for SEO that can help improve a site's rankings. Having relative and useful content on your website is essential for Google to believe that your site is related to that topic. Google also prioritizes quick loading sites. Websites bogged down with slow loading images, videos, and bulky code will get penalized by Google. Google also favors sites that have higher domain authority. Domain authority is a measure of how much people trust your website. The more backlinks (links from other websites to yours), the better. As Google (and other search engines) have evolved, they have all gotten smarter. Long gone are the days when you could trick a search engine into thinking that your website was the most relevant one to a specific topic by cramming it with keywords and rendering them in the same color as the background so that a casual user would not see them, but a search engine would read them. There are other tricks that website owners use to try to improve a site's Google ranking. For example, some website owners will try to pay for backlinks to their site or stuff their content with irrelevant keywords. Tactics like these may work initially, but will likely get a site banned by Google for these "unethical" practices (Lahey 2020).

Social media

For many businesses and organizations, social media can be an effective way to generate traffic to a website. The key with social media is finding the right channels and creating content that appeals to your target audience. For example, some businesses sell products and services that are inherently more visual so they may thrive on platforms like Instagram or Pinterest where images and videos are the primary means of communication. Pinterest is an especially powerful driver of traffic to a website because the images link back to the original source. In other words, if someone pins an image from your website and someone else clicks on it, they will be brought right into your website. Driving traffic to your website from Instagram is a little bit trickier as you can't incorporate URLs into your posts. You can, however, include a URL in your profile. One common tactic that many marketers do is to use a link to a Linktree site as their profile URL as opposed to their website home page. Linktree is a third-party application that lets you build a family of buttons that link to all the important pages and sites associated with your brand.

Paid advertising

Another way to generate traffic is through paid advertising. This can be done easily through Google Adwords, or Meta (Facebook and Instagram) Ads which are the most dominant type of ads you see on the web. With these types of campaigns, you can target your audience and create ads that are specific to them. You can also have control over how much you spend, when the ads are displayed, and what kind of results you get. Paid advertising campaigns can be very effective, but they can also be expensive and may not yield results if the strategy is not implemented correctly.

"Essential ingredients of a website" by web developer and professor Scott Granneman

Every webpage ever made uses only three languages: HTML, CSS, and JavaScript. Those are the foundations that every web developer has to know. If you are a cook, you understand that there are only five basic tastes: sweet, sour, salty, bitter, and umami. If you study color, you learn that our brains process yellow/blue and red/green into every color we can see. Likewise, the core to all web development is just three things: HTML, CSS, and JavaScript.

Study questions

1) What do you need to do on your website before you can start selling product?
2) What is SEO and how can it help drive traffic to your website?
3) How does social media play a role in generating traffic to a website?
4) Why was the internet more heavily used after the web was invented?
5) What are the core web languages and what do they do?

Exercises

1) Research website-building platforms and recommend one to a small startup business that wants to start selling product online.
2) Research the latest SEO best practices and make five recommendations to a website of your choice to improve its search engine rankings.
3) Identify a client and make recommendations on paid advertising opportunities on the internet.
4) Practice coding in HTML, CSS, and JavaScript by building a simple personal portfolio website from scratch.
5) Identify a social media platform and create a series of posts that promote your website in a manner appropriate for the platform.

References

"About Drupal." n.d. drupal.org/about.

"About WordPress." n.d. Wordpress. https://wordpress.org/about/. Accessed May 2, 2024.

Duk, S., D. Bjelobrk, and M. Čarapina. 2013. "SEO in E-Commerce: Balancing between White and Black Hat Methods." In *2013 36th International Convention on Information and Communication Technology, Electronics and Microelectronics (MIPRO)*, 390–95.

Lahey, Connor. 2020. "What is Black Hat SEO? 9 Risky Techniques to Avoid." https://www.semrush.com/blog/black-hat-seo/. Accessed May 11, 2024.

Raza, Syed Hassan. 2019. "10 Most Popular Websites That Use Joomla." Cloudways. https://www.cloudways.com/blog/popular-joomla-websites/.

"WordPress Archive." n.d. Wordpress. https://wordpress.org/showcase/archives/. Accessed May 2, 2024.

Yantsan, Ellie. 2023. "Top 15 Magento Stores: Best Websites Using Magento in 2023." Mageworx Blog. https://www.mageworx.com/blog/top-world-brands-on-magento.

12 Writing for media production

When you are expressing your ideas though media, it may feel like writing as a form of communication is no longer relevant. However, this could not be further from the truth. Writing plays a major role in all aspects of media production. Before you can even begin to produce media, you must often write a proposal to get your ideas off the ground. Writing is also essential in media production as it helps to structure and organize ideas. Whether it's creating a script for a film or developing an outline for a blog post, writing allows us to clarify our thoughts and present them in a cohesive manner. Writing is also an essential aspect of storytelling in media production. It allows us to convey emotions, set the tone and mood, and captivate our audience. Written content takes center stage on the web. The rise of social media, blogs, and other online platforms have made writing a crucial skill for anyone involved in marketing and promotion. The words are often what prompts the viewer to take action, whether it be purchasing a product or sharing a piece of content. In almost any media production project, writing also serves as a means of documentation. From recording interviews to transcribing videos, writing allows us to preserve information and share it with others. It is through written words that we can accurately convey the thoughts and ideas of others, making it an essential skill for all media professionals.

In this chapter, we will explore the various roles that writing plays within media production. We will discuss how to craft effective proposals for different types of media projects. Next, we dive deeper into effective scriptwriting. Finally, we will examine different forms of writing used on social media posts and websites.

Proposal writing for media projects

Almost any media-related project begins with a proposal. Whether it is pitching an idea to a potential client or seeking funding for a film, writing a proposal is the first step in turning your ideas into reality. A well-written proposal can make or break the success of your project. It serves as a blueprint for your ideas, outlining the objectives, target audience, budget, and overall vision for your project.

DOI: 10.4324/9781003462200-12

A proposal for a media project is crucial for a multitude of reasons. First, it aids in providing a clear understanding of the project's vision to all stakeholders, usually directed towards investors or clients who could potentially fund the project. Secondly, it serves as a roadmap guiding the project's execution, breaking down the workflow into manageable tasks and milestones. Additionally, the process of writing a proposal facilitates critical thinking, prompting the author to identify potential challenges and devise strategies to overcome them. The proposal also allows for a thorough examination of the project's feasibility, helping you to consider factors such as cost, time, resources, and market demand. Ultimately, a well-crafted proposal enhances the likelihood of a project's success by encouraging meticulous planning and clear communication.

Proposals for media projects can take different forms depending on the type of project you are proposing and to whom you are proposing it. For example, a proposal for a film would differ greatly from one for a digital media marketing campaign. Similarly, the language and tone used in the proposal will vary based on your audience.

Creative project proposals

When it comes to producing film and television content, "a proposal is, first and foremost a device to sell" your project (Rosenthal and Eckhardt 2016). You use this document to convince the funding organization that the project is interesting and would appeal to a broader audience. Unlike a proposal for a client-driven project, a proposal for a creative project has not been requested by the reader. It is unsolicited and possibly unexpected, so the reader needs to be tantalized into learning more. The opening paragraphs are critically important as they must explain the project while exciting and intriguing the reader. The content of this type of proposal should contain a working title, a rationale, a research outline (if it is a documentary), a list of subjects or characters, locations, and a description of content and style, budget, audience, and details about the creators.

In the film world, proposals for new projects are often called one-sheets. These are single-page documents that include a brief synopsis of the project, key creative elements such as cast and crew, target audience, and budget. One-sheets are often used to pitch ideas to potential investors or distributors.

Client-driven proposals

Client-driven proposals, on the other hand, are directed toward clients or businesses seeking media production services such as social media management, advertising campaigns, content creation, and/or website development. These types of proposals are usually requested by the organization (solicited). Public organizations often put out an RFP (request for proposals) when seeking a company to take on a project. The RFP outlines the client's expectations, and it is up to the bidding companies to respond with a well-written proposal that showcases their capabilities and why they are the best fit for the job. These types of proposals should address the client's needs directly and provide solutions to potential challenges.

This type of proposal should clearly demonstrate an understanding of the client's needs and how your company can meet them. Common elements include:

- Executive summary: A brief overview of the project, highlighting the key points and objectives.
- Introduction: The why behind the project. What is the problem and the project background?
- Objectives: The goals and aims of the project. This may be a reiteration of what the client has asked for, but it demonstrates that you understand their needs. The objectives should be framed in terms of what the project will accomplish.
- Target audience: Who the project is intended for? Show your understanding of the industry by researching the target audience and identifying their interests, behaviors, and preferences.
- Methodology: Outline the process you will use to achieve the project's goals, including any specific tools or techniques you will utilize.
- Budget: A breakdown of the costs associated with your project. It is important to be realistic and detailed in this section.
- Deliverables: List what you will deliver upon completion of the project. This could include specific types of media content, such as videos or images, as well as any additional services, such as social media management or website maintenance.
- Timeline: Outline the timeline of the project, including start and end dates, as well as any milestones along the way.
- Credentials: The team's relevant experience and the company's portfolio to showcase your expertise. You can also include testimonials from previous customers to highlight your recent successes.
- Conclusion: Summarize your proposal and reiterate the importance of your project.

Ingredients of effective proposals

Regardless of these differences in proposal types, there are certain qualities that all media project proposals should embody.

Grammatically correct

As with any written document, grammar and spelling errors can reduce the credibility of your proposal. Make sure to proofread carefully for any mistakes or consider having someone else review it before submission.

Understandable

A well-written proposal should be easy to understand. If the reader cannot understand the project, the proposal will be dismissed. Avoid technical jargon or convoluted language that may confuse the reader. Use clear and straight-forward language to get your point across effectively. Avoid ambiguity as it "forces the reader to select a meaning from among various choices—and the wrong one can be selected" (Pfeiffer and Keller 2000, p. 80).

Persuasive

The language used in a proposal should convey confidence and enthusiasm for the project. Strong language can help convince the reader of the project's value and potential success. Avoid using weak words like "hopefully" and "should" as they can weaken the proposal's impact. Instead, use confident language and back up claims with evidence.

Concise

The length of your proposal will depend on the project's complexity, but it is important to keep it as concise as possible. Avoid including unnecessary details or information that does not directly relate to the project. Your reader has a limited attention span.

Thoroughly researched

A good proposal demonstrates a deep understanding of the project and its goals. Make sure to conduct thorough research on the topic, target audience, and any potential challenges before drafting your proposal.

Lawfully and ethically sound

Ensure that your proposal follows all legal and ethical guidelines. Any copyright infringement or unethical practices can harm your credibility and potentially lead to legal consequences. Make sure to properly cite any sources used and adhere to industry standards.

Focused on benefits not features

Instead of simply listing what your project can do, focus on how it will benefit the client or audience. This is especially important in client-driven proposals, as the client wants to know how their investment will pay off. Remember, "customers don't buy features; they buy the benefits provided by the features of your product or service" (Pfeiffer and Keller 2000, p. 87).

Visually appealing and organized

A well-structured proposal will make it easier for the reader to follow along and understand the project. Use headings, subheadings, and bullet points to break up large chunks of text and make important information stand out. An attractive proposal also shows that you put effort and care into your work.

Scriptwriting

Scriptwriting is a crucial step in the production of several different types of media projects including animations, videos, and podcasts. We have touched on the importance of screenwriting as it relates to different disciplines in previous chapters. While the script form and style varies based on the project being produced, the key purpose remains the same. The role of a script is to guide yourself as well as any other people involved with your production such as actors, directors, and crew members in bringing the project to life.

A film or a television script might be what most of us visualize when we hear the term scriptwriting. It is a multi-page, highly detailed document that outlines dialogue, action, and setting for the scenes of a movie or TV show. This type of scriptwriting is a discipline in itself and is outside the purview of most communication professionals. Nevertheless, other types of projects that we are more likely to encounter require scripts as well.

Scriptwriting for podcasts

Podcasts have become a popular medium for sharing information and storytelling, and scriptwriting plays a crucial role in creating engaging and well-structured podcast episodes. Unlike traditional scripts, podcast scripts are less formal. However, they still need to follow a structured outline to ensure that the content is organized and flows smoothly. Podcast scripts also tend to include references to sound effects and music, adding an additional layer of creativity to the writing process.

While podcasts can be delivered in a variety of formats such as interviews, hosts bantering, or monologues, a script is still essential. For more freeform style podcasts, having a script that simply summarizes the topics at hand can help the presenter stay on track. In the case of an interview, all questions should be outlined. Podcasts that feature two or more hosts bantering back and forth should also have a general outline to keep the conversation flowing. For monologue-style podcasts, a more traditional script may be necessary.

Organizing the script in a two-column table using a document editor is a simple way of blocking out a narrated podcast episode. On the left, indicate who should be speaking, when music should commence, and what sound effects should be played in the background. On the right, write the corresponding text.

When writing a script for a podcast, be mindful of your language. Write for the ear, not the eye. Unlike a written document, intended to be read, podcasts are meant to be heard. Use language that is easy for listeners to understand and follow along with. And use descriptive language to create a vivid listening experience for your audience.

The tone of a podcast should be conversational. Write your script like you talk. "Audio is inherently an intimate form of communication, and podcasts take that intimacy even further" (Euritt 2023, p. 2). Stodgy, formal, and unnatural language detracts from the connection that the podcaster is striving to foster with his audience. For example, change phrases like "are we acquainted?" to "do I know you?" (McHugh 2022, p. 16). At the same time, the content should be grammatically correct. Common errors such as the improper use of "I" and "me" can turn off and offend listeners and make you sound unintelligent. While your content should be informal, always avoid using filler words such as "like" and "you know" in your writing as well as your delivery.

Consider the structure of your podcast script. To hook your audience from the beginning, start with an attention-grabbing intro so that they want to hear more. Get to the point quickly. "Don't make your audience wait for the meat" (Morris et al. 2007). Throughout your script, use transitions and segues to connect different segments and keep the flow of your podcast.

When it's appropriate, incorporate music and sound effects. Adding in music or sound effects can help break up the audio and add depth to your podcast. Just be sure to use them sparingly and make sure they enhance, rather than distract, from your content.

Scriptwriting for YouTube videos

Creating content for YouTube has become a common practice for businesses and organizations. They often produce short-form videos like product demonstrations, company stories, and live-streaming events to showcase and market their brand. Therefore, it is crucial to ensure these videos are of high quality, and the key to a polished and professional presentation on YouTube starts with a well-crafted script.

Scripts for YouTube videos can vary in style and level of detail. Some videos may only require bullet points as a guide, while others may need a more detailed script. Regardless of the style chosen, it is essential to have a clear structure and flow to your video. Even for live-streaming events, you will want to "prepare a detailed outline for what you'll discuss or cover within your program" (Media and Rich 2018, p. 199).

Before writing a script for this type of video, you should have a clear goal that is consistent with your current marketing and advertising messages in other forms of media. You should also be aware of your target audience. What existing knowledge do they have? What points might your audience need clarified? What do they hope to learn? Understanding your objectives and target audience will inform the content of your script.

Once you are clear on your purpose and audience, craft a script that contains the following sections.

- A hook: An attention-grabbing statement or question to immediately engage the audience and entice them to continue watching. Consider starting with an interesting fact, question, or statement.
- Introduction: Introduce yourself, your brand, and what the video is about. Keep it concise but informative.
- Main content: This is where you present your main message or idea. Use a logical flow, supporting evidence, and examples to get your point across effectively. Take advantage of the visual nature of the medium and incorporate graphics or B-roll footage to clarify points. In your script indicate when these will appear.
- Call to action: What do you want your viewers to do after watching your video? End with a clear call to action such as subscribing to your channel, visiting your website, or purchasing a product. This can help foster a relationship with your audience and keep them coming back for more.
- Conclusion: Summarize the main points and leave a lasting impression on the audience.

As with podcast scripts, a simple two-column table structure can be used to script your video. On the left, clarify who is speaking, the type of shot you will use, and any graphics, B-roll, or audio clips integrated. The right side of the table should contain the text.

To enhance understanding and connection with your audience, be mindful of your writing style. Use short sentences as they are easier to follow and understand. Vary your sentence structure to make your speech sound more conversational. Always write in the present tense to keep the focus on the here and now. Use active voice more than passive voice to create a sense of action and movement. Additionally, injecting humor and showing your personality when appropriate can make your content more relatable and engaging for viewers.

After writing your script, it's a good idea to get feedback from someone not familiar with your topic. This can help you identify any areas that may be unclear or need improvement. Remember, the key to a successful script is to make it informative, engaging, and easy for your audience to follow.

When you actually record your video, it's not necessary to follow your script word for word. In fact, you will sound much more natural if you are able to deliver your content in a conversational manner. However, having a well-written and well-planned script will serve as a helpful guide and ensure that you (or your subjects) cover all the important points in the video.

Writing for websites

Writing for the web encompasses various styles, as websites serve diverse purposes. However, certain fundamental principles apply to all web writing. When creating content for any type of website to be read by a diverse audience, the challenge is capturing and maintaining their attention. On the web, there is always more compelling writing just a click away. Writing techniques that aid in achieving this goal include organizing and structuring the content effectively, choosing words strategically, and integrating devices to break up text.

Content structure

The structure of content on a website should differ from the structure of a magazine article or a research paper. On the web, it's advisable to follow a top-to-bottom hierarchy where you put the most important information first. This hierarchy helps readers focus on the information that matters most without getting lost in a sea of text.

Reading on a screen takes 25% longer than reading a printed page (Mizrahi 2013, p. 48). To make content on the web more reader-friendly, use shorter sentences (no longer than 20 words) and paragraphs. Shorter paragraphs provide visual breaks for readers, making the text appear less dense and overwhelming, and shorter sentences enhance readability by presenting information in smaller, more easily understandable components.

Word choice

On the web, it's important to choose words carefully to ensure your message is clear and easy for readers to understand. This means avoiding jargon and technical terms unless they are necessary for your specific audience. Define any unfamiliar language the first time you use it or take advantage of the interactive nature of the web and link the term to another page on your site that addresses it more in-depth. Be consistent when choosing your words to describe the same thing or action and always spell it the same way. While you may know that the variations in your language have a similar meaning, it could be confusing to your user. This is especially true when writing "how-tos."

Voice

Whenever possible, write in the active voice. Sentences written in the active voice are stronger and more concise. The active voice is also more engaging for readers, making them feel like you are speaking directly to them. Passive sentences can sound distant and detached. However, when you can't name the subject, or the action is more important than the person completing the action, the passive voice may be a better choice.

Formatting

In addition to short paragraphs and sentences, employ formatting techniques to make your content easier to scan. This includes using headings, subheadings, bullet points, and numbered lists. These devices help break up text and make it more visually appealing, as well as making it easier for readers to find information quickly.

Visual aids

Incorporating visual aids, such as images or infographics, can greatly enhance the impact of written content on a website. These visual elements can help break up text and add visual interest, as well as providing additional information or context to the written content. However, these aids should support your written content and not detract from it. Visuals should always be relevant and enhance the overall message of the website.

Writing for different types of websites

Different types of websites have specific content needs. For instance, crafting content for a news website requires a different approach compared to an e-commerce site. To effectively convey your message and captivate readers, it's crucial to comprehend the website's purpose and target audience. This understanding will improve communication and engagement.

In addition to creating well-crafted content with a clear purpose, in most cases you also want to create content that will be recognized by search engines. The language that we use and the frequency in which we use certain terms on a website effects how and if people find our web pages. The practice of crafting content for optimal search engine recognition is called search engine optimization.

Although there are entire courses on how to write content for search engine optimization, some of the basic principles include focusing your page content on a specific keyword or phrase then incorporating these keywords into your content, especially in your page title, headings, and subheadings. You will also want to incorporate these keywords into your ALT tags—the hidden text that is associated with the images you use on the page. When incorporating your keywords, avoid overdoing it. You can get penalized by search engines if your content looks too loaded with a keyword. Search engines want to deliver high-quality content to searchers, so your main priority should always be creating valuable and engaging content for your audience that is relevant to your chosen keyword. Keep in mind that even the most well-optimized, search-engine-friendly writing is not a guarantee that Google will serve up your site on page one of their results. The algorithms that a search engine uses to evaluate a site or page consider other factors such as the amount and type of incoming links there are to your site, the quality of the incoming links, the age of your site, and its load speed and mobile friendliness.

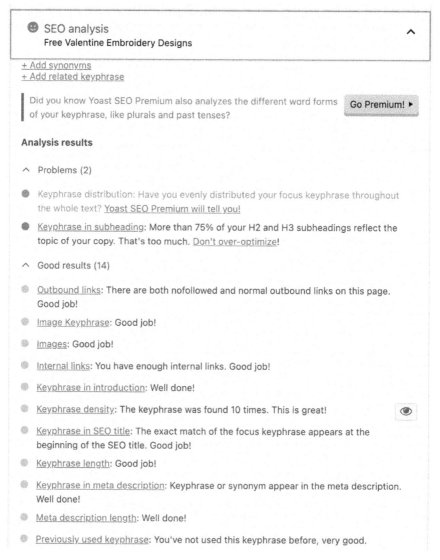

Figure 12.1 The Yoast SEO plugin will analyze the writing on a page and assess SEOs

Business and organization informational site

Many businesses and non-profit organizations have websites yet don't sell any products or services through the web. The purpose of their sites is to strengthen their brand identity, show off their work and provide an easy way for potential customers to get in touch. These types of sites typically have (at a minimum) pages with a company/organization description, team-member bios, case studies or portfolios, and a contact page.

Because the audience of these types of sites can be quite broad, the tone should be professional and convey credibility and trust. For larger organizations, the tone of the writing is dictated at a corporate level to ensure consistency among various writers. As the web has evolved, the tone of corporate website content has as well. Many sites have moved from a less lecture-like style "towards a tone that engages the reader by employing more of a 'we are all in this together sensibility'" (Mizrahi 2013, p. 43).

While sites of this ilk don't typically have as many pages as a blog or an e-commerce site, there is still potential for capturing user queries via search engines. Most businesses or organizations would expect that a Google search for a company's name would lead a searcher to their home page, especially if the company has a unique name. However, a company could capture searches for some of the products or services by crafting their content differently. Consider how a business or organization could write more search-engine-friendly content by framing their writing in a different way. Instead of writing a case study focused on a customer or client, the writing could be centered on the problem the company solved. If this problem was the target key phrase on the webpage and integrated strategically throughout the content, the page could gain traffic when users searched for that phrase.

Blogs

Blogging is a popular way to share information, opinions, and experiences on the web. Blogs were once seen as personal journals but are now frequently used as a powerful marketing tool. Many modern blogs are a collection of articles, each focused around a keyword or phrase. They strive to show up in search results for the keywords they are targeting and entice users to click on the link and visit the site. When visitors come to the site, the blog earns revenue via advertising, affiliate marketing, or other means. Because blogs are typically very content rich, crafting a blog that is associated with a company or organization's site can be a way for a company to get additional traffic to their website.

Writing for a blog is different than writing for an organization's informational website because the goals are different. Blog writers should establish their own unique voice and style in order to stand out among the vast amount of content available online and encourage visitors to explore other areas of the site. This means writing with authenticity, personality, and passion about topics that are relevant and interesting to readers and developing a rich system of cross-links to make it easy for readers to discover other relevant pages on the blog. Short paragraphs are also highly desirable on blogs because it yields more breaks within the text and more opportunities for advertisers to insert ads.

E-commerce sites

E-commerce sites have specific goals compared to other types of websites. These sites aim to provide an online shopping experience to users, with the ultimate goal of yielding a transaction. Content on these websites has the primary purpose of selling, showcasing products or services, and persuading customers to make a purchase. The writing on these websites needs to be "colorful, descriptive and specific," highlighting the benefits of the product or service being sold (Mizrahi 2013, p. 50). The focus of the writing should be on the potential customer transformation. For example, instead of highlighting that a book has a certain number of pages, focus on the transformation that the customer will make from the lessons in the book.

Writing on e-commerce sites should also be optimized for search engine discovery in order to increase visibility and attract potential customers. This includes incorporating relevant keywords in product titles and descriptions on the product pages. Building content-rich keyword-focused category landing pages can also be a good tactic for attracting search engine traffic.

Social media writing

Like writing for the web, writing for social media should adhere to some fundamental principles while considering the unique characteristics of the social media platform. Social media posts are shorter and more concise compared to traditional web content, with character limits depending on the platform. This means that every word counts and should be carefully chosen to ensure maximum impact.

Social media posts also have a more conversational tone, reflecting the informal nature of social media platforms. Brands and organizations can use this to their advantage by connecting with their audience in a more personal and relatable manner. However, it's important to maintain professionalism and align the content with the brand's overall voice and message.

In addition to written content, social media also relies heavily on visual elements such as images, videos, and graphics. These visuals should be carefully selected and edited to enhance the message of the post and capture the attention of users scrolling through their feeds.

Another key aspect of writing for social media is understanding the platform's algorithms and utilizing them to increase visibility. This includes using relevant hashtags, posting at optimal times, and engaging with other users through replies and comments.

Overall, writing for social media requires a balance between creativity, strategy, consistency, and understanding of the platform's unique characteristics in order to effectively reach and engage with target audiences. By leveraging these principles and adapting writing styles to different platforms, businesses and organizations can effectively utilize social media as a powerful marketing tool.

"Creating value through your writing" by chief product officer Christy Pogorelac

Whether you're writing content for a website, script, or social channels, the opportunity to connect with your audience in a memorable and lasting way exists in the relevance of the topics and the language you choose. Not only does it make it much easier for your content to find an audience's feed and search results, but it creates the framework for you to create useful content in a consistent voice. When you're not sure where to begin or how to prioritize the content you're writing, it's helpful to think of it as a physical product. Understanding how, when, and why your audience will use and interact with your work will help you craft something that provides value on its own while complementing content across multiple platforms.

Study questions

1) Why is proposal writing important for media projects?
2) What are some differences between writing a script for a podcast vs. a video?
3) How can businesses and organizations write more search-engine-friendly content on their informational websites?
4) How is writing strategy different for different types of websites? How is it the same?
5) What are some key considerations when writing for social media platforms?

Exercises

1) Create a product description for a new e-commerce website selling sustainable clothing. How can you make the product page search-engine friendly?
2) Compose a series of social media posts promoting an upcoming webinar on digital marketing strategies. Make sure to include relevant hashtags and visuals.
3) Write a blog post on a niche topic focusing on a particular keyword or phrase.
4) Write a script for a podcast episode of your choice.
5) Craft a proposal for a media project, outlining the objectives, target audience, and proposed budget.

References

Euritt, Alyn. 2023. *Podcasting as an Intimate Medium*. Routledge Studies in New Media and Cyberculture. Abingdon: Routledge.

McHugh, Siobhàn. 2022. *The Power of Podcasting: Telling Stories Through Sound*. New York: Columbia University Press.

Media, The Staff of Entrepreneur, and Jason R. Rich. 2018. *Ultimate Guide to You-Tube for Business*. 2nd ed. Ultimate Series. Irvine, CA: Entrepreneur Press.

Mizrahi, Janet. 2013. *Web Content: A Writer's Guide*. 1st ed. Corporate Communication Collection. New York: Business Expert Press.

Morris, Tee, Evo Terra, and Ryan C. Williams. 2007. *Expert Podcasting Practices for Dummies*. Hoboken, NJ: John Wiley & Sons.

Pfeiffer, William S., and Charles H. Keller. 2000. *Proposal Writing: The Art of Friendly and Winning Persuasion*. Upper Saddle River, NJ: Prentice Hall. https://worldcat.org/title/41641287.

Rosenthal, Alan, and Ned Eckhardt. 2016. *Writing, Directing, and Producing Documentary Films and Digital Videos*. 5th ed. Carbondale, IL: Southern Illinois University Press.

13 Soliciting and using audience feedback

Business success relies on understanding the needs and preferences of your audience. Listening to feedback and incorporating it into your growth strategy is a powerful way to stay ahead of the competition. Actively soliciting feedback offers us valuable insight into what our audience thinks about our work and helps us better tailor our offerings to meet their needs. Feedback can come in the form of reviews, surveys, polls, or just direct conversation, and it allows us to learn from our successes and mistakes. We can also gain insight into our customers' mindsets by leveraging digital tools to study their behavior. By taking the feedback we receive seriously, paying attention to our audience's behavior, and doing our best to implement positive changes, we can open ourselves up to new opportunities, improve our skills, and create more loyal followers.

In this chapter we will explore the various ways to receive audience feedback and how to use it to enhance our business strategies. We will cover some of the conventional methods of soliciting audience feedback, what has changed, and what channels we can now use to receive audience feedback. We will also discuss methods of analyzing and implementing both quantitative and qualitative audience feedback and how to respond to the feedback we receive.

Conventional methods of soliciting audience feedback

Prior to the dawn of the internet, it was almost impossible to determine how your messaging resonated with an audience. TV ads could only be measured by the number of people who watched them. The impact of a newspaper or magazine ad was assessed based on the number of copies typically sold. But in either of these cases, as an advertiser, you had no idea if your ad was working. Only crude metrics of effectiveness were possible. For example, you could advertise to an audience in a specific geographic area and track sales in the corresponding area to gauge efficacy.

Companies and organizations came up with different solutions to learn from their audiences. Surveys have been around for decades and were the primary tool for soliciting audience feedback. Focus groups where companies collect representative target audience members to discuss their feelings about

DOI: 10.4324/9781003462200-13

a product, service, or marketing campaign can be a valuable method in providing insights. While both of these methods are still used as a means of collecting audience feedback, they can be expensive and time-consuming. With the help of modern technology, new options are available to solicit feedback from audiences more quickly and with less expense.

Soliciting audience feedback from different channels

On a website

There are a number of ways you can solicit audience opinions on a website by integrating different feedback devices. First, create a contact form on your website where your audience can submit their comments and suggestions. Encourage specific feedback by asking targeted questions and providing multiple choice options. Any website-building platform has built-in tools to create such forms that you can customize to suit your needs.

If you are looking to get feedback on the website (or an app), itself, you can conduct a usability test to determine whether your website is easy to navigate and understand. Usability testing involves observing users as they navigate through your website or app, noting any difficulties they encounter. By conducting usability tests regularly, you can identify problem areas in your website and improve the overall user experience. Inexpensive services like UserTesting, Userlytics, and UserBob provide insightful observations and user reactions to your website or app.

Surveys

Surveys are still a great tool to better understand your audience's wants, needs, and preferences. With the rise of online survey platforms like SurveyMonkey, it has become easier than ever to create and distribute surveys. If paying for a survey platform is beyond your budget, you can easily build a survey using Google Forms. Any survey tool (including Google Forms) will allow you to export your data as a spreadsheet so that you can thoroughly analyze your responses. A common technique to maximize your response rate is to provide some type of reward for completing your survey such as a product your company makes. Or, if you are an influencer and companies send you free product, you can use these as a raffle prize to those who completed your survey. Gift cards are always a winner as an incentive for a user to complete a survey. Providing rewards for survey completion is such a common tactic that some online platforms even have a built-in incentive system for survey respondents.

Getting your audience to participate in a survey can be a challenge; however, getting them to finish it can be a struggle as well. Edit and simplify your survey as much as possible, as "there is a negative relationship between completion rate and survey length and question difficulty" (Liu and Wronski 2017). If a survey takes too long to complete, your audience is less likely to finish it. Secondly, if a survey looks too complicated, your audience may feel intimidated and abandon it. To avoid these issues, it's important to keep surveys short and simple, using clear language and avoiding jargon or complicated questions.

Social media

Another way to solicit audience feedback is by using social media platforms like TikTok, Instagram, Facebook, and X. You can post questions or polls and invite your followers to share their thoughts and opinions. This method not only allows you to gather valuable information, but it also encourages engagement with your audience and creates a sense of community. Instagram actually has a poll feature where users can vote on a specific topic, giving you quick and easy feedback. TikTok also has a polling feature that works in a similar way. By customizing polls to showcase results exclusively from chosen participants, you can gather focused information that is pertinent to your specific niche or audience.

Social media has other built-in tools that allow you to learn more about your audience. Hashtags play a vital role in monitoring social media conversations. They not only help organize posts into categories, but also provide insights into specific topics. By utilizing hashtags, you can effectively track mentions of your brand and identify any positive or negative feedback patterns that require attention. Third-party tools like Mention or Hootsuite can be used to track mentions of your brand across all social media platforms.

Social media can also be an effective tool to request feedback. You can ask customers to leave reviews on Facebook or Google, or you can create a hashtag for customers to use when sharing their experiences with your brand. For example, UK-based stationery company Papier "encourages all [their] customers and followers to use #lovepapier so [they] can see what they're posting" (Cook 2020). These reviews and user-generated content can provide valuable feedback and also serve as social proof to attract new customers.

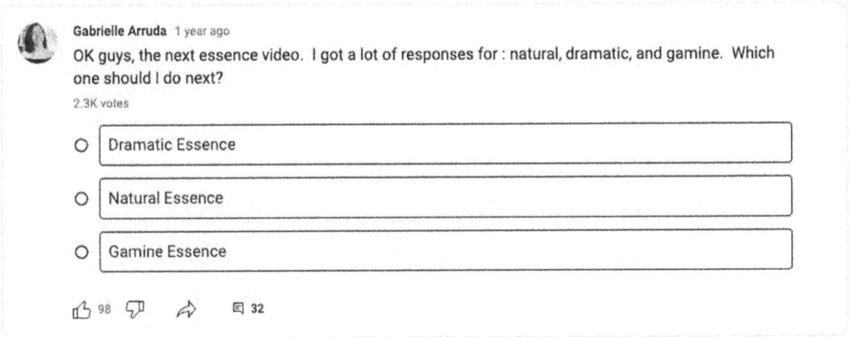

Figure 13.1 YouTube content creators can create polls to get feeback from their audience

Private communities

Invite your customers to join a closed community such as a Facebook group dedicated to the issues your company is addressing. This will provide you with a wealth of feedback and give your customers an opportunity to ask questions, share their experiences, and interact with other like-minded individuals. Private communities also have the added benefit of creating a sense of exclusivity for members, making them feel valued and part of something special.

A great example of how a company uses a Facebook group to get feedback from their customers is the fitness company Tonal. With their 54,000-member Facebook group, they have a built-in mechanism for receiving feedback from their customers. To keep the group active and engaged, while also gauging customer satisfaction, Tonal uses weekly group polls as well as other initiatives and events to communicate with their audience ("Tonal Success Story: Building an Engaged Community" n.d.).

Direct communication

Sometimes, the best way to receive feedback is through direct conversation with your audience. Whether it's in person at events or conferences or through email or phone calls, having one-on-one conversations with your audience can provide valuable insights into their experiences and preferences. This method also allows for personalized feedback and shows that you value each customer individually. Depending on the industry, industry-related conferences can be an ideal opportunity to have these conversations.

Blog comments

If you have a blog on your website, you can also use it as a platform to solicit feedback from your audience. Encourage readers to leave comments and engage in discussions about your content. This not only allows for direct feedback but also creates a sense of community and encourages interactive conversations with your audience. If you don't have a blog, you can also participate in discussions on other blogs or industry-related forums to receive feedback and engage with your target audience. This can also help establish your brand as an authority in your industry.

Leveraging digital platforms for passive audience feedback

The previous examples for soliciting audience feedback pertained to a more proactive approach—engaging with your audience and asking for feedback. Other techniques for collecting feedback are more passive in nature, utilizing digital platforms to gather information without directly interacting with your audience.

Website analytics

Tools like Google Analytics provide highly detailed insights into the behavior of your website visitors. By tracking metrics such as traffic sources, bounce rates, and time spent on each page, you can gain a better understanding of what content is resonating with your audience and what may need improvement. You can also use heat maps to see where visitors are clicking and scrolling on your website, giving you an idea of what areas are drawing their attention.

Social media analytics

Similar to website analytics, social media platforms have built-in tools that allow you to track the performance of your posts and content. By analyzing metrics such as engagement rates, reach, and click-through rates, you can learn which types of posts are most effective in engaging your audience. This information can help guide your content strategy and improve the effectiveness of your social media presence.

A/B testing

A/B testing involves creating two versions of a webpage, an ad, or a marketing email with a slight variation, then tracking which version performs better. This technique allows you to test different elements such as headlines, images, or call-to-action buttons to see which resonates better with your audience. By continuously A/B testing, you can gather feedback on what content is most effective in engaging your audience and make adjustments accordingly.

Google Alerts

Google Alerts are an excellent tool to gain insights from your audience. With Google Alerts, you can monitor the web for new content about any keyword or phrase (typically your brand, products, or related industry term), directly receiving updates to your inbox anytime your alert phrase gets indexed by Google. This allows you to gauge public sentiment and spot any concerns.

Online forums

Online forums and chat rooms are often a goldmine of candid feedback where users discuss their experiences, issues, and solutions. Participating in these platforms not only provides you with valuable information but also gives you the opportunity to clarify misconceptions and provide support. Enthusiast pages, such as fan-created Facebook groups or subreddit threads (niche communities focused on specific topics), offer a unique view into your most engaged audience members. Observing and interacting in these spaces lets you understand your audience's needs and pain points and may provide inspiration for new ways to connect with them.

Analyzing and implementing qualitative feedback

After soliciting feedback from your audience, the next crucial step is to analyze it and implement any necessary changes. But doing this type of analysis can be quite challenging for a number of reasons. First, the sheer quantity of data that you might have collected can be a bit daunting to sift through. Secondly, the language that people use to give feedback may not be consistent or straightforward. People often say the same thing in different ways. And finally, people's opinions might be conflicting or unclear, making it difficult to determine the best course of action.

Despite these challenges, it is still possible to make sense of qualitative feedback and streamline the implementation process. Allow the feedback you collect to dictate the overarching themes. Keep in mind that some comments you receive may apply to multiple themes. It can be helpful to create theme "buckets" in which you deposit comments (or portions of comments) into each of your theme buckets.

Once you organize the information you have received into theme clusters, you can start to analyze each one and look for common threads. What do people seem to be saying the most? Are there any clear patterns or trends emerging? Take note of both positive and negative feedback, as well as suggestions for improvement. This process will help you prioritize which changes need to be made and guide your decision-making moving forward. This could include adjusting messaging, improving products or services, or changing marketing tactics.

Remember to also communicate any changes or updates made based on audience feedback. This not only shows that you are listening and actively working to improve their experience but also builds trust and strengthens the relationship with your audience.

Analyzing and implementing quantitative feedback

Quantitative feedback refers to data that can be measured and expressed in numbers. This includes metrics such as website traffic, engagement rates, click-through rates, and customer ratings or reviews. Analyzing quantitative feedback is often more straightforward than qualitative feedback since the data is already organized into measurable categories. However, it's easy to get overwhelmed with all of the data that is available. How do you know what numbers are meaningful to you? And how do you use that information to make informed decisions?

The key is to focus on the metrics that align with your overall business goals. For example, if your goal is to increase website conversions, you would want to pay attention to metrics like conversion rates and bounce rates. If your goal is to improve customer satisfaction, you would look at customer ratings and reviews.

Once you have identified the relevant metrics, track them over time to see any trends or patterns. Are certain metrics consistently improving, while others are declining? This can give you an indication of what strategies are working and where improvements are needed.

When it comes to implementing changes based on quantitative feedback, consider A/B testing as mentioned earlier. By testing variations in elements such as website design, ad copy, or email subject lines, you can gather data on what resonates best with your audience and make data-driven decisions.

Responding to audience feedback

Receiving feedback from your audience is just one part of the equation—it's equally important to respond and communicate with your audience about their feedback. This not only shows that you value their opinions, but also demonstrates your commitment to continuously improving and providing a positive experience for them.

When responding to feedback, be sure to acknowledge and thank the person for taking the time to share their thoughts. If the feedback is negative, try to address their concerns and offer a solution or explanation. If the feedback is positive, express your gratitude and let them know that their support means a lot. It's also important to be transparent about any actions you plan to take based on the feedback received. This not only keeps your audience informed, but also shows that you are actively listening and taking their opinions into consideration.

Don't be afraid to ask for clarification or follow-up questions if needed. This not only shows that you are engaged and interested in understanding their feedback, but also allows you to gather more specific and detailed information that can further inform your decision-making process.

Lastly, be sure to follow up with your audience once changes have been implemented. This not only closes the feedback loop and shows that their opinions have been heard, but also allows you to gather further insights on the effectiveness of your changes.

"Filtering data through empathy" by chief insight officer Bob Cuneo

When trying to change people's behavior, remember—data is not insight. Data provides the "what." It tells us what people did. Data does not provide the "why." It does not tell us why they did it. Getting someone to do something requires insight. Data is easy. Insight is hard. Insight is a fresh, intimate understanding of people's beliefs that has the power to genuinely change behavior. Insight requires filtering data through empathy, feeling what another person feels. To achieve insight, you must scour data to deem what is important. Plus, and here is the part many businesses avoid, you must have real conversations with people. Insight is not concrete. It is messy. You have to argue about which actions and beliefs are critical to effecting behavior. Then commit your insight to paper. Argue again. And maybe, you will have the insight you need to make your communication significant.

"There is nothing wrong with needing improvement" by president and chief creative officer Heidi Singleton

As AI becomes ubiquitous, human-centric experiences will become more and more valuable to consumers. Active listening is a form of emotional intelligence, one that enables brands to be more human in the way they interact with their users. Understanding what customers want and need, and using that data to improve the user experience, shows the audience they are valued. And when they feel valued, they are more likely to stay loyal to the brand and share their positive experience with others. There is nothing wrong with needing improvement, as long as you are always improving. That is a fundamental human truth.

Study questions

1) Why is it important to regularly track and review feedback from your audience?
2) What are some tools or methods for collecting audience feedback without explicitly asking for it?
3) How can you use data from website analytics to improve your business strategy?
4) Why is it important to identify relevant metrics when analyzing quantitative feedback?
5) How can A/B testing help in making data-driven decisions based on quantitative feedback?

Exercises

1) Choose a company and research what people are saying about it online. What sources did you use? Could you identify any common themes?
2) Set up an A/B test. Design two different ads and ask a sample of your audience which one is more effective. Test the winner against a third ad and repeat the test.

3) Reach out to a brand or company you have recently interacted with and provide them with feedback, whether positive or negative. See if they respond and how they handle the feedback.
4) Create a survey for an audience that all use a particular product or attend the same institution. Ask what they like and what they don't. How could you improve that product or institution based on what you learned?
5) Conduct a usability test on a website or app and gather both qualitative and quantitative feedback from users.

References

Cook, Jodie. 2020. *Instagram Rules: The Essential Guide to Building Brands, Business and Community.* London: Frances Lincoln. https://library3.webster.edu/login?url= https://search.ebscohost.com/login.aspx?direct=true&db=nlebk&AN=2707993& site=ehost-live&scope=site.

Liu, Mingnan, and Laura Wronski. 2017. "Examining Completion Rates in Web Surveys via Over 25,000 Real-World Surveys." *Social Science Computer Review* 36 (1): 116–24. https://doi.org/10.1177/0894439317695581.

"Tonal Success Story: Building an Engaged Community." n.d. Meta. https://www. facebook.com/business/success/tonal. Accessed February 9, 2024.

Index

For Product Safety Concerns and Information please contact our EU
representative GPSR@taylorandfrancis.com
Taylor & Francis Verlag GmbH, Kaufingerstraße 24, 80331 München, Germany

www.ingramcontent.com/pod-product-compliance
Ingram Content Group UK Ltd.
Pitfield, Milton Keynes, MK11 3LW, UK
UKHW021031180425
457613UK00021B/1122